ENTREPRENEURSHIP
AND
INNOVATION

ENTREPRENEURSHIP
AND
INNOVATION

An
Economic Approach

Bruce A. McDaniel

M.E. Sharpe
Armonk, New York
London, England

Library of Congress Cataloging-in-Publication Data

McDaniel, Bruce A., 1946–
    Entrepreneurship and innovation : an economic approach / Bruce A. McDaniel.
      p. cm.
    Includes bibliographical references and index.
    ISBN 0-7656-0708-5 (cloth: alk. paper) — ISBN 0-7656-0709-3 (pbk: alk. paper)
      1. Entrepreneurship. I. Title.

HB615.M3732 2002
338′.04—dc21   2001057687

Printed in the United States of America

The paper used in this publication meets the minimum requirements of
American National Standard for Information Sciences
Permanence of Paper for Printed Library Materials,
ANSI Z 39.48-1984.

BM (c)   10   9   8   7   6   5   4   3   2
BM (p)   10   9   8   7   6   5   4   3   2

This book is dedicated to my parents, Hatti Marie Stidham McDaniel and Maurice Maynard McDaniel. To my mother, who during my early childhood, youth, and adulthood has always encouraged me, believed in me, and tried to convince me that no task was too large for me to accomplish. Although at the writing of this book, she resides in a nursing home with advanced dementia, she remains one of the kindest persons I have ever known. And to my father, who was always there to support whatever task I undertook or venture I decided to pursue. In my adulthood I returned home to the family business for eight years following his heart attack. During those years he taught me the true spirit of entrepreneurship. As he recalled his many experiences innovating to make changes, he helped me understand by example the nature and drive of entrepreneurs. He remains my best friend, my mentor, as well as my best example of what human caring is all about.

Contents

List of Tables and Figures

Tables

Figures

Acknowledgments

I would like to thank the eleven entrepreneurs in the entrepreneurial biographies for their time and willingness to help others understand entrepreneurship. Several of these entrepreneurs have taken the time to meet with me to explore areas of entrepreneurship, as well as to meet with students in my entrepreneurship classes and seminars to help them develop a better understanding of entrepreneurship and innovation.

I would also like to thank Linda Jack for her kind friendship and cheerful willingness to read my notes and type the manuscript. I would like to thank the many participants of the conferences and seminars in which I have organized and participated for their insight, inputs, and encouragement to pursue ideas about entrepreneurship and innovation. I especially appreciate Wali Mondal, Director of the American Society of Business and Behavioral Sciences (ASBBS), for his tolerance and encouragement to allow me to organize and participate in sessions on entrepreneurship at the annual ASBBS meetings. Also, I would like to acknowledge the Sponsored Programs and Academic Research Center at the University of Northern Colorado for financial support for travel to conferences during the development stage of papers on entrepreneurship and innovation that were the basis of this book.

Finally, I wish to thank the Colorado Council on Economic Education for financially supporting my development of a regional conference on entrepreneurship to further explore ideas and concepts with speakers and participants.

ENTREPRENEURSHIP
AND
INNOVATION

1

Introduction and Overview

The Transformation of Human Activity

One of the great transformations of humankind in the past several hundred years has been a change in human nature as the result of the Industrial Revolution. Somewhere in the early to mid-1700s, the transformation, which began in England, changed human activity from agrarians to assemblers; from working by the sun to working by the clock; from tasks according to the season to tasks according to production processes. This great transformation cannot be overstated, for it affected virtually every aspect of human activity. In the process of this transformation, three major changes in human activity occurred. The first, as mentioned above, was the very definition of work transformed from a natural to a non-natural setting. Artificial light, exclusions from weather and seasons, as well as mechanical operations replaced activities revolving around flora and fauna.

The second major change was an almost immediate and severe decline in the standard of living for all day laborers. This included virtually all citizens except for a very privileged but small number of the elite. This decline covered several decades where it was possible for husbands and wives to toil eighteen to twenty hours per day yet not earn enough income to provide even the barest essentials of food, clothing, and shelter. Much literature exists,

3

painting a very bleak picture of the helplessness and hopelessness of these workers. Most children were forced into day labor by the age of five, and a common practice was to chain them to the machine where they were to work, lest they forget their assigned task. Sleeping quarters for the four to six hours daily spent not working often accommodated as many as twenty people in a small room with workers queued in rows on the floor attempting to sleep. With no sanitary facilities and the closeness of human flesh, one can only imagine the stench in such places. This incredible decline in the common lifestyle was followed by an ever-so-slow reversal in this trend, and today's industrial capitalist economies in no way resemble that bleak beginning. The average citizen in today's western industrial economies lives with a drastically higher standard of living than the kings and queens of royalty just a meager 100 years ago.

The average U.S. citizen in today's capitalist market industrial economy awakens in a heated and air-conditioned house, takes a hot shower, and eats a warm breakfast. He rushes to work in several minutes using a climate-controlled transportation system, works in a climate-controlled environment (within a few degrees of ideal), and performs operations that not so long ago would not even qualify as "work." All of these comforts were not remotely available to royalty in the not so distant past.

The third part of this transformation, and the major focus of this book, was the development and refinement of a sociologically distinct group of individuals known as "entrepreneurs." The concept of the entrepreneur will be defined succinctly and developed in chapters 2 and 3, but here a brief description is needed to begin the explanation of entrepreneurship.

It is important to note that there is not a specific beginning for entrepreneurs. Prior to the Industrial Revolution, it is generally thought that the serfs who left the manors in medieval Europe were entrepreneurs of a type. These individuals who escaped the manor and were away for one year and one day were termed "freedmen." These individuals generally joined the traveling carnivals that moved from manor to manor and began selling and trading various wares. The desire to "change the way things are done," which is a characteristic of entrepreneurs, has long existed in history. Very simply, today's entrepreneur is a person who makes a change in the type of good or service available for sale or in the way goods and/or services are provided in order to make the production process work more smoothly. The result of the efforts of the entrepreneur is some form of innovation. In other words, if an innovation has occurred, an entrepreneur was at work and succeeded in making some form of change. The workings of the entrepreneur as well as the resulting innovation will become much clearer in chapters 2 and 3. The entrepreneur in the early stages of the Industrial Revolution made the early production process work more smoothly.

Adam Smith's classic pin factory example in *The Wealth of Nations*[1] is an example of the entrepreneur speeding and smoothing the production process. As the example of the pin factory suggests, a craftsman making pins one at a time could complete, for example, fifty pins with one day's labor. However, if tasks were divided and repetition could be used to speed the process, production could be increased. By using one worker to cut the pin shaft, one worker to sharpen one end, one worker to form the pin head, and another to attach the shaft to the head, an assembly-line process could be formed. Using this innovative process instead of four craftsman accounting for 200 pins (50 x 4) in one day's time, possibly 1,000 pins could be made by the four workers joining their activities together. This was part of the process that started the Industrial Revolution. Once the Industrial Revolution began in England and was soon transplanted to the United States, entrepreneurs began a never-ending process of a smoother, faster production line with ever-increasing amounts and different kinds of material goods.

A Brief Economic History of Entrepreneurship in America

The most often-cited example of entrepreneurship in the early industrialization of the United States is Henry Ford's production of the Model T. Fordism, as it is often referred to, is no more than Henry Ford using Adam Smith's pin factory example and applying it to the assembly-line production of automobiles.[2] In fact, in the early stages of the assembly line, men with leather harnesses pulled auto frames from station to station. This concept of continuous-process assembly lines will be more fully developed in chapter 6. The fact that what Henry Ford did was not at its basis overly complicated does not detract from the enormous consequences of Fordism on the U.S. economy.

There were several factors leading the way to the assembly-line production of automobiles. The innovation of interchangeable parts was a very significant factor allowing the concept of assembly-line production to occur. Eli Whitney made the development of interchangeable parts. Although Whitney is given little credit and is not usually remembered for this development, it remains one of the most significant innovations in the American history of entrepreneurs. The labor transition from skilled workers to much less skilled assembly workers allowed immigrants with little or no specific skill to begin assembly production work with ten or fifteen minutes of minor explanation of job requirements. Also, the innovation of a management-level operation was required to orchestrate the assembly of the parts into a complete unit. Finally, there were ongoing innovations creating the machinery and tooling to make the various and sundry parts of the automobile. Fordism remains the most classic example of all entrepreneurship in U.S. economic history leading to successive innovations.

Although Fordism was a remarkable feat of entrepreneurship with its resulting innovations, it was neither an isolated nor an independent development in United States economic history. Parallel innovations in oil cracking and processing were occurring simultaneously. Oil refining was being transformed from a batch process to a flow process, a concept that will be fully developed in chapter 6. Likewise, innovations in the steel industry greatly enhanced the automobile industry. Refinements in the quality of steel, the scale of production for ever increasing demands for larger quantities, the technology for both quantities of steel as well as increases in the high quality of steel were made at a parallel time to great expansions in the auto industry. Andrew Carnegie was one of the major innovators in the steel industry, and he actually enhanced the success of Henry Ford.

Innovations were limited not only to the ancillary industries of the automobile. Innovations in road building and bridge construction, as well as advancing technology regarding highway mapping, traffic flows, and connecting highway systems, aided both the automobile industry as well as the western expansion of the U.S. economy. These roads were built by the U.S. government and were offered to the public free of any use charge; in the process, they pushed the U.S. economy to new heights in terms of economic growth, encouraged westward expansion, and opened vast new areas of productive resources.

It seems important here to at least briefly identify the result of entrepreneurial behavior, that is, innovation. Innovation will be more clearly explained in chapter 3, but innovation is most simply the application of an idea or concept to the production of goods and services. To partially distinguish an innovation from an invention, an invention is the development of an idea or concept, and an innovation is the use of that idea or concept. From the standpoint of economics, we can reasonably assume that innovations rather than inventions are the central point of interest. Chapter 4 more fully differentiates the concepts of innovation and invention and further explains why innovations are the focus of economic inquiry.

These innovations in the automobile industry, steel industry, and petroleum industry led to great economic expansions in the early 1900s. This major economic expansion and its corresponding development of entrepreneurial innovations were followed by a major collapse in the U.S. economy (as well as economics worldwide). There appears to be a strong connection between economic growth and expansion and continuing development of innovations. Likewise, there seems to be a strong connection between a decline in entrepreneurship and innovative activities and the resulting decline in economic growth and expansion. Although the entrepreneur and innovations remain largely outside mainstream micro- and macroeconomic theory, there is a very strong historical connection to validate the need for economic theory to incorporate both entrepreneurial behavior and its resulting innovative activity into the mainstream body of economic analysis.

After the Great Depression and World War II there was another major movement of entrepreneurship and innovation. Innovations led to more efficient production, advancements in almost every aspect of technology, and a host of new and improved products that were not even in the imagination only a decade earlier. The source of these innovations is the focus of chapter 10 and how they affect production is the focus of chapters 5 through 9. However, it should be clear from casual observation that these post–World War II innovations catapulted the U.S. economy into a position of international world trading dominance. This world trading dominance continued unchallenged for almost four decades. Again, a decline in innovations (the use of inventions by entrepreneurs) to change and expand the production of goods and services led to a toppling of the United States as the dominant international trading country. The result was a major U.S. economic recession with a compounded dilemma of double-digit figures for both inflation and unemployment, as well as increasing importation of foreign goods and a very large and growing deficit in the international balance of trade. As other countries began using the inventions of the United States and turning them into marketable innovations, the United States continued to see a declining status as a world trader of marketable goods. Our inventions were taken abroad, turned into marketable goods, and then shipped to the United States and sold to waiting consumers, which further increased the trade deficit in the United States.

The following story will help to illustrate the lack of entrepreneurship and innovation in a capitalist market economy leading to a decline in international balance of trade. Apparently, several decades ago the Japanese government wanted General Motors Corporation to build automobiles for their growing domestic market, so the Japanese government invited a large entourage of General Motors executives to Japan. These executives were wined and dined on saki and sushi, given a first-class tour of Tokyo, and then invited to a closed meeting between the General Motors Corporation and diplomats of the Japanese government. The Japanese spokesmen told the group from General Motors that Japan wanted General Motors to produce their domestic automobiles. The Japanese diplomats reasoned that since General Motors was the world's largest automobile producer, they were best suited to produce automobiles for Japan.

The story progresses: The Japanese officials explained that there were two problems that General Motors would need to accommodate in order for Japan to purchase automobiles. First, because the Japanese drove on the left side of the road, General Motors would need to produce automobiles with a steering wheel on the right side of the car. Secondly, because the streets in Japan (and especially Tokyo as observed from the guided tour) were quite narrow, General Motors would need to build a much smaller automobile than their current production in order to accommodate the narrower streets and roads. The story concludes with a short caucus by General Motors followed by an official General Motors statement informing the diplomats that when Japan started building wider streets and roads, and the country learned the correct side of the street on which to drive, then General Motors would gladly start selling automobiles to Japan.

The rest, of course, is history, with General Motors, the largest single corporation in the United States, almost declaring bankruptcy. The attitude that if we are good capitalists, we need not concern ourselves with entrepreneurship and innovation was prevalent in much of corporate America during the time period from the late 1960s through most of the next two decades. Research and development of many of the inventions sponsored by both the U.S. government and many larger U.S. corporations were never turned into products, as the role of the entrepreneur and the resulting innovations went unexplored. When foreign entrepreneurs took these U.S. inventions and developed products that were sold back to markets in the United States, many citizens complained that the products should be U.S. products because that was the origin of the invention. There was an outcry claiming unfair competition. In fact, the products were foreign because that was the source of the entrepreneurial effort and the home of the innovation. As this fact was fully recognized in the U.S., the entrepreneurial effort and skill was rekindled and product innovations began to dominate U.S. production as well as world trade.

Entrepreneurship and the resulting rapid development of innovations became a worldwide phenomenon in the 1980s as market capitalism became the ideology espoused by Margaret Thatcher, prime minister of England, and Ronald Reagan, president of the United States. This movement was enhanced by the declining acceptance of socialist-based economies worldwide. Exact reasons for the timing and fervor of this movement remain unclear, but in the United States the drive to regain recognition as a world trading power, the downsizing of inefficient plants, opportunities for small start-up firms, and the need for innovations leading to better efficiencies have certainly helped propel this movement. Innovation has become a necessity as well as the hallmark of any quality business venture.

In the 1930s and 1940s it was Joseph A. Schumpeter who attempted to define the entrepreneur as a distinct social being. Schumpeter saw the drive of the entrepreneur as having three primary parts: (1) the desire for power and independence; (2) the will to succeed; and (3) the self-satisfaction of getting things done. Schumpeter argued that money and profits were not per se what ultimately motivated the entrepreneur.[3] However, successful innovations most often bring both money and profits to the successful entrepreneur. That is, money and profits follow success, but they are typically not the motivators. This book will attempt to explore and analyze many different facets of the entrepreneur, including motivation, characteristics, and actions, as well as the role of the entrepreneur in a modern economy.

Once again as American entrepreneurs began innovating in the areas of product and processes of marketable goods, the United States started regaining international trading status. New products, new production processes, and the development of new markets, as well as new and varied inputs in the production process, all contributed to the resurgence of innovations in U.S. economic activity. As we move into the twenty-first century, the U.S. entrepreneur and the resulting innovations are the envy of other world economies. Many countries are strongly supporting their own emergence of modern entrepreneurs in an effort to expand economic activity, domestic economic growth, and a substantial increase in the material standard of living for their respective nations. This book attempts to explain this economic phenomenon in terms of the entrepreneur and the resulting innovations using the United States as an ongoing example.

A Brief Outline of the Remaining Chapters

Chapter 2 attempts to concretely differentiate between the economic activities of the capitalist and those of the entrepreneur. This attempt will be supported with a distinction between the types of risks taken by the capitalist and those risks taken by the entrepreneur.

The importance of this distinction is to prevent the generalized assumption that capitalists are entrepreneurs and entrepreneurs are capitalists, lest we repeat mistakes like the one General Motors made with Japan. An explanation of risk analysis will be included in this chapter. Chapter 3 attempts to develop the inseparable link between entrepreneurship and the resulting innovations. A Schumpeterian view and analysis of the entrepreneur is included in this chapter. Also, an attempt is made in this chapter to show the differences as well as the connections between evolutionary and revolutionary innovations.

Chapter 4 evaluates the process of developing a marketable product. Research and development in both the private and public sector is evaluated in terms of the successful commercialization of products and processes. The role and analysis of demand for products that drives innovations and assures the success of marketable products is included in chapter 4. Chapter 5 continues this product development by analyzing the temporary monopoly control that results from successful innovations. After an analysis of temporary monopoly control, this chapter develops the drive of competitors to reintroduce competition into the production and marketing of goods. The analysis includes a simultaneous push by the monopolizing entrepreneur to maintain some degree of monopoly power using innovations as well as a push by competitors to eliminate that monopoly power.

Chapter 6 expands on the drive for continued monopoly control by elaborating on process innovations. These production process innovations lead to expanded efficiencies and decreased production costs in an attempt to dominate product markets. Different methods of accomplishing this product dominance are also explored in chapter 6. Chapter 7 attempts to integrate product as well as process innovations into a smooth, ongoing innovative process in the development and refinement of goods and services. The economies of scale, economics of scope, and economies of integration are explained and developed in this chapter.

Chapter 8 views innovations as a multidisciplinary approach using technology and management as well as economics to better understand the process by which new marketable products are developed. Time lags, the infusion of technology, and product improvements are viewed in terms of the entrepreneur and innovations. Chapter 9 attempts to critically evaluate the omission of the entrepreneur in much of microeconomic theory. Different approaches to include the entrepreneur into microeconomic theory are suggested.

Finding the source of innovations is the focus of chapter 10. Most innovations are either user-led or producer-led. This chapter attempts to define each type of innovation and build a rationale for deciding which is the source of the innovation. This becomes important as one views the historical government funding of research and development and attempts to define a more productive result of such funding. Chapter 11 attempts to summarize the economic analysis of the entrepreneur and the resulting innovations developed throughout chapters 1–10 in this text. A host of suggested readings to further explore entrepreneurship concludes the last chapter. It is hoped that this text will begin to open a large area of unexplored ideology about the role of the entrepreneur in the economic workings of capitalistic market economies. The readings as well as this text are a start to that exploration.

To aid the reader in analyzing the true nature of the entrepreneur, I have included an entrepreneurial biography at the end of each chapter. Although these individuals have quite different occupations, produce quite different products, and have vastly different experiences, there are common threads that tie each individual to the umbrella of entrepreneurship. Each individual entrepreneur possesses most of the characteristics outlined in chapter 3. The entrepreneurial biographies will enhance the reader's grasp of that unique set of people that Joseph A. Schumpeter described as sociologically distinct individuals. These entrepreneurs in the biographies are not the nation's largest entrepreneurs nor are they widely known for exceptional innovations. Rather, they are everyday entrepreneurs running successful enterprises and are not attempting to say "look at me and look at what I've done." These are typical entrepreneurs who have succeeded and go to work every day thinking up new innovations just like the majority of all entrepreneurs in the world. The following questions were asked of all eleven entrepreneurs to show similarities of views and contrast responses and types of business endeavors of each entrepreneur:

1. What events and/or people were present in your youth or early adulthood that you now realize influenced your becoming an entrepreneur?
2. Describe some of your early efforts at entrepreneurship.
3. What were some events or projects that were not successful, but contributed to your success as an entrepreneur?
4. What project stands out as one of your major entrepreneurial successes?
5. What event stands out as a major stumbling block that you needed to overcome as an entrepreneur?

6. What advice could you give someone who has aspirations of becoming an entrepreneur?
7. Describe your current enterprise.
8. Describe your feelings toward your enterprise. Would you sell your enterprise? Would you work for a new owner? Would you take on a partner?
9. How do you stay competitive with other firms in your industry?
10. What innovations have you implemented to improve your enterprise?

Entrepreneurial Biography 1: Robert Walker

Name:	Robert Walker
Company:	Walker Manufacturing Company
Number of Employees:	145
Annual Sales:	$41 million

What events and/or people were present in your youth or early adulthood that you now realize influenced your becoming an entrepreneur?

There are two people. I quickly would mention my father. He was a farmer over in Kansas back when I was a young man in grade school, and he made a very distinct decision to leave the farming operation in 1957. I got to see firsthand what it looked like to start a business from scratch and living that experience, of course, had a great impact on me personally. I saw my dad learn many lessons from those early experiences, and also there were some inspiring things that came out of that. I saw how an idea could be turned into an opportunity if you were willing to go through all the effort that it took.

Another person would be an industrialist and manufacturer, Mr. Robert LeTourneau. He was a well-known entrepreneur who got started as a young man in the 1930s building large earth-moving equipment. . . . Some of his inventions were eventually sold to Caterpillar. But across the years he was very much an inventor and entrepreneur, and I heard him speak, as well as read a couple books that were written about him when I was a teenager, and I have to say that he really inspired me. As it turned out, he had started a technical college as part of his program where he would train engineers and technicians to work in his company. When I graduated from high school, I went to his college in Longview, Texas. That's where I got my engineering degree. Mr. LeTourneau was a big influence on me.

Describe some of your early efforts at entrepreneurship.

Those efforts would include working with my dad and living the experiences of my grade school and high school years. My dad was involved in starting the company and building a line of golf cars and then little off-road trucksters. That was the earliest effort. It was my dad that was really heading it up, and I got to observe and work with him as a young fellow right in that environment.

You also at one point built some evaporative coolers.

Yes, that was after I went to college. My dad sold the company and moved to Wyoming, and after a few years the company actually went completely out of business, and my dad lost everything. That was about the time I got out of college, and he was able to start over again with a new product based in Colorado building an evaporative cooler. After he restarted in the early 1970s, he invited me to work with him in 1975. We worked with that particular project, which was something completely different than he'd been in before, and it definitely was an entrepreneurial experience early in my career.

What were some events or projects that were not successful, but contributed to your success as an entrepreneur?

One of the key things that we learned points back to the first efforts with the golf car and the truckster. My dad always took the track that he could design, build, and manufacture products, but he wanted other people to be involved in the marketing. He really had the view that people involved in sales and marketing were a different breed of people, and he really didn't want to be involved in that. So he found other people to do it. We think what ultimately brought that project down, where it didn't ultimately succeed, was the lack of control over the marketing process. We were doing okay on designing, developing, and producing the product, but we just weren't getting them sold in the right way. That was the failure we realized when the company was sold and ultimately went out of business. As far as contributing to our success today, that was a lesson that we felt we learned the hard way.

When we started the lawn mower project, which is our product today, we [were] determined to do the marketing ourselves even if we weren't particularly specialists in marketing. We decided we wanted to control the whole project all the way from the very design of it all the way through to the end customer. That's a great lesson we learned.

Probably the other aspect is going through the process of selling the company and losing the actual control of the company financially. We also learned a great lesson about keeping control of your company and all the investment. If you're not going to be in control, you should probably just go out and get an eight-to-five job and not try to be an entrepreneur. Quite often, control is through finances. So that's an important lesson that we learned, again through a failure; we try to remember that lesson today.

What project stands out as one of your major entrepreneurial successes?

This lawn mower project has been the greatest opportunity that we've ever worked on. We can look back with hindsight; we were at the right time and the right place with the product concerning the market. We were early in a market that has evolved in a very strong way, in a very favorable way, towards our kind of product. So there's no question about it, we've had a great opportunity to develop an opportunity that was not visible at the time we started.

You want to describe your early lawn mower and the evolution into your current manufacturing company?

The first mower project was really started as a hobby project and as a challenge. My father and I had been using push mowers, and we purchased a couple of riding mowers in the Spring of 1977 for our own personal use. We bought a couple little riders right off the showroom without even trying them. After a few weeks of using those mowers, we found that they didn't work as well as we thought they would; they weren't very maneuverable; they didn't do as nice a job of cutting as the push mowers and weren't saving us any time. We thought we would save time with those riding mowers and make it more enjoyable to mow. We began to talk to each other and thought we could build a machine that would work in an environment that was a landscaped, private-type residence; one that would be maneuverable and compact enough to replace a push mower. My brother, who's the third part of the company, began work to design our first prototype mower in 1977. After a few weeks we were mowing grass with our own riding mower. We thought the first machine was working pretty good, but then we built another machine in 1978 and one in 1979, each one being somewhat of an improvement over the one before.

By 1979, we began to realize that we had a pretty good design, and we decided it was time to show it to some other people to see what they thought about it. Since our background was from Kansas and a farming background, we decided to go to a farm show in the Spring of 1979 and show our machine to the farmers there. We always felt that farmers were good judges of equipment. Sure enough, the farmers liked the machine. There was enough interest that we decided to take some risk and build twenty-five machines. We proceeded to do that in 1980. We built twenty-five of them; they were nearly hand-built, and it took us virtually all year to build twenty-five of them. We began to sell them; we had no dealers or distributors, so we just sold them like a peddler. We would go to some farm shows and state fairs and take the orders and sell machines.

It took us two years to sell those first twenty-five, but by the end of 1981 something else had happened. A magazine that had shot a photograph at one of the farm shows put it in their trade publication as a new product announcement. They didn't tell us they were doing this, but on their own initiative they exposed the product to the whole country. From that, we were thrust into a situation where we hadn't really planned to move that quickly. All of a sudden we began to get inquiries from all over the United States; people wanted to see this machine. We took a couple of the machines that were left from that first twenty-five and began to make some trips around the United States. My parents traveled and began to show the machine, and from those early trips we had gotten enough interest and some orders from people that allowed us to build 125 machines in 1982. One of those trips ended up in Florida. We met some people there who were contractors. We had originally thought of the machine mainly as a private homeowner application, but when we met those contractors, they told us the kind of work they were doing in Florida around retirement homes. They'd been using push mowers. They were so enthused with the product that they ordered forty-eight machines and gave us money down. They even bought the trailer that my parents had pulled down hauling those machines. My parents came home empty handed with an order for forty-eight machines. A few other orders were accumulated, so we weren't taking a big risk when we decided to build 125 machines. From there we really began to do some advertising and marketing in 1983 and 1984.

Our other manufacturing business, the evaporative coolers, which had been a contract-type business for a company in Greeley, came to an end in 1983 because the company changed ownership, and they decided they wanted to manufacture for themselves. So we were forced to go full time into lawn mower production, the first year being 1984. We didn't know if we could make it because financially we had been depending on that contract business. We actually turned a profit in 1986 and 1987; the first year we actually went in the black and have been on a climb ever since.

How many mowers did you build in the fiscal year that just ended?

We built 6,000. When we passed August 11, 2000, we built our 50,000th machine, so we had a celebration. When we remember how slowly we had started off, it's a remarkable journey we've been on.

What event stands out as a major stumbling block that you needed to overcome as an entrepreneur?

Money is always a problem. In fact, the people who stand around and tell you money is no problem are usually just not telling the truth. Money always is a problem to start a project like this. The only thing that's seen us through to get started is the idea of what we call "the poor boy project." That means that you're willing to take what you have, the resources you have available to you to get started. No matter how slowly you need to start, it's better to do that than to try to bring in a bunch of outside capital and risk the loss of control of the project. That's really the tradeoff, and we keep seeing that ourselves. When my dad lost control of the business, or gave away control of the business, we saw how destructive that can be to a business. It's not that the other people who invest are always wrong or have the wrong ideas, but so often investors are people who want quick results. They want an almost immediate return if they make an investment, and the kind of compromises that creates for the entrepreneur is oftentimes fatal.

Where an idea is not allowed to develop at a more natural pace and mistakes are made, where short-term decisions are made to thrust products onto the market before they're ready to really be marketed, where there's inadequate quality control, inadequate sales and support; all those things can create quick results, but in the process of doing that, you can fatally flaw the project. If you're humble enough and don't let your pride get in your way, you will admit that it may take a long time to get started "poor boy" style. If I don't have a lot of money, but I'm willing to just keep working at it, then that's the way to launch these things. If you're going to start a restaurant, some people would say, "Location, location, location," and "We've got to get some high-priced real estate to start our restaurant." Maybe the poor boy approach is, "We've got great food, I'll be the waiter, the cook, the washer, I'll do everything, and I may not have a great location, but I'm going to have great food, and that is how I'll attract people. I'll start in a little garage if I have to get my restaurant started because I happen to have a garage!"

What advice could you give someone who has aspirations of becoming an entrepreneur?

Use the poor boy approach; don't risk large amounts of capital because oftentimes, it's not necessary. In fact, money in itself oftentimes doesn't accelerate the real process. For example, trying to gain a reputation for a good product or a good service takes time to do, and it doesn't matter if you have a lot of money. It is not going to accelerate that process. In fact, a lot of money can be wasted in something like that. So, my first advice is to use the poor boy approach; that means you start with what you've got. In fact, that's also my second point; use the resources that you have at hand. Take a look at what you have right now that you could use to get started. A point that is well known is oftentimes your best opportunities are those that are disguised as small and unimpressive, while some of your big ideas may just evaporate when you get right down to it. So many times those opportunities are right in front of you; they don't look very big or very impressive, but get started with what you have, and see where it will take you. And that's my third point; get started. Small resources shouldn't stop a project. The people that keep putting off starting until they have lots of capital or lots of resources behind them probably are never going to get started. As I've already alluded to, outside capital doesn't mean it's going to be successful. The people who think their success hinges on having a lot of money behind them are probably never going to get started and realize the success that they could.

The fourth point in minimizing risk is to use a trusted outside financial advisor. And this can be somebody you know that works in the financial side of things, such as a banker, maybe a retired banker, a CPA, or a person with some business finance experience. Let this person help you review your plans and progress and develop accurate financial reporting. Even if you're starting out with very little money, in order to do the best you can, it's important to have someone help you make that money go as far as possible and avoid the mistakes. Many times people work for a whole year or two years and then run out of money and find out the reason they ran out is because they didn't have a good handle on their expenses. They could have avoided that whole mistake and minimized their risk by having good financial reporting. You don't have to spend a lot of money with a professional CPA. For example, I believe you can usually find some acquaintances or somebody that has some background that will be willing to help you get your financial reporting in order as you start. So these are my points on minimizing risk for this entrepreneur.

Describe your current enterprise.

We are a manufacturing company. One of the things we are doing that's perhaps somewhat against the trends is that we are trying to be fully engaged in manufacturing. If you look at manufacturing, quite often these days it is more or less an outsourcing of all aspects of fabrication and production and then simply an assembly operation and warehousing. For us, we've tried to design our product and design our facility to do as much of the manufacturing of the product as we can in house. We literally bring in raw steel, about ten to fifteen thousand pounds of steel per day, and cut it up to make the parts that are used to manufacture our frames and working parts of the equipment. We do buy a lot of component parts. About 60 percent of the dollar value of the machine are such purchased components as engines, transmissions, seats, wheels, and gearboxes. The rest of the machine is all done under our roof; virtually all of the fabrication except molding plastic is done in our factory. In addition to the fabrication department, we have a welding department where we weld the assemblies. Approximately twenty-six welders are required; it takes one welder per machine per day, and we're building twenty-six machines a day, and we have twenty-six welders. We have a finishing area where all the welded and metal parts are cleaned and painted. Then parts go into assembly operations where there are assembly lines. There is a warehouse operation where component parts are stored upon receiving them and then distributed and brought into assembly. There is a shipping area where the machines are staged and shipped out in typically truckload quantities. That comprises our operation.

We work with independent distributors. We don't have our own marketing group, such as marketing employees that are physically outside the company. We work with fifty independent distributors who, with their own operations, purchase the product from us and distribute them to dealers who in turn sell the product to the end customer. The control that we maintain is over the process of how our equipment is sold. We have a single channel of marketing that we think is important as a servicing channel. We believe that this type of equipment needs to be serviced through a single channel.

Where are your fifty distributors?

We have thirty distributors in North America, which includes the United States and Canada. Twenty are in Europe, Australia, and New Zealand, and there are a few more remote locations such as South Africa and Israel.

Describe your feelings toward your enterprise. Would you sell your enterprise? Would you work for a new owner? Would you take on a partner?

One of the first things that we feel about the enterprise is that this enterprise is much more than just us, the original owners. It is a family business, and we own the company, the facility, and the basic manufacturing operations. But this project and this enterprise are an investment that has been made beyond just us, and I'm primarily referring, first of all, to our employees. We have an average employment length now of around six years for 145 people, so we have 700 or 800 years of experience here. We believe that these people have put a lot of their lives into this enterprise, and that's a concern to us. In addition, a lot of investment has been made by the people who have created the marketing channel: the distributors and the dealers. These people are independent from us, and I would like to say that for every dollar we've invested, there's at least $2, $3, or $4 that other parties have invested to help get this product to the market.

When we look at the enterprise, we try to look at it as a whole circulation process that starts with our suppliers, our employees, the distributors and dealers, and the customer. And all of that is a process that, again, goes way beyond just us as owners. So when you ask the question, "Would you sell your enterprise?" one of the first things that would come to mind is that we could say we could cash out of this thing and walk away. But we feel a sense of responsibility towards other people who have invested. We haven't seen too many cases when companies are sold that the investment of some of these other people is really being protected. The story told by new owners is to leave everything the same, and all these people will still have the same opportunity that they have right now, but the truth and practical experience suggests that's usually not the case. Usually these opportunities are in one way or another lost to the people who invested, and that would be a great concern to us in thinking about selling the enterprise and walking away.

"Would you work with a new owner?" Again this issue of control is a big issue with us. Remember my dad's experience years ago giving control to other people and staying on with the company and seeing what happens with other people in control? One of the problems we find with new owners is that constant battle between long-term and short-term thinking. This kind of enterprise is based on long-term thinking, or should be, in order to continue to succeed. So often new owners will come in, and their designs and their ideas are involved in short-term results. So in that sense, "Would we work with a new owner?" I would say no. If we felt we had to sell and give up control, then really we wouldn't want to stay and assist in the continuing of the operation.

"Would we take on a partner?" Again, some of the very same issues would be the control aspects. Not to say that all these other people would have wrong thinking, and we're the only people that think right, but a lot of the ideas that have helped us succeed are those having the right perception of who we are and how we got here and where we're going. When you begin to bring in other people and give them control, they may have a whole different view. They can come in with a real distorted view of how you got there and therefore have a distorted view of where you want to go.

How do you stay competitive with other firms in your industry?

I've talked a little bit about being a self-contained manufacturing company, and one of our ideas as a smaller company is to be an active company and an agile company in the sense of being able to be very responsive. We're going against some giant competitors. We've got John Deere and Toro; Textron has Jacobsen and several other turf equipment companies under one of their divisions. These are huge companies. How do we compete with people like that? We believe we need to play to our strengths. We believe our strengths are to be able to move quickly, to keep our product well attuned to where the market's at, to have a better customer service and support available by working with people that are specializing in this kind of equipment. They're very specialized in what they are doing; that's the people we're trying to work with in the marketing side.

My brother and I typically try to attend quite a few of the trade shows and dealer meetings where we can talk face-to-face with customers. We feel that this allows us to keep well attached to the end customer so that we can hear what they're saying and what they're thinking and keep our product responsive to what people are looking for. Many of our big competitors try to do all these same things, but they're rather insulated by their sheer size and numbers of people who are involved in shaping products and markets. They tend to get bogged down so that they're behind a smaller, more aggressive and agile company.

Are they the companies that are producing bulldozers, farm tractors, and mowers maybe in the same shop?

Sure. In fact, some of our competitors' strategy recently seems to be acquisitions. Toro has been very active in that. One of the theories seems to be that the company is going to be the one-source supplier for everything the buyer needs, for example, as a landscape contractor. "Come to us, and we have everything." That's quite a strategy, and some companies are big enough to do it. But we feel the specialist (and we think of ourselves as a specializing company) provides a certain kind of equipment for a certain kind of customer, and that allows us to be very good at what we do. A company like Toro, or some of those that are trying to handle a broad range of products, tends to be compromised. It's hard not to be average when you're doing so many things.

What innovations have you implemented to improve your enterprise?

I've alluded to the fact that we've been able to bring as much of the production of the product under our roof as possible. That again allows us to be very quick and responsive to changes. For years our company has continued to follow a pattern. We don't make a lot of parts drawings unless we go to an outside vendor. If it's done in house, most of our parts are produced by patterns, and that sounds in some ways kind of backwards. However, it actually works very well and allows us to quickly make design changes and improvements in our product. While the competitors are still making drawings and trying to circulate them through their approval process, we've already got the part on the assembly line and have made the improvement. That kind of manufacturing has been innovative but not a highly technical approach. We're not afraid of technology, but we haven't been awestruck by it to the sense of saying, "Well

I guess if we can afford one of these robots, we'd better get one because it's a high-tech product." We've tried to put these things to the end of a pencil and make sure that the technology would pay for itself. We have not been afraid of technology and have begun to move some technology into our process that's helped us. I think it's an innovation to take that viewpoint and try to not get either over- or under-zealous in the use of technology products in manufacturing.

What are some special innovations in the Walker mower itself?

We tried not to copy what had been done before, and we were able to come up with several innovations that we were able to patent or get some patent claims on. Several machines were on the market with lever steering or steering levers rather than a steering wheel. We looked at those machines back in the 1970s and at that time, all these machines were large machines. They were physically pretty big. Our innovation was to think in terms of making a machine that would be compact enough to fit into a tight area. The theory was that a small machine can fit in and do the tightest work and also some of the bigger work, but the big machine can only do one kind of work—big work. It can't do the small work. That's a simple idea, but very few companies that have tried to compete with us have tried to design compact machines. They have ended up with machines a little bit bigger than ours. That has helped us because every degree of increase in size is a loss of versatility and the ability to fit in and do the mowing that we're able to do. So that's given us a real competitive edge, and it's innovative to be able to design something compact. Anybody can put together a big contraption, but to be able to design a very small, compact machine requires a lot of skill in the design process.

All of our competitors collect grass clippings with an attachment on an existing side delivery mower deck and have some kind of a hopper or catcher on the back of the tractor. For our design, we looked at some farm harvester equipment, hay cutters, and so forth, that had a rear discharge that would go into a blower similar to a hay cutter we were familiar with from our days on the farm.

We miniaturized that idea and brought the grass clippings right through the middle of the tractor into a blower that blew into a hopper and that allowed us to keep the machine quite a bit more compact. Again, the idea was to make it as compact as possible. We eliminated any side chutes and any apparatus hanging off the end of a mower deck and that was a great innovation. Several competitors now have borrowed that idea. We didn't get a patent on that, so it's been used several times. That has been a great innovation for us, and we were pioneers of that. An extra part of the grass collection system is an oscillating delivery spout inside the catcher. That was something we got a patent for because the spout would oscillate back and forth and spread the clippings inside and deliver a full load of clippings. Otherwise, it would tend to pile up in one corner, and you'd have to stop and empty the hopper or it would clog up. Along with that we came up with a "full" signal, which again was another patent. A little vane was put on the end of the moving spout, and as soon as that began to touch the grass clippings, a horn signal would tell the operator it was time to stop mowing or otherwise they were going to overfill the catcher.

A number of other competitors have tried to come up with something that would work better than that or at least match that performance. There have been several pretty interesting designs, but ours has proven to be very effective. For example, Toro has a machine with an electric eye in their grass catcher, but that hasn't really proven to be as durable or reliable as our system. The last innovation is a system on a steering lever type machine which we call forward speed control. With our competitors, in order to operate the steering levers, you actually hold the levers forward to go forward and hold them back to go backwards and pull one or the other to turn. On our machine with the forward speed control, the levers are actually positioned forward by an extra control lever and that allows the machine to simply cruise forward without your hands on the controls eliminating a lot of tedium of sitting there holding levers to keep the machine going. This really functions like a cruise control on an automobile.

Explain your offset transmissions that allow you to narrow your width.

That was an innovation when my brother first designed the machine that allowed us to reduce the width of the machine. Our competitors had basically stacked their transmissions side to side, which defined the width of the machine. In our machine we put one transmission ahead of the other one and drove them with a common drive belt and that shaved several inches from the width. This allowed us to have a thirty-four-inch width and be able to run a thirty-six-inch rear discharge deck. Most of our competitors who have tried to design these kinds of machines have ended up more in the forty-inch range. We're six inches more compact with that concept.

Is there anything you want to add to this?

I have talked in the past about some of the responsibilities that come with being an entrepreneur. I've already alluded to the fact that the company is not just you. Sometimes it may start out as just you, but pretty quickly you have employees that come to work with you. They begin to put their lives into the project and their talent; you have people who invest in helping you market the product; customers who invest in your product; and suppliers who are supporting you. For all of these people, in one way or the other, you have some responsibility. A lot of times that's not understood. It's something to think about; whether or not you want to have that kind of responsibility. The network again can surprise you, be overwhelming sometimes.

I've talked about the importance of integrity. On a long-term basis you're not going to operate a business unless you operate with integrity. Some businesses have been operating for a while on a dishonest foundation, but have no long-term prospect. Ultimately you need to ask yourself as an entrepreneur, "Am I a person who's willing to operate with integrity and make the hard choices that are going to be faced?" It's not easy. I think one of my biggest challenges is just telling the truth. There's a lot of pressure on you in a business to not always tell the truth, and yet that's the very foundation of a long-term business; the willingness to tell the truth no matter what the cost. That's something an entrepreneur needs to look at and see if they can be honest enough with themselves to ask, "Am I a person who has the training and the ethics that will allow me to operate my business in this way?" Otherwise, you have no long-term future as an entrepreneur. It's interesting to look at how freely investment towards you will flow if people can trust you and rely on your character and person; people like bankers who are asked to underwrite in helping you accomplish your goals. It's interesting how freely investment flows if they feel like they can depend on your integrity.

Notes

1. Adam Smith, *An Inquiry into the Nature and Causes of the Wealth of Nations* ([n.p.], 1776), Book 1, Chapter 1.

2. Chris Freeman and Luc Soete, *The Economics of Industrial Innovation,* 3d ed. (Cambridge, MA: MIT Press, 1997), pp. 137–139.

3. Joseph A. Schumpeter, *The Theory of Economic Development* (Cambridge, MA: Harvard University Press, 1934), Chapter 2.

2

Capitalism and Entrepreneurship: Economic Differences

The Use of the Term "Entrepreneurship" in Economics

It appears that one of the earliest uses of the term "entrepreneur" (see Table 2.1), a French term for risk taking, was Richard Cantillon in the 1700s.[1] Cantillon correctly separated the activities of the capitalist from those of the entrepreneur. By the end of the 1700s, the French economist Jean-Baptiste Say had developed the term "entrepreneur" to mean the changing of resources from a lower productive use to a higher productive use. By the mid-1800s, John Stuart Mill started associating the risk of the entrepreneur to make changes with the risk of the capitalist in hopes of a profit. Mill rightly recognized both endeavors as taking a risk; but he confused the underlying issues by combining both endeavors as if there was only one activity, and the risks in each were seen as a collective risk.

Much of economic theory has failed to accommodate the contributions of the entrepreneur. Risk is assumed to be the domain of the capitalist, with profit as the most important and only reward for taking risks. Adam Smith, often referred to as the father of

Table 2.1

Timetable for Early Economists Using the Term "Entrepreneurship"

Year	Economist	Contribution
1725	Richard Cantillon	Separated activities of capitalist from entrepreneur
1776	Adam Smith	Discussed entrepreneur but associated activities with the capitalist
1803	Jean-Baptiste Say	Defined entrepreneur as improving the state of resources used in production
1871	John Stuart Mill	Associated capitalist and entrepreneur together through risk
1934	Joseph A. Schumpeter	Defined entrepreneurs as sociologically distinct individuals; separated entrepreneurship from the role of the capitalist

western economics, referred to the entrepreneur as a capitalist in his classic writing, *The Wealth of Nations*. Although Smith adequately described the activities of the entrepreneur, he missed a great opportunity to emphasize the entrepreneur and instead credited the capitalist for taking risks and attempting to attain profits in the process.

Neoclassical economics developed an entire theoretical body based on the efforts of the capitalist with the complete absence of the entrepreneur. This theoretical framework went unchallenged until Joseph A. Schumpeter reintroduced the entrepreneur and the related activity of innovation into economic analysis in the 1930s. While his descriptive definition seems to explain both an application of innovation as well as a role for the entrepreneur, this definition was a source of much published criticism. Many economists, including P.M. Sweezy,[2] W. Leontief,[3] J.W. Angell,[4] D.M. Wright,[5] O. Lange,[6] and W.W. Rostow[7] began a professional debate about innovation and its relevance to economics. Some writers thought Schumpeter's definition was too narrow; others, too broad. Some critics thought this definition to be a tautology explaining very little, while others thought it was so open and "all encompassing" that it explained everything and therefore added little useful knowledge to the field of economics.

The attention received by Schumpeter, both critical and in support of his works, helped define innovation as an economic tool. This academic interchange led to the transfer of the concept of innovation from the realm of speculative reasoning in the scientific laboratory to a functional model of the capitalist process allowing for both new firms and the rise of new men to business leadership. This appears to be the real meaning of entrepreneurship. Innovation is, therefore, the function of a sociological type of individual known as the entrepreneur.[8] Although the entrepreneur has not become a part of microeconomic analysis, the innovative changes as outlined by Schumpeter are today recognized as a major driving force in any dynamic capitalist economy.

Among the early U.S. entrepreneurs and one of the most notable was Eli Whitney. Although Whitney is most well known for his development of the cotton gin, it was neither his greatest contribution, nor his most profitable. Supposedly, after watching a cat reach through a fence, attempt to catch a chicken by extending its claws, and end its pursuit with a paw full of feathers, Whitney envisioned the cotton gin. The gin (short for engine), consisting of a drum with metal wires protruding outward, was rotated against the slats of a bin of cotton. This process separated the cotton fibers from the seed. The gin immediately increased the labor productivity in the cotton industry by a factor of ten. Whitney, for many reasons and a lengthy story, never financially benefited from the development of the cotton gin. However, the gin greatly increased the profitability of cotton farming and increased the demand for slavery, one of the worst social events in U.S. economic history.

Whitney's greatest innovation and best entrepreneurial contribution to the ongoing Industrial Revolution in the United States was the development of interchangeable parts for the production process of assembled goods. Originally the U.S. government contracted with Whitney to produce guns for defense purposes that had interchangeable parts to aid soldiers on the battlefield. This concept of interchangeable parts was quickly transposed to all areas of economic production and the mass production assembly line soon followed.

Like capitalists, entrepreneurs were involved in taking risks in the economy. However, these risks were much different for each of the two groups, and both the endeavors and the rewards were quite contrasting for capitalists as opposed to entrepreneurs. One must understand the varying types of risk before a delineation of capital risk and entrepreneurial risk can be assessed.

Evaluating Risk

A common myth is that because capitalists, producers, entrepreneurs, and in general, business people take risks in order to accomplish tasks, they are therefore risk seekers. This group of individuals—and in fact most individuals—do not seek risks. In fact, most people are risk averse by nature. Buying a $1.00 lottery ticket may be a fun, recreational way to gain enjoyment, but it is a terrible investment since failure has an extremely high probability. If buying a lottery ticket leads to excitement about the numbers drawn for the winner, fun conversation about the ticket purchase, or in general a fantasy about "what if," then the purchase has little harm. If however, the intent of the purchase is to win and not winning is a great disappointment, then the lottery possesses potential harm. This risk seeking leads to addictive gambling where increasingly larger amounts of money are wagered at extremely high probabilities of loss. Capitalists, entrepreneurs, and business people in general do not and will not buy a lottery ticket as an investment.

Sound economic decisions may include some degree of risk, but this risk, unlike a lottery ticket, is balanced against successful rewards and risk is always minimized whenever possible. Therefore, these decisions are made by individuals who are risk averse. It is sometimes mistakenly stated that an individual with a variable mortgage interest rate (one that will increase with increases in general interest rates) must be a risk taker or risk prone. This is an incorrect analysis of risk because it mistakenly views potential

Table 2.2

Risk and Outcome Table for Evaluating Types of Risk Takers

	Investment I	Investment II
Risk of loss	10 percent	20 percent
Required investment	2,000	2,000
Outcome if successful	10,000	11,000
Probable success	90 percent	80 percent
Net outcome if successful	8,000	9,000
Average value of investment	7,200	7,200

changes as high probabilities. In fact, there are three distinct groups of risk takers: (1) risk prone—individuals who seek out risky choices with potentially high gains, but low probabilities of success and higher probabilities of failure; (2) risk neutral—individuals who have no preference for more or less risky choices; and (3) risk averse—individuals who attempt to lower the probability of failure whenever possible. Most individuals fall into this third group and compulsive gamblers fall into the first group.

To determine if an individual is risk prone, risk neutral, or risk averse, several criteria must be met. First, the average outcome (probability of success times value if successful) must be identical for the proposed choices. Second, there must be different probabilities of success and failure for the choices. Also, the choices must be made clear to the risk taker such that the degree of risk becomes the choice. Table 2.2 meets this criterion and can be used to determine the type of risk taker for any individual.

From Table 2.2 it can be seen that Investment I has a risk of loss of 10 percent and an outcome of $10,000 if the investment is successful. Likewise, Investment II has a risk of loss of 20 percent and an outcome of $11,000 if the investment is successful. Because each investment in Table 2.2 is the same ($2,000) and the average value of each investment over time is the same ($7,200), an investor's choice between Investment I and Investment II can be used to determine the type of risk taker an investor would be. A person who would consistently choose Investment I would be classified as risk averse because the risk is lower, and the outcome of investment is equal. A person who would consistently show no preference between Investments I and II would be considered risk neutral, and an individual who would consistently choose Investment II would be considered risk prone. Again, most capitalists, most entrepreneurs and most individuals are risk averse. The purchases of health insurance, home insurance, and automobile insurance are examples of individuals attempting to lower the risk of loss while at the same time accepting some degree of risk, which is inevitable if one owns a home, drives an automobile, or just lives in a populated area.

Risk of the Capitalist and Risk of the Entrepreneur

Because both capitalists and entrepreneurs are, in general, risk averse, a different method of evaluating risk is needed to differentiate the two groups. Capitalists and entrepreneurs can be distinguished by the particular type of risk taken by each group. This is a very important distinction and helps separate capitalists and entrepreneurs. The capitalist takes a risk of potential loss of finances, with the possibility of gaining profits if the event is successful. This is a common capitalist venture where some degree of risk is incurred for some level of profits if the venture is successful. The risk is loss of investment compared to the possibility of profits if the event is successful.

The entrepreneur takes a risk, but that risk is quite different from risk for the capitalist. The entrepreneur takes a risk of change to make some process work more smoothly or more efficiently. Likewise, an entrepreneur may have an idea for a new product that will work better or be more useful. The entrepreneur may have no capital investment, the entrepreneur may not share in any profits if the change is successful, but nonetheless the entrepre-

Table 2.3

Comparing Capitalist Risk and Entrepreneurial Risk

	Capitalist	Entrepreneur
Type of risk	Financial	Change in process or product
Risk of loss	Lose invested money, dollars	Lost time, increased inefficiency; lack of acceptance of a new product
Potential gain	Profits	Smoother process, more efficient method of production; general acceptance of a new or improved product

neur is willing to change the way things are being done currently in an attempt to make the process work better or the entrepreneur may be willing to develop a new product. Thus, both the capitalist and the entrepreneur take risks, but the type of risks is different for each group. Table 2.3 attempts to summarize these differences.

Some examples of entrepreneurial activities may also help differentiate the activities of the capitalist from those of the entrepreneur. A plant manager, floor supervisor, or maintenance person may not be an investor in the company, may not have a chance to share in the company profits, and therefore would not be considered a capitalist. However, these individuals may be driven by a desire to make the plant, production floor, or assembly operation run more smoothly and efficiently. These individuals may constantly keep a watchful eye on ways to speed production, eliminate bottlenecks, or make the assembly process move more evenly with fewer stops, less slowdowns, and/or less downtime. The nature of each of these activities is entrepreneurial. Further, an entrepreneur may be driven by a desire to make a product that is useful to a large number of users or an improved product that is more useful.

Individuals who look at a common way of doing business and envision a smoother, better way and then implement necessary changes to accomplish that goal are entrepreneurs. For example, accounting firms for decades figured taxes payable for individuals as well as businesses using the same income minus allowable expense methods. An entrepreneurial tax accountant challenged this long-standing method by envisioning inputting all income and all allowable expenses into a federal tax code computer program that would try every different tax method and automatically choose the method that would tax the individual or business the least amount. This entrepreneurial effort has dramatically transformed tax accounting.

Another example of entrepreneurial behavior at this point may be helpful. The floor supervisor in an assembly plant may be confronted with a bottleneck problem where stations A, B, and C perform assembly processes. However, by noon Station A is far ahead of Station B, Station B is taking up floor space with unprocessed parts, and Station C is waiting for inputs from Station B. An entrepreneur may find a way to redesign the product, reorganize the assembly process, and/or restructure the floor assembly area to make the assembly line run more smoothly, more efficiently, with fewer slowdowns, less downtime, or at a faster rate. The end result might entail placing Station C after Station A and before Station B. Thus, the flow process of the assembly would likely work much more smoothly. An entrepreneur works to change the system to make it work better, likely with no thought or promise of profits. The individual is not a capitalist, but most certainly is an entrepreneur.

Pioneers, sod busters, prairie farmers, and most self-employed workers in the late 1800s and early 1900s were entrepreneurial because of a need to make do with what they had and a drive to make their operation work better. There is an old story of a banker, a cheese salesman, and an entrepreneur traveling west on a stagecoach. In the middle of Nebraska, fifty miles from the nearest outpost, a wheel lost its grease lubrication and was in danger of falling off the axle. In disgust, the banker told the driver, as well as the other two passengers, that if he did not arrive in Denver within two days that he stood to lose several hundred dollars. The driver explained that he had no grease and could not continue until the next stage came by their location in about four days. The entrepreneur learned that the cheese salesman had a 15 lb. block of cheese valued at twelve dollars. The entrepreneur convinced the banker to buy the cheese and have the driver pack the wheel with cheese, and they arrived in Denver in time for the banker to make his profit of several hundred dollars. This old example illustrates the role of the entrepreneur: make changes to get things done and make things work better. Obviously, the banker portrayed the role of the capitalist who risked twelve dollars with the possibility of making the trip to Denver within the allotted time for a large financial gain.

In today's world, an individual may be both a capitalist and an entrepreneur. However, it is very important to separate the tasks and risks, as well as the rewards, for each individual role in an effort to more clearly distinguish the capitalist part of the efforts from the entrepreneurial part of the efforts. If this separation is not made distinct, it becomes mistakenly easy to associate, mix, and confuse the role of the capitalist with the role of the entrepreneur. The danger in this confusion is that the perspective and importance of the entrepreneur can be lost, and in the process an important ingredient is missing from the formula that keeps the economy prosperous.

It appears that it was John Stuart Mill, one of the great classical economists, who began associating and interchanging the terms "entrepreneur" and "capitalist."[9] Mill viewed each as being associated with risk taking and, therefore, began associating the two terms as one endeavor. By associating the entrepreneur with that of the capitalist, the distinct activities and outcomes from each endeavor became blurred, and the entrepreneur and the capitalist were assumed to incur the same risk and attempt the same activities. This combining of the terms has more recently been compounded when journalist news reporters and other writers use the terms "capitalist" and "entrepreneur" interchangeably to make their use of vocabulary more varied and their articles more interesting.

It was the notable economist Joseph A. Schumpeter who succinctly defined and separated the domain of entrepreneur from that of the capitalist. While each takes a risk, that particular risk, the rewards as well as the endeavor, is quite different for the entrepreneur as distinguished from the capitalist. Schumpeter explained that the risk of the capitalist is one of finances for the gain of monetary profit if the individual is successful and one of monetary loss if the venture is unsuccessful. On the other hand, the risk of the entrepreneur is one of change to make the product or process better. The reward for the entrepreneur is the satisfaction of improving the product or the level of production, creating less downtime, fewer bottlenecks, or less inventory buildup, or in general, making the production process run more smoothly.

The capitalist may also be an entrepreneur, but in each case, there are separate activities and risks associated with the capitalist and activities and risks associated with the entrepreneurs. Joseph A. Schumpeter clearly distinguishes those activities of the capitalist from those of the entrepreneur. Schumpeter further separates the two activities when he states that the entrepreneur is a sociologically distinct individual. Schumpeter's analysis of the entrepreneur is the focus of the next chapter.

Entrepreneurial Biography 2: Barbara Houghteling

Name:	Barbara Houghteling
Company:	Alpine Ventures
Number of Employees:	7
Annual Sales:	$1 million

What events and/or people were present in your youth or early adulthood that you now realize influenced your becoming an entrepreneur?

That would be both of my parents, my grandparents, as well as the neighbors. I lived in an area where very few people were employees; they were almost all business owners. In my family, my grandparents, my mother, and my father were all self-employed with their own businesses. My grandparents had a baby bootie business that they started. I watched them, and they definitely influenced what I wanted to do. My father was an attorney with his own firm. My mother, when she was ready to start working, started a natural food store. It never even dawned on me that I might work for someone else.

Describe some of your early efforts at entrepreneurship.

When I was working for my mother at her natural food store, she gave me part of the storefront, and I opened up a little resale clothing store called Steppin' Out. I bought clothing from estates, and since this was in the 1970s, the retro look was very popular. I also sewed a few things and put them in the shop and took in a few other items on consignment. I discovered, though, that I didn't like having to man the retail shop. Shortly after that I married, and I realized that I wanted a manufacturing company. I liked what my grandparents had done with manufacturing the baby booties. I was trying to figure out which way to go, and because we were in a recession, there was not a lot of disposable income. I thought, babies and weddings were two things that can't wait for another day. So I focused on baby things, and I made quilts. I took leftover fabrics that I had and made them into pretty little baby patchwork quilts. I took them around to gift shops, and they sold them as baby quilts and also as lap quilts for people in wheelchairs or the elderly. It actually brought in enough money that I got going a little bit on my own. I didn't have to work quite as much, and I could think about other things to do.

Then I started to get a little bit more creative about the baby things I was making. I developed a baby bib that had an elephant's head on it and held a pacifier with its trunk. A major bib company later successfully marketed a similar product. However, I couldn't get liability insurance for it. I was a small company and since the bib was an item that went around the neck with something hanging from it, I had to get liability insurance. So it was a lesson learned that whatever I was going to do, I had to be able to afford the liability insurance. Just to get some perspective of how my quilts and bibs were selling, I offered to work one day a week for free in the one baby shop in Winter Park where we were living. As I watched what people said and thought about different products, I tried to get an idea of pricing. There were some adorable baby booties in the shop that people kept looking at and saying, "Oh, I love these. I just wish they weren't so expensive." I went home and decided I was going to develop a bootie that could be made more quickly than those but had the same kind of appeal and that's how Scootees® were born.

When I was first married, my husband and I came up with a product called Ho's Honey Corn. It was a honey-based caramel corn made for my mother's natural food store. At the same time, we also had a tea that we sold at the restaurant at the natural food store called New Moon tea. People loved it, and we tried to figure out a way that we could actually bottle it. Now it's more commonly known as Chai. We made a spiced blend that people could make at home, and that was our first lesson in dealing with the food industry. To get our product into grocery stores, we had to pay for the space, and that was really difficult. The caramel corn, however, was literally the lowest profit margin item of the grocery store. Pet food was the highest.

What were some events or projects that were not successful, but contributed to your success as an entrepreneur?

That was definitely the tea and the honey corn. We lost money on them, but I sure learned a lot about pricing and checking out a market before I went forward with an idea. I learned that you didn't have a product until you could produce it at a price that people were willing to pay and that you could actually get on the market. I barely broke even on my early baby products. They certainly couldn't be considered a success, but I learned about the market. For instance with the quilts, by talking to people in the shops, I learned I was in a higher priced category. Even though they loved the quilts and they sold, they told me that when people had that much money to spend on a gift, in the $30 retail range at that time, they had a lot of choices. However, if they had only $10 to spend on a gift, their choices were limited. If I could come up with something in that price range, they could sell them all day long. So I learned from all of those experiences, and it helped me narrow down what I wanted to do.

What project stands out as one of your major entrepreneurial successes?

That would definitely be my booties, Scootees®. During the time I was working in the store, I came up with a better baby bootie. I woke up about 4 A.M. and had an idea in my head as to how I could make them. I have no idea to this day where the idea came from. It was a one-piece pattern that was very simple. With a picture of it in my head, I traced it out, made a pair, and then had to wait for my neighbor to wake up so I could try them on her baby, Dustin. They looked adorable and fit him perfectly. They stayed on his feet when he crawled, and when I went to take the booties, his mom said, "You can't have them." I realized then that I had something. From there I wanted to get them going as a real business. I met with a man from the University of Colorado's small business enterprise department who came up to Winter Park to talk to me. He gave me some ideas about how to get the business going. I started out with quilted fabric because I could buy it retail. I didn't have the money to buy wholesale fabric. I made a pattern, my husband traced them at the table and cut them, and I took them downstairs, bound the edges and put the elastic on. I brought them back upstairs, and my husband took a hammer and pounded snaps on them. When I had six pairs made, I sneaked into the Denver Merchandise Mart using our natural foods business card and posing as a buyer. I went straight upstairs to the baby floor looking at showroom windows until I found one that had small infant accessories. The store happened to be Baby Needs, which was a national chain of distributors at that time. They loved the booties, took them, and the next thing I knew they were in our first department store, and the business grew from there.

Your first large order was a semi truckload that you had to ship?

It was our first real order. The largest order we ever had was for about four dozen pairs of booties to a single Joslins store. I sent out press releases. I had a friend take black and white photos of Dustin wearing the booties and sent them to some trade publications. A man in Cherry Hill, New Jersey, saw it and called me to tell me he thought he could sell the booties for me. I sent him some samples, and he called me back about three days later and told me to sit down. He had taken them to Kids "R" Us. He had never had it happen before, but the manager ordered 17,000 pairs on the spot. We had no production, and no fabric. I hung up the phone and went to find my husband, a builder, who was doing a remodeling job. I told him to finish the job quickly; I needed help! We had a cancellation date three months later.

We started hustling as fast as we could to come up with money, production, everything. It was a crazy nightmare. We were literally hiring people out of parking lots to come and help us pack and tag booties. If we didn't meet the cancellation date, the entire order would be canceled. We'd put our house on the line with a home equity line of credit, and we finished the order just in time to put it on the truck. The truck driver had to get to the weigh station by 5:00 P.M. to say that they were shipped that day, and he took a nap in the truck waiting for us to finish boxing and making the last pair of booties. We got them on the truck, and he pulled out and got to the weigh station at five minutes until five. It was absolutely insane.

What event stands out as a major stumbling block that you needed to overcome as an entrepreneur?

I think the first major stumbling block was coming up with a way to be able to afford to spend the time to come up with a product and get it going. For that, my husband and I just worked together. We were never afraid to risk every penny we had to get something going. He believed in my idea that I could someday get a company going, which was a huge leap of faith. Then there is the fear of trying something and failing. I found that the first time I tried something and failed and walked away and tried something else, I was over that fear. I knew there was another day and another product and I learned something positive each time. I learned a lot. I could easily have just gotten completely discouraged and why I didn't, I really don't know.

There was a major stumbling block with a fire if I remember correctly.

We had shipped our first order to Kids "R" Us, which took an entire summer and everything we had. We were literally rationing our sleep; we were sleeping five to six hours a night because we didn't have time to even sleep. We got the order out and had just heaved a great sigh of relief. We had found a new building to move into because the building we were in was crumbling beneath our feet. We bought a little house and remodeled it and put our business into it all in one week. Our first order had only been in the stores for three days when they called us for a reorder. They had sold 500 pairs the first day. We were thrilled with the reorder for 9,000 pairs. We started hustling to get that order out. We had three distribution centers and had the order to the first distribution center in California ready to ship. We called the company on a Friday for a pickup on Monday, went home Friday night, and got a call at 1:00 A.M. Saturday that our building that housed the business was on fire. It was a faulty chimney; it was a heat-o-later fireplace we used for heating. The entire structure burned down, and we thought it was the end of everything. Fortunately, our insurance covered us at the wholesale price of the booties, not our cost, because every bootie in the building was sold. They were all waiting for delivery, so they gave us the wholesale cost.

In the end the fire, even as much as we were devastated and really didn't know if we could recover from it at first, turned out to be a good learning experience. It forced us to update everything. In a way, the booties that were the sizes and colors that could have been better were destroyed, yet we were paid for them. Then we were able to update everything. It allowed us to get rid of our antiquated accounting system and switch to a computer. It was a huge stumbling block to get over, but we learned from it. I called Kids "R" Us Monday morning—this was right before Christmas—and told the buyer we had had a fire. I could tell she really didn't believe me and thought it was just an excuse. I offered to ship the sizes and colors she needed most, and I would send them second day air UPS at my expense. We didn't make a lot of money on that order, but I won a true client. I knew she would stick with us forever, and she really appreciated what we did. Winning the Kids "R" Us account was our big break.

What advice could you give someone who has aspirations of becoming an entrepreneur?

I thought about this question for a long time. When I meet people who are thinking about doing something like this, they are generally already people who have the same kind of drive that I have or they wouldn't be thinking that way. They're not happy working for someone else or doing what they have been doing. One looks for inspiration. I checked a lot of books out of the library and read every success story I could find. I found the people around me, for whatever reason, were always naysayers. It was always, "What makes you think you can do that?" My answer was always, "How do you think every product out there on the market got there?" Anybody can do it. I needed something to counteract that.

One of the stories that really inspired me was about a man named Harry Coffman. He had different mail order companies . . . [that sold] inspirational tapes about how to get going in your own business. His approach was so much "you can do it," and that really helped. Don't share your idea with people who aren't going to be supportive. Don't become married to your first idea. Your first idea may be a learning experience. If you don't succeed the first time, try again. Start small at the beginning to give your idea a try. For instance with the booties, we started out by making a dozen and taking them to the baby stores to see if I could even sell them. When you enter a business, you must be honest with the owner. Tell them that you're just starting and think that you really have a good idea and ask them what they think. Ask them for their advice and if they would be willing to try them and give you some feedback. Take a leap and try.

Describe your current enterprise.

I have a lot of things going on. First and foremost, I have the booties. After selling those to a large company, I repurchased the rights in the Winter of 1996, and we started selling them mail order. I've recently licensed those to another company that's going to be selling them wholesale again to catalogs and stores. I don't even have a name for that business; it's just something I do myself. I developed baby products and licensed those for royalty deals with baby companies. I love that because it allows me to be totally creative, and I don't have to think about the marketing end. If I come up with a creative idea, I only have to make the prototypes and make sure it's something that they can produce and sell. Then I have another company called Loveland Creations, LLC. With Loveland Creations we produce personalized paper products. We have a poem that is used with the child's name, and then each poem is also personalized with the child's full name and birthdate, and each letter of the poem is given a rhyming phrase. The poem is for wishing the child all the good things in life and all the things you want for them in the future. With that, my role was that I came up with the idea and developed all the phrases. The last time I looked we had over 1,500 names in our database for poems, although we still get anywhere from six to twenty-five new names each week. My partner runs everything else including production and order fulfillment.

The other business I'm involved in is Colorado Creative Concepts, and I'm much more personally involved in this business. The product was brought to me. It's the only product I'm involved with that I didn't develop. It's a tote bag that zips into a five and one-half inch pouch. We call it a Bag-Along™. When you unzip it, the pouch actually becomes the bottom of a full-size tote bag. We started with some beautiful decorator fabrics that we found from an affordable source. I cut the decorator fabric and then send them to a factory to get them produced. We take them to gift shops and specialty stores. We have thirty theme groups with four or five fabrics available for each. We focus on museum gift shops and tourist venues. We're in Denver's Butterfly Pavilion and Ocean Journey, Colorado History Museum, and other museums around the country. It's an interesting niche because it's the tourist venue. Price wise, the tote bags are all made here in the United States, and they're not competitively priced with other products, but what we offer can't be made overseas because you can't afford to do all those different prints.

We're really focusing on making our product something really special, so when someone wants a purchase that will remind them of their visit, what we offer is both beautiful and useful. In two weeks we're going to be giving away 900 bags to each of the buyers who are attending the museum gift shop association trade show. Some of the fabrics we get now are beautiful tapestries, and I developed a product to use them in book covers for paperback books. We have strips of fabric left over that we use to make holders for credit cards or business cards called a card cache. The operator at the factory that makes most of my products came up with a triangular-shaped scarf with a brim on it that you tie over your head and makes a great fun hat. We also offer this Head Tog® to our accounts.

You have a very unique way that you have done your market testing at malls.

When I was coming up with ideas for the baby products, we needed a way to find out if people liked what we had. One licensed product of mine, the Tag-Along®, is a fanny pack with a leash attached. My daughter disappeared at a store one day, and I needed to develop something to keep track of her since there was nothing on the market that worked very well. I came up with a little fanny pack for her. Basically, it's an elaborate pocket with a belt and a stretchy leash that I can attach to it. I put it on her, and she loved it, but I didn't know what public perception would be toward it. So we went to the mall—she was a year and a half—and I walked through the mall with my daughter, while my husband walked perhaps a hundred steps behind us in order to catch comments from shoppers. He heard all positive comments, and that showed me that product testing doesn't have to be elaborate. Don't ask friends for opinions, however, because for some reason you will hear the negatives more than the positives. I also learned to never go up to anybody and say, "Oh, that's my product" because they never believe it. I'm always exploring for new ideas.

Describe your feelings toward your enterprise. Would you sell your enterprise? Would you work for a new owner? Would you take on a partner?

I don't think I'd sell my enterprise. I initially sold the booties business because it was a good time in my life to sell and have some time to myself. I'm much more inclined now to develop my enterprises in such a way that they don't take all of my time, and I still have time to be creative. But I like to remain active in my enterprises; I was very upset at the way the booties were handled, even though we had a great contract. When a huge baby products company contacted me about purchasing my booties, I later learned that one of the vice presidents had seen them on a baby at a family function and really liked them. So they researched my booties and knew exactly what they wanted to do with them before they contacted me. I was at my very first trade show—and the only one I ever attended—with the booties. The company contacted me and said they wanted to work out a contract to acquire the product. From there we met in Denver once, and they also flew us to the East Coast a couple of times. We hammered out a deal, and then when we were leaving, the man who I have great admiration for and who was president of the company at that time, looked at me and said, "Now we'll turn it over to the attorneys and see if they can ruin the deal." They very nearly did. I had our attorney do a rough draft and then their attorney did another one. They started making changes to it. Some things happened that I feel were pretty unscrupulous, and I called and actually said that I was pulling out of the deal. We were not going to be able to come to terms on the legal agreement.

After about three months we ended up with a whole book that was the agreement, and it was a good one. However, there was an administrative change at the company that made the division less of a separate entity and instead brought it more into the whole of the corporation. We lost the advantage of having the company functioning almost as a small company within a large company. Some decisions were made at that point that really destroyed the booties, although that certainly wasn't their intent. They wanted some huge retailers to take the booties and in order to do that they tailored the booties to meet their expectations of pricing.

They started making the booties overseas, and the quality of the fabric decreased, as did the quality of the nonslip soles. The overall quality of the product declined until they lost their market share. They could have been just as profitable, if not more so, making and selling the booties through different avenues. They then decided that the company was coming to an end itself. In fact, the company is now defunct. However, they discontinued the baby booties along with a number of other products. I had a buyback clause in my agreement, and I bought back the rights at a tiny percentage of what they had paid me. I worked trying to get them marketed again, but at that point the booties had developed a bad reputation, so now we're about five years after the buyback. The buyers have changed. The people who had babies at the time have changed, and there are enough people out there with good memories of the booties that are still looking for them, so two years ago we reintroduced them in their original form. We've heard from a lot of people who are thrilled to find the same booties and had wondered what happened to them. So we had a lot to overcome this time, but it looks like we have. It has just taken time while the market changed over.

I could never work for a new owner, though. I don't like to work for anybody. I like to make and implement decisions. I go crazy when people think they need to discuss things for three weeks before they make a decision. When I see something that needs to be changed, I like to make the change right now. I think you can miss so many opportunities by playing around trying to pretend you're a big business when you're not. I saw the company functioning so well because they ran it like a small business. I would go nuts if I saw somebody making a decision, and I didn't have any way to say that it shouldn't be done that way.

If I worked for someone, they would have the ultimate say. As close as I have ever come to that was with the company that acquired the booties when I had agreed to still consult. As long as we were working with the original team, that was a wonderful experience, but as soon as I wasn't working with the same team, I went out of my mind. I saw them making decisions that I knew were going to ruin the product. I knew that product inside and out. Somehow I had a good intuition about that product.

I have said I really didn't want to take on a partner, but I have three small children, and I still enjoy having businesses, so I need to spread my time around. I do have a wonderful partner in Colorado Creative Concepts, someone I know I can trust completely. She's very willing to get out and work, and she knows that I have the experience that she doesn't. We certainly consult on things but come to the same point of view very easily and that's worked out very well. My partner in Loveland Creations is the same situation. I really can't have a new business now without a partner.

But you share different responsibilities in that partnership, don't you?

Totally. In both businesses I told them I have the creativity, the experience, and the money to put into the business, but I don't have the time, and I hate sales. So in both cases, they are responsible for the organization of sales, the bookwork, the paperwork, and any employees we have, but I am the creative end. I like the marketing end, just not the sales.

How do you stay competitive with other firms in your industry?

That's a big issue right now because there's so much competition with prices from overseas. Part of the reason that I went into personalized paper goods was that there's no way to do that except here domestically. So we're competing with people on the same level as we are. We all have to deal with the same cost factors. I can't afford to make the booties the same way I used to when I had the company here, and I was having them made domestically. They're being made in Mexico, and the company that I'm working with works on a very small profit margin in comparison to what I was accustomed to when we did domestic production. I don't even want to try to compete with foreign manufacturing with the Bag-Along™. By targeting the tourist venues, we're not interested in the huge retail chains; we're not interested in any place that's selling anything cut-rate. We're making a very high quality product that is very appealing; a competitive product to ours that isn't nearly as attractive, but has the exact same function, retails for $8.40 at a local store in Fort Collins. I found out about that when I took ours in. Ours wholesales at $6.90. That's a big difference in price yet when I told them that I had a competitive product that they might like better, they bought mine immediately even at the higher price. So the way we're competitive is that we just simply make a more appealing product, and people pay for something more appealing.

Part of your competitiveness is also your creativity for those new products.

Absolutely. My products are problem-solving products. I like market-driven products where people see it and know immediately why they need it. I don't have to convince anybody. My newest product that I've just licensed is a sunshade that fits into strollers and car seats. It's unique and much different than other products out there; you have to keep safety in mind, especially with something being used in moving vehicles. The other new product is used for storing or toting baby supplies on car seats and strollers. Those are products that I wish I had had with my twins; they simply were not available. I didn't have time to develop them then, but now that my children are a little bit older, I took the time to produce them because I know they would have helped me and that they will help other people.

I've come to understand that products have a life cycle. Once products are developed and are new and unique, they sell very well. Then sales level off and maybe you have a nice steady product for a number of years, but they really only "hit" for a period of time. So I'm always coming up with new ideas. I realize that I don't have to have a patent on everything or be the only person out there with something. People are always so concerned that somebody is going to compete with them. Somebody is going to compete with you someday and a patent is only good if you have the deep pockets to defend it anyway. People are also frequently concerned that as soon as they show the product to someone, other people are going to use your idea and copy it. You have to get over that and go ahead with your idea. You need to do the best you can and if someone does copy it, maybe you can compete very well with them. If you can't, then maybe you can come up with the next idea.

What innovations have you implemented to improve your enterprise?

The first improvement I can think of revolves around the personalized paper products. For instance, when we first started, we just used the first name, and it turned into a poem with a little verse that I wrote. The verse was always the same with the name inserted. We found that due to our response rate on the mail order, we needed to increase the price slightly. In order to do that we needed to give more perceived value without increasing our own cost. The creative person at the company that produces the flyers for us suggested we add an area for a photograph. The problem with that is that it adds cost, and it is a hassle. Also, not everybody wants to add a photograph. But she said I needed to make it more personal in some way. So we added the first, middle, and last name plus their birth date. Therefore, when the poem is for Kyle or Michelle, it's only for one Kyle or Michelle. We did that and raised our price by an average of $3.00 per poem, which was significant, and our response rate stayed just the same. So that was an innovation that really helped. The price increase made it profitable at the response rate we were getting.

With the booties, nothing changed for a long time. The earliest change we made, before we really got going, was switching from quilted fabric to sweatshirt fleece. Sweatshirts were just becoming very popular, and I was looking for a fabric that was less troublesome than quilted fabric. I found a really heavy weight sweatshirt fleece much too heavy to make a shirt or pair of pants from but perfect for booties. People loved them because they had a really nice clean look, soft and thick on the inside, and had that feel that you would want to put on a baby—soft and durable. My booties were also the first booties with a snap on them. They've been copied at times since then, but my thought was that it was hard to tie a bootie on a crawling baby, and ties come undone. Velcro isn't a good alternative because babies can easily open it, and it makes a neat sound, so they're enticed to keep taking their booties off. Another innovation occurred when we first started selling our booties that were wholesaling at $4.00 a pair. The most expensive bootie retailed at $3.95 a pair. We were very expensive. Our booties were retailing at $7.95 when other booties were selling mostly at $2.95, some $3.95. Our booties are a comfortable alternative to shoes so I coined the term "soft shoes." I wanted people to understand that this was an alternative to a pair of shoes, and even though $7.95 was expensive for a pair of booties, it was inexpensive for a pair of shoes, and they were easy to walk in. I read some articles written by pediatricians telling people that babies need to be able to grasp with their feet when they walk, and so we used that in our marketing. Changing to the sweatshirt fleece, adding the snaps, and coining the term "soft shoes" really made a difference.

With the bag, the innovation was definitely coming up with our unique way of sourcing fabric. In fact, that's what sold the manager of the store I took them to in Fort Collins. She said her mother was a decorator and that these were really beautiful fabrics. So that was our little trade secret; we came up with something that really works. When anyone else wants to know how we did it, our answer is that we came up with the idea by chance and saw the opportunity. Another idea was the idea of using themes. The Museum of Nature and Science in Denver wanted dinosaurs and Egyptian prints because those are two of their most popular exhibits. We took swatches of Egyptian, dinosaur, and Vikings fabric to them and showed that we could tailor to their needs and go the extra mile to come up with something for them. It works with their venue and won't be the same as what people are seeing someplace else. We try to come up with things for people that are not intimidating so they know right away how it's going to work and how they're going to use it. They don't need an instruction manual, and they usually don't want one.

Notes

1. Jacob Oser and William C. Blanchfield, *The Evolution of Economic Thought*, 3d ed. (New York: Harcourt Brace Jovanovich, 1975), p. 39.

2. P.M. Sweezy, "Professor Schumpeter's Theory of Innovation," *Review of Economic Statistics* (February 1943): 93–96.

3. W. Leontief, "Implicit Theorizing: A Methodological Criticism of the Neo-Classical School," *Quarterly Journal of Economics* (February 1937): 337–351.

4. J.W. Angell, *Investment Business Cycles* (New York and London: McGraw-Hill, 1941), p. 332.

5. D.M. Wright, *The Economics of Disturbance* (New York: Macmillan, 1947), p. 34.

6. O. Lange, "A Note on Innovations," *Review of Economic Statistics* (February 1943): 19–25.

7. W.W. Rostow, *British Economy of the Nineteenth Century* (New York: Oxford University Press, 1948), p. 29.

8. Joseph A. Schumpeter, *The Theory of Economic Development: An Inquiry into Profits, Capital Credit, Interest and the Business Cycle* (Cambridge: Harvard University Press, 1934), p. 66.

9. John Stuart Mill, *Principles of Political Economy*, 7th ed. (London: [n.p.], 1871).

3

Entrepreneurship and Innovation

Schumpetarian Analysis of Innovation

As was pointed out in chapter 2, Joseph Schumpeter classified the entrepreneur as a sociologically distinct individual. This person is characterized as one who sees an opportunity, seizes that opportunity, and creates a new product, changes a production process, or otherwise creates a new marketable contribution to the economy. Schumpeter termed this activity "innovation" and claimed innovation as the sole domain of the entrepreneur. Schumpeter defined innovation as activity that leads to a new production function, and he listed five specific acts where innovation would lead to a new production function. These are listed in Table 3.1 and are described as follows:

1. *The introduction of a new good*—that is, the entrepreneur would find a potentially saleable good that was not currently available to consumers and provide it in the market;
2. *The introduction of a new method of production*—this innovation would typically involve a different production scheme where changing the existing inputs could lead to greater output, the per-unit cost of production could be lowered, or new inputs could be used in place of existing inputs;

Table 3.1

**Joseph A. Schumpeter's Five Innovations Leading to
a New Production Function**

1. The introduction of a new good

2. The introduction of a new method of production

3. The opening of a new market

4. The conquest of a new source of supply of a raw material

5. The carrying out of a new organization of an industry

---

3. *The opening of a new market*—this innovation might en-
    tail sales to a new region, sales to consumers or consumer
    groups not previously thought to be potential buyers, or
    renaming or viewing the product as a new market product;

4. *The conquest of a new source of supply of raw materials*
    —oftentimes as a resource supplier becomes comfortable
    with supplying raw materials to a product producer, there
    is a tendency to decrease the raw material quality or in-
    crease the price of the input resource. As new resource
    suppliers are developed, the increased resource quality or
    decreased cost will be reflected in the new production
    function;

5. *The carrying out of a new organization of an industry*—
    Schumpeter described this as an entrepreneur breaking into
    a monopoly market where prior competition did not exist
    or creating a condition where the entrepreneur could enter
    into a monopoly market position.

Any one of these cases was considered by Schumpeter to be innovation and was, of course, brought about by an entrepreneur.[1]

Some of these five cases will initially affect the supply of products, while other cases may initially influence the consumer or
demand for products. While this distinction has created much con-

troversy about demand-induced or supply-induced changes in the market, it is clear that eventually all five cases will affect the production or supply of products.

Schumpeter viewed these changes as not having a continuous flow in a market economy but, rather, lumpy or big jumps in the economic changes that come about in a market. These changes would occur together and create an expansionary economic cycle where one innovation would lead to others and set off a chain reaction of innovations. These innovations would likely be related and set off an expansionary phase of a business cycle. Once the new markets were opened, new material supplies found, new methods of production realized, and so forth, the old methods of production and old markets would become obsolete. Schumpeter referred to this process as "creative destruction." That is, innovation leading to new products and new ways to produce would render obsolete the old products and old ways to produce.

Schumpeter also made a clear and strong distinction between invention and innovation.[2] Invention was referred to as creating ideas or visions, including ideas and visions about products and production. This is quite different from innovation, where the entrepreneur would "do" things differently. Innovation is the act of using an invention to make new things or to make things differently. Again, the entrepreneur's activity is called innovation, and it is the act of getting things done.

Invention is usually associated with discovery of new ideas, concepts, or material items, but is normally confined to the realm of speculative reasoning in the scientific laboratory. Once this invention is transferred to the business sector and put into place to change the production function, it then becomes innovation. This is the real meaning of entrepreneurship. Innovation is therefore, as Schumpeter stated, the function of a sociological type of individual known as the entrepreneur. That is, the entrepreneur takes an invention (simple or complex), applies it to an industrial process and the new production function that results from this application demonstrates the presence of innovation.

Innovation is commonly associated with a change in technol-

Figure 3.1 **Per-Unit Losses for a Firm in a Purely Competitive Industry**

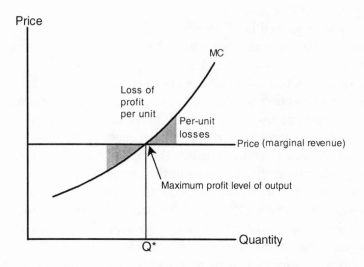

ogy, and there are four stages of development through which technology must progress to become an innovation. These four stages include research, development, demonstration, and commercialization and can generally encompass all activities from the scientific laboratory to the marketplace. These four stages will be more fully discussed in chapter 4.

There are four broad areas where much of the economic rationale for implementing innovations with a firm rests. The first area is that of a firm in a heavily competitive market where price is established not by the firm but rather by the industry. In this case increased profits require cost reductions and, likewise, innovation is a key to reduce costs. To explain, if a firm is selling product at a price equal to marginal cost, increased sales will only reduce profits while reducing per-unit cost of production will increase profit. This reduction in profits can be seen in Figure 3.1. Implementing innovation to reduce cost of production will lead to success (profits) for the entrepreneur. This was referred to by Schumpeter as a new method of production that is one result of innovation.

To summarize, a firm facing a competitive market as described

Figure 3.2 **Comparing the Use of Innovations in Competition and Monopoly**

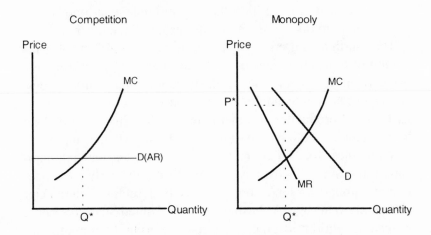

in the above competitive figure will maximize profits at Q. That is, at $MR = MC$ (in this example $AR = MR$) maximum profits for this firm will be realized. If there is an attempt to gain market share and quantity is increased (pushed rightward), then $MC > MR$ and total profits will be reduced. Therefore, market share is not a legitimate concern in a competitive market whereas decreases in per-unit costs of production are legitimate avenues to increase profits. Innovations can yield these results.

In the second area, one in which there is less competitive markets, market share becomes more important. In these markets, marginal cost is less than price and therefore an increase in sales will increase profits. This can be seen in Figure 3.2. Innovations leading to improved products, improved delivery timing, reduced pricing, and so forth will gain market share through increased sales. If market share is important and increased market sales is an objective, then implementing innovations in the above areas is an obvious choice for the entrepreneur.

The third area used as an economic rationale for implementing innovation is to meet the objective of creating, maintaining, or increasing monopoly control. A firm that has sole control of a new product, a new technology, or a new production process has usually ensured monopoly control. It is not uncommon to find companies that incur a large financial cost to implement innovations in an attempt to discourage new entrants into the industry.

The fourth area used as an economic rationale for implementing innovation is to reduce or eliminate control of input suppliers over a firm. New methods of production, new input combinations, or new production technologies can reduce input use of a particular factor of production. Furthermore, at times this can even lead to the complete elimination of the need for a particular input.

While these four areas are currently accepted as paths to innovation in business today, they originate from the early classification of rationale for innovation explored by Joseph A. Schumpeter some sixty years ago. As businesses in the United States reemerge as leading world traders, they are rediscovering the role of innovation as a path to profits.

Evolutionary and Revolutionary Innovations

Innovations in products and production processes can be categorized into two broad areas: evolutionary innovations and revolutionary innovations.[3] Generally, innovations occur within a firm and progress incrementally, allowing the firm to adjust to each small change. These innovations are referred to as evolutionary changes. In the automotive industry, a new, more efficient carburetor system for the engine would be considered an evolutionary innovation. A more fuel-efficient transmission, less polluting emissions, and electronic ignition are other examples of evolutionary innovations in the automotive industry. These innovations allow the firms to adjust to new products and new production processes without major transitions in their product assemblies.

Another example of evolutionary innovations would be in agriculture. Improved planting and harvesting machinery has allowed for increased labor productivity and decreased per-unit production costs. Improved commercial seeds have led to higher yields and increased resistance to insects and spring frosts. These evolu-

Figure 3.3 **Innovations Leading to a Decrease in the Average Cost of Production**

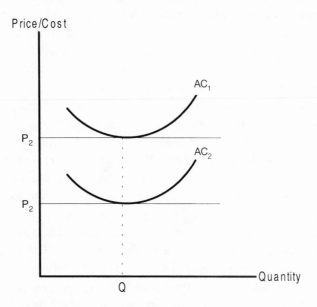

tionary innovations occur incrementally over time; they allow firms to adjust to the improved methods and, over time, become a necessity for the survival of the firm to remain competitive in that industry. Firms that do not, over time, adopt these evolutionary innovations will be forced to exit the industry because falling costs of production experienced by other firms and the resulting decrease in commodity prices will force the firm into economic losses. Evolutionary innovations occur quite often and are a normal process of change in virtually all industries.

Figure 3.3 can be used to describe the outcome for three different competitive firms in the presence of an evolutionary innovation. First, the firm that develops the innovation will be able to lower per-unit costs as depicted by a move from AC_1 to AC_2 in the figure. This development will allow the firm to experience short-run excess profits (which are per-unit profits of $P_1 - P_2$). As the second group of firms attempts to stay competitive, they will implement the innovation and will also move from AC_1 to AC_2. These firms will receive less or possibly none of the excess short-run profits as competition drives the price to the minimum of the lower average cost curve (AC_2). Third, those firms that do not implement the innovation will remain on the first average cost curve (AC_1). As competition drives the price to the minimum of AC_2 (P_2), these firms not implementing the innovation will experience economic losses and be driven from the industry.

On the other hand, revolutionary innovations are not part of the normal process of change and create major upheavals within an industry and generally spread to multiple industries. Revolutionary innovations represent major breakthroughs, create new industries, have drastic changes on existing industries, and often render some existing industries obsolete and doom them to failure and extinction.

The most obvious recent revolutionary innovation has been the development and realignment of the computer. The electronics industry's move from tubes to transistors to digital circuitry (which were evolutionary innovations) enabled the widespread use of computers. The revolutionary innovation, which was the widespread use of computers in virtually all areas of decision making, has not only changed the whole computer industry with more powerful units and units in almost every home, office, and school, but it has also influenced almost every aspect of economic activity. CAD-assisted design for new products, computer-generated inventory and orders, computer diagnostics for problems with products as well as the Internet use of advertising products and doing business (e-commerce) are but a few examples of the drastic, major changes brought about by the widespread use of the computer. The computer has revolutionized the way business is done across almost every industry in the economy.

Another revolutionary innovation was the automobile. The automotive transportation industry changed the whole American way of life. The advent of the suburbs, cross-country travel for vacations and family visits, movement of resources from suppliers to producers from coast to coast are but a few examples of the revo-

Table 3.2

Evolutionary and Revolutionary Innovations

Evolutionary	Revolutionary
Incremental changes to industry	Major changes to industry and usually inter-industry changes
Maintain competitive position within the industry	Creates new industries and destroys other industries
Relatively common within an industry	Rare and results in large-scale transitions
Short-run economic changes—temporary monopoly control	Long-run economic changes—in the structure of the firm or industry

lutionary change from innovations leading to the modern automotive transportation industry. Again, this innovation has changed almost all other industries and rendered some (like the livery) obsolete and extinct.

Once the distinction between evolutionary and revolutionary innovations has been made, it is also necessary to link the two types of innovations. Firms are required to make changes brought about by evolutionary innovations to remain competitive through improvements in products and production operations, yet this can lead to standardized products as well as standardized production methods. Once this happens, it opens the vast area of revolutionary innovations making the current standardized methods and products obsolete. This paradox bridges the ongoing evolutionary innovations (which are quite frequent and common) with the revolutionary innovations that create major changes across many industries. Table 3.2 helps identify some basic characteristics of evolutionary and revolutionary innovations.

As described in the previous section, a firm facing a monopolistic market will experience a downward-sloping demand curve. In this case MC < Price, and therefore, an increase in quantity at the same (current) price will increase profits. The firm in a monopolistic market will find market share important and increasing demand would be one way to increase profits. These changes (innovations) that are incremental and may lead to short-run excess profits are described as evolutionary innovations. Revolutionary innovations are generally longer term and will be discussed using long-run cost curves.

Historically, the long-run cost curve has been defined as changes in the size of the firm where an increase in size would lead to a decrease in per-unit cost when the firm was operating to the left of the minimum of the long-run average cost curve. However, even though this explanation was true in the 1950s and 1960s as firms continually pushed for larger operating facilities, it explains little in today's economic activity.

For example, an entrepreneur may be located in a small office building, with one computer and no additional employees, providing a service to area customers. A major change in the firm's operations may occur (a new computer program, a new advanced computer, a new market not previously serviced) that drastically changes the operation, the long-run average cost, and so forth but does not change the physical size of the plant, the amount of equipment, or the number of employees. This results in a larger long-run quantity of product or service.

This revolutionary (long-run) change cannot be explained with the traditional textbook explanation of moving downward along the long-run average cost curve by expanding the capacity of the firm, larger plant, more employees, more machines, etc. That is, the traditional explanation of a 10 percent increase in capacity leading to a more than 10 percent increase in output does not explain today's entrepreneurial firms in the long run.

Figure 3.4 helps connect short-run evolutionary innovations to the long-run revolutionary innovations. The firm always begins production at the tangency point between long-run average cost and short-run average cost (point A in the figure). As the entrepreneur makes evolutionary innovations, the firm lowers short-run costs per unit and consequently moves to the minimum point on the short-run average cost ($SRAC_1$ or point B). At some point the entrepreneur makes a revolutionary innovation and sees a drastic

Figure 3.4   **Comparing the Impact of Innovations in Short-Run and Long-Run Reductions**

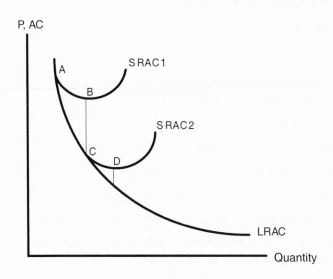

reduction in per-unit costs of the firm that moves the firm to a lower point on the long-run average cost curve (point C). Historically, this has been explained by an expansion of the firm (making the production facility larger). However, in today's modern firms this same result is possible with a revolutionary innovation and no change in productive capacity.

This process of moving from point A to point B through evolutionary innovations and from point B to point C through revolutionary innovations is known as the ratchet effect of cost reductions for a firm. However, the process of cost reductions is quite different from the historical explanation of building a larger plant, hiring more employees, and buying more machines.

Characteristics of the Entrepreneur

Joseph A. Schumpeter described an entrepreneur as a sociologically distinct individual. But, what is this sociologically distinct individual who innovates really like? There is much literature and

---

Table 3.3

Characteristics of an Entrepreneur

Self-esteem/self-confidence

Determination to finish a task and succeed

Persistence/diligence to keep trying

Willingness and ability to take calculated risks

Optimism about success of efforts

Creativity: Ability to see a need and end result of efforts

Focus: Orientation to continuously pursue a goal

Foresight/insight: Ability to see the future as it might be

Unwillingness to accept failure and the ability to learn from mistakes

Responsibility/ability to accept control and willingness to accept results

---

a very large array of characteristics trying to describe the activities of this type of person. Although no set of characteristics can describe all entrepreneurs, not all entrepreneurs exhibit the same exact set of characteristics. However, there are some similar characteristics that seem to be present in most entrepreneurs. This list of ten characteristics in Table 3.3 will be discussed here.

Self-Esteem/Self-Confidence

Most entrepreneurs are sure enough of themselves and their abilities to honestly believe that they can and will succeed at the task. This is not expressed as arrogance, but rather as a belief in oneself. Most entrepreneurs believe that if they work hard enough, long enough, and push the envelope of success, they will break through and succeed. Most entrepreneurs that succeed do not think that the act of succeeding was spectacular or extraordinary, but rather as another day's work.

Determination to Finish a Task and Succeed

Most entrepreneurs can singularly focus on a task and continue diligent effort until the task is finished and success accomplished. Most entrepreneurs can shut out the outside world (television, radio, and idle conversation around them) and solely focus on the task at hand. This single-mindedness can often lead people to assume entrepreneurs are unfriendly, rude, and/or self-centered because entrepreneurs often do not involve themselves in their surroundings and the people around them. However, it is this ability to be determined to succeed that allows entrepreneurs to finish the task at hand.

Persistence/Diligence to Keep Trying

Most entrepreneurs have the attitude that they will/must keep trying until they succeed. The old saying, "If at first you don't succeed, try, try again," is quite characteristic of entrepreneurs. Henry Ford had not been successful in previous ventures with machine shops and small engines when he decided to build an automobile. Colonel Sanders came out of retirement to start and build the most successful quick-food chicken restaurant franchise in the United States. Most successful entrepreneurs do not get it just right on the first attempt, but persistence allows changes that ultimately lead to success.

Willingness and Ability to Take Calculated Risks

As seen in chapter 2, the risk taken by an entrepreneur is for change to make a new product or change to make a production process work more smoothly and efficiently. However, entrepreneurs, like most people, are risk averse and minimize risk whenever possible. On the other hand, when risk is required in order to undertake a task, the entrepreneur stands ready and willing to accept this calculated risk as necessary to be successful. People who hesitate or worry about taking risks when necessary do not fit the characteristic of an entrepreneur.

Optimism About the Success of Efforts

Optimism is described as the belief that actions will lead to the best possible event or outcome. Most entrepreneurs have the confidence that their efforts will yield success. This confidence is coupled with the willingness to keep working until success is achieved. Most entrepreneurs have the belief that I can, I will, and I will keep working until I do. Entrepreneurs do not accept failure, but see failed attempts as "temporary setbacks" on the road to success. Entrepreneurs do not see problems as obstacles, but rather as "opportunities" to solve as part of the drive toward success.

Creativity: Ability to See a Need and the End Results of Efforts

The single most described characteristic of entrepreneurs is creativity. In general, this characteristic is the ability to see things differently, to see a product that is not currently available but would be viewed positively by consumers. It is the ability to see the end result of a production change in order to make the production process run more smoothly. Entrepreneurs take a risk to make a change, but normally they have the insight to see the end result of this change. This insight or creativity allows the entrepreneur to be the first to make changes and push toward a successful result.

Focus: Orientation to Continuously Pursue a Goal

There are many people in society who get an idea, get quite excited, and pursue that goal, but somewhere along the path they lose interest and stop pursuit. This is not the path of the entrepreneur. The ability to keep focused on the end result and the ability to continue pursuing that end is a common characteristic of an entrepreneur. College students that lose focus of a college education and stop pursuing that goal will drop out of college. Statistically, the most recognized common trait of an entrepreneur is a college degree. It appears that the focus and pursuit of a college degree is quite similar to the focus and pursuit of goals that are required of successful entrepreneurship.

Foresight/Insight: Ability to See the Future as It Might Be

It would have been quite difficult to live in the late 1800s in a world transported by horse and carriage and to envision a world being transported by the automobile. However, Henry Ford did just that. Entrepreneurial foresight/insight is not always that grandiose, but entrepreneurs possess the ability to see how ideas could be turned into products to make the world around us different—even in quite small ways. In order for entrepreneurs to make changes to products and production processes, they must first possess the foresight and insight to see how those changes will impact the future.

Unwillingness to Accept Failure and the Ability to Learn from Mistakes

Most entrepreneurs look at failure as simply part of the learning process toward achieving success. Instead of being viewed as a failure, entrepreneurs analyze the process and results and use that information and knowledge for continued attempts at success. A typical response from entrepreneurs is that "I see what I did wrong and I will do much better on the next try." This unwillingness to accept failure is part of the reason that entrepreneurs eventually succeed. This learning process is repeated until there is a satisfactory outcome. This is often part of a continuum where each trial event is made better by correcting prior mistakes.

Responsibility/Ability to Accept Control and Willingness to Accept Results

Entrepreneurs generally have the characteristic that allows them to take control of a situation and then accept the end results. They do not rationalize the situation in an attempt to blame the lack of success on someone else or some other event. The prevailing attitude is that "This is my responsibility; I will take control and success or the lack of it will remain on my shoulders." In choosing which of three actions people need to take—lead, follow, or get out of the road—entrepreneurs are the leaders who take the responsibility to push ahead.

These ten general characteristics do not describe superhumans. These characteristics are not uncommon to many individuals in society. However, the combination of these characteristics together is common to most entrepreneurs. The combination of these characteristics gives the entrepreneur the essentials to envision change, make changes and work with those changes until success is achieved.

Entrepreneurial Biography 3: Maurice McDaniel

Name:	Maurice McDaniel
Company:	Mac's Eggs, Inc.
Number of Employees:	20
Annual Sales:	$2 million

What events and/or people were present in your youth or early adulthood that you now realize influenced your becoming an entrepreneur?

My first entrepreneurial effort occurred when I was eight or nine years old during the Summer of 1928. I lived in northern Indiana about one-half mile from the construction of U.S. 30, a transcontinental highway, which at that time was a gravel road. About the only soda available for sale was made by Nehi. As the construction of the New York to California highway neared the area of Indiana where I lived, I would put Nehi soda in my wagon, walk to the construction site, and sell a bottle of Nehi for five cents. The

wagon contained no ice, so the soda was warm, but the construction workers would quickly purchase my entire wagonload of Nehi.
Today it doesn't sound like very much money, but that summer I
made a lot of money by 1928 income standards. My mother, who
taught school, always encouraged me to try new ideas.

When I was sixteen, I left home and lived with a farmer named
Tracy Cochran. By helping him farm, including morning and
evening chores, he financially supported me so I could finish high
school. After high school, Wallace Anglin took me on as a partner
in growing vegetables and selling them in the Indianapolis farmers market about 100 miles from where we lived. Most restaurants
and grocery stores in Indianapolis would buy their produce from
this market, and I learned many entrepreneurial skills from that
partnership and Wallace Anglin.

Describe some of your early efforts at entrepreneurship.

When I decided to be an independent farmer, I first worked in the
steel mills in Chicago to earn money to buy land and equipment.
Then I worked nights in Indiana steel mills and began farming
during the days to finish paying for my investments. Most of my
additional farming turned to cash renting farmland as I quickly
learned that share farming gave most of my efforts to the landlord.
It was during this time that I realized I did not want to work for
someone else but, rather, I had a strong drive to be an independent
entrepreneur.

**What were some events or projects that were not successful,
but contributed to your success as an entrepreneur?**

From 1937 to 1959 I had many different jobs and made many
moves from farm to farm and in the end, I had very little to show
for my efforts. Winter jobs included truck driving, custom trucking, and a day laborer of many different types. This included many
different bosses, and I quickly learned how to treat people and
how not to treat them.

What project stands out as one of your major entrepreneurial successes?

In 1959, with a loan from an entrepreneur named Hobart Creighton, I built a large poultry barn, and with equipment and laying hens, that mounted to a staggering cost of $80,000. This project paid back the loan to Hobart Creighton in just over two years and has led to four poultry barns and an egg grading and packaging plant that constitutes Mac's Eggs, Inc.

What event stands out as a major stumbling block that you needed to overcome as an entrepreneur?

In the 1950s, I could not get any bank to loan funds for agricultural production. After spending several years with little success in expanding my small egg production operation, Hobart Creighton agreed to finance my proposed expansion. I had once worked for Hobart, and he believed as much in my honesty and willingness to work hard as he did in my proposed expansion. Without his financial help and constant advice, I would likely have never been able to expand the business.

In addition, as I began the expansion of the business, I needed to hire employees. I was fortunate in that many employees were hard working, sincere employees, but some were not. One of my biggest stumbling blocks, in addition to financing, was to learn the difference between desirable and unacceptable workers and be able to hire good employees and say no to applicants that were not acceptable.

What advice could you give someone who has aspirations of becoming an entrepreneur?

To be an entrepreneur, there are at least three factors that must be considered. First, an entrepreneur must be willing to work much harder than if that person was an employee working for someone else. If you want to work only nine to five, then you should be an employee, not an entrepreneur. Second, as an entrepreneur, you should give employees and fellow workers credit for successes that are achieved. You need to let them know that they are an important part of the enterprise and therefore responsible for its success. And third, the entrepreneur must be willing to personally accept the responsibility for failures in any entrepreneurial endeavor. After all, if I am in charge, then I am responsible if the project is not successful.

Describe your current enterprise.

Mac's Eggs, Inc. has capacity for one quarter of a million laying hens in three poultry barns. It has an inline egg grading and packaging plant, it has a contract pullet growing facility, it produces about 20 percent of the annual grain required for poultry feed, and it produces about one million eggs each week. It is located on a homestead farm that has been in my family since 1836. I contracted to buy it from my stepfather in the early 1960s as my father, Joseph McDaniel, died when I was two years old.

Describe your feelings toward your enterprise. Would you sell your enterprise? Would you work for a new owner? Would you take on a partner?

At eighty-one years of age, I have realized that I cannot keep expanding the way I did in the 1970s and 1980s. This past year, I agreed to sell the egg production facility, but I still own the rest of the homestead farm. I agreed to work for the new company but soon realized that working for another company was very frustrating. I now run errands and do odd jobs for the company, but I do not take an active role in the operation.

In my experience as an entrepreneur, I have had the opportunity to be involved with various partners. Outside of family members, I have generally thought that partners end up with most of the benefits and less of the burdens than I was willing to accept. There are some good exceptions to this, but it is very difficult to end a partnership after it has been formed.

How do you stay competitive with other firms in your industry?

My firm experienced both very profitable years as well as years of great financial loss due to the very volatile prices in the commodity market. There have been three keys that have allowed me to survive in this business. First, being efficient is a mandatory part of staying in business. A firm must be able to produce with small amounts of labor and material inputs per unit of output to be successful. Second, per-unit cost of production must be below the average in the industry, especially a competitive industry if the firm is to stay in business. Innovations can lead to this lower per-unit cost. And last, if a firm is not expanding, it is going backward. That is, if it is not expanding, it is losing its competitive edge over other firms. To be successful, the firm must expand both horizontally as well as vertically with the newest innovations and know that this process must continue if the firm is to stay competitive in an industry.

What innovations have you implemented to improve your enterprise?

Mac's Eggs, Inc. was an early user of cages to house laying hens to increase the capacity of the poultry barns. Also, the company experimented at an early date with forced molting of flocks in order to rest the laying hens and maintain a higher level of egg production. Early experiments with molting were a disaster, but continued efforts led to an efficient process and higher overall production.

In the 1950s, before commercial manufacturing of four-wheel articulating tractors for farm tillage, I experimented with that concept. With the help of Virgil Wise, a local welder and fabricator, I put two tractors together so it could be operated with one driver. It looked rather crude, but it did twice the work of one tractor and could be separated after the spring tillage was completed. Also, this tractor combination was used to experiment with the concept of minimum tillage agriculture. The tractor combination was hooked to a five-bottom molboard plow and a two-row planter. This was the only operation performed until harvest. This was very crude, but it caught the attention of other innovators in agriculture. Purdue University spent time observing and measuring the crude tractor and the minimum tillage operation. Purdue sent several observers over two or three years to study the innovation. Also, a group of agricultural experts from Russia toured the United States during this era and filmed and observed the innovation as it was used in the field.

Notes

1. Joseph A. Schumpeter, *The Theory of Economic Development* (Cambridge, MA: Harvard University Press, 1934), p. 66.

2. Joseph A. Schumpeter, *Business Cycles: A Theoretical, Historical and Statistical Analysis of the Capitalist Process* (New York: McGraw-Hill, 1939), p. 84.

3. Hamio Noori, *Managing the Dynamics of New Technology* (Englewood Cliffs, NJ: Prentice-Hall, Inc., 1990), p. 103.

4

Economic Development
of a Product

In Search of a Product: Research, Development, Demonstration, and Commercialization

Innovation is frequently part of the development of technology that is applied to a new product or a change in a production process. There are four stages of product or process development through which an invention or technology must progress in order to become an innovation. These four stages occur in specific order and are research, development, demonstration, and commercialization.[1] This process moves from a concept or idea (possibly in a scientific laboratory) to a commercialized product or production process where the end result is offered for sale in the marketplace. Each of these stages will be explained as an idea or concept as it is transformed into a product or production process.

Research accounts for 3 percent of gross domestic product, and it is estimated that one-fourth of current sales of U.S. companies are from products and processes that were developed within the past five years. Research is scientific investigation that normally leads to an idea or a concept if it is successful. Research is often separated into two different categories: basic and applied. Basic research is, most simply, scientific investigation with no preconceived outcome or direction for the research results. Applied research is research with a specific product or process as the goal, and applied research is often referred to as new product research or business research.

The second stage to which an invention or technology must progress is the development stage. This stage explores the actual potential of a product or process, but within a laboratory environment. This development stage is the process of moving the theoretical idea or "set of blueprints" from the research stage to an actual example of the physical product or process. The result of this stage is sometimes called the "prototype." Sometimes the research and development stages are combined, and the process becomes one of a continual progression that results in a prototype from the combination of several research and development attempts.

The third stage in this progression toward an actual product or process is the demonstration stage. Once the development stage has produced a product or process in a laboratory setting, the next stage is to build a functional model in a real workplace environment to prove operational success. Thus, the demonstration stage becomes one of "demonstrating" a real-world application. This stage attempts to show the usefulness of a product or process of the size and under the conditions that would exist if the technology or the invention is to prove a real-world use to society.

Commercialization is the last stage of moving scientific discovery through the methodical development of becoming an innovation. This stage launches the scientific or demonstration model into the marketplace. Commercialization duplicates the prototype in larger numbers in an attempt to offer the product or process for sale. The current literature differs on the requirement for profit at this stage. Some literature suggests that it is sufficient at this stage to offer the product or process for sale, while others require a profit in the course of action to complete the commercialization stage.

Regardless of the inclusion or exclusion of the profit requirement, this commercialization stage is the critical link in current technology and product development that Joseph Schumpeter addressed some sixty years ago. The commercialization stage separates invention from innovation and seems to be the missing link to much of the research activities in the United States in the 1960s and 1970s. That is, Schumpeter's insistence that an entrepreneur must innovate seems to have lost its importance in the two decades of declining U.S. dominance in world trade. Let me explain this in the following manner.

Many of the great scientific inventions in the United States in the 1960s and 1970s remained as only inventions because of a lack of implementation into the production stream of goods. That is, there was an absence of the utilization of the commercialization stage of product development. As discussed in an earlier chapter, the Japanese utilized many of these inventions as they moved the scientific invention into the realm of business innovation. There was an often-heard cry from the United States that those were U.S. inventions and that the Japanese were therefore practicing unfair competition. In reality, full credit for the innovation into products is due to the Japanese entrepreneurs. If capitalism is to fully function, the entrepreneur must be given full credit. This process of innovation is exactly what Schumpeter outlined as the role of the entrepreneur in the 1930s, and it appears to have been lacking in U.S. commerce in the era of the 1960s and 1970s.

Figure 4.1 briefly summarizes the flow of the development process of products and processes. The end result of research and development is commercialization, and commercialization is defined as the "production for sale" of a product. Obviously, if more commercialization is desirable, then more research and development is required. However, more research and development has not historically been directly proportionate to the increases in new product development. This less than proportional increase in new products can be attributed to government policies concerning government-funded research and development.

Historically, increases in gross domestic product have been directly linked to the material standard of living. Concern with maintaining and improving the standard of living has led to public sector

Figure 4.1 **Development Process of Products**

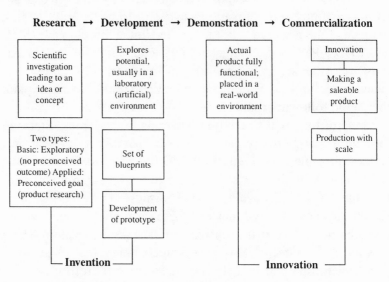

involvement in stimulating economic growth through research and development. This participation has been justified in the past, largely on economic and political grounds, and revolved around welfare and equity issues.

A general area justifying government intervention into market processes through research and development is the case of public goods. Research and development appears to meet the nature of a public good. There is a demand for it, which, for largely economic reasons, is not being met by the private sector. More precisely, research and development is a mixed good that is provided to a very limited extent by the private sector but which, at least initially, needs the stimulus afforded by the public sector.

In the development of research and development in general, public issues lend support to the argument in favor of government action to develop the potential for new products. There are two areas in which the public goods nature of research and development requires governmental intervention in the market economy. The first area relates to governmental policies concerned with national security, foreign policy, and public welfare and equity. In these matters the government must coordinate the outcomes of the research and development with national priorities set by explicit national policies. For example, the government may decide, for national security reasons, to decrease the amount of imported goods that are strategic in our national defense. This decision may involve government support to encourage the production and use of particular domestic goods. Most federal programs, to date, have been ad hoc and difficult to relate to the needs of society.[2] An attempt must be made to relate the changing needs of society to an overall research and development at the national level.

The second area in which the public goods nature of research and development requires governmental intervention in the market economy is in cases where the market fails to allocate resources in a socially desirable way. From an economic point of view, research and development involves an investment in which the knowledge of the outcome from that investment is largely unknown. An investment in research and development involves a commitment of resources to an exploratory process in which the outcome may be a large number of dead ends rather than profitable economic applications. This high degree of risk that is inseparable from the investment activity causes a downward bias to the willingness of private firms in a competitive market to undertake investments in the research and development. Since it is impossible for risk averters to shift these risks completely, society as a whole will underinvest in such activities. The topic of federal government involvement in research and development will be more fully explored in chapter 10.

The Role of Research and Development

The purpose of research and development is to identify, investigate, and implement innovations in the new product spectrum. However, the function of any government research and development activity is to provide a climate for private research and development, share risks with the private sector, and conduct research and development that is deemed important, but is not being carried out by the private sector. The private sector is now and will continue to be the major source of goods production and consumption. Thus, research and development carried out by the government should be aimed at eventual implementation into the private sector.

It is appropriate at this point to identify the risk involved in developing new and not yet proven products in the economy. An example would seem most appropriate at this point, and photovoltaic electric power systems will be used as the example here.

There are very few commercial producers of photovoltaic electric power systems in the United States at this time. Investment in photovoltaics is required to find ways of producing solar cells at costs that are competitive with existing electric rates. Since many of these potential cost-reduction methods must be eliminated by trial and error methods, investments in photovoltaics at this time are quite risky. Firms acting separately to find better production methods cannot relieve themselves of risk bearing in this potential industry. "Hence any unwillingness to bear risks will give rise to a nonoptimal allocation of resources, in that there will be discrimination against risky enterprises as compared with the optimum."[3] Because of this, resources will be underemployed and there will be less than optimal investments in risky enterprises such as the development of photovoltaics.

Because private enterprise will likely underinvest in photovoltaic research, the government sector is required to increase such investments. The government has superior risk-bearing ability, and so the burden is shifted to it. Risk is a major rationale for federal government support of research and development in new areas of invention. The government is needed as well because of misallocation problems that arise from the nature of the information generated. Any information generated from innovation in photovoltaics should be made available at zero cost to potential users to attain a level of investment that is socially desirable. This, however, is from a welfare point of view and ensures the optimal utilization of the information but provides no incentive for investment in research by private industry. Thus, the role of government research and development in this case is to encourage investment in research to fill the void that exists with the private-sector investment.

The present energy situation in the United States can be used to build a case for a positive role for the public sector in shaping the future course of solar energy in this country. This case is based on four existing conditions. First, there are demonstrated cases where markets inherently fail to provide efficient resource allocations (e.g., externalities discussed in previous sections). Second, previous government policy seriously limits the effectiveness of the market in the solar energy area. Therefore, the public sector must either remove or modify these impediments or seek ways to give equal support to the development of solar energy. Third, there are multiple objectives for energy policy, and for many of these objectives, the public sector is the only logical magistrate (e.g., foreign policy, national security, alienation and the facilitation of changing social values discussed above). Fourth, the government currently owns the major portion of the remaining nonrenewable energy resources. Since this is the case, the public sector must make the ultimate decision of whether to use these resources and, if so, when. In an attempt to promote wise use over time, the public sector can use solar energy to expand the time horizon of available nonrenewable energy resources.

Historically, government-sponsored research and development had a funding requirement in which firms that received research and development funds from government could not benefit financially from the use of that research. Therefore, firms that developed ideas and concepts were forbidden by government from developing and selling products that were the outcome of federally supported research and development. As a result, many ideas and concepts (inventions) have historically not resulted in new products but, rather, were left in some obscure government report and were never rediscovered by firms that wanted to innovate. Or historically, the research and development was developed into products by foreign countries and then they were resold into the United States, which created balance of payments problems.

The rationale for not allowing research and development firms to profit from the sale of products (outcomes) from government-funded research and development seems at first to be quite logical. If the government financially supported the research and development and then the firm also profited a second time through the sale of the products developed from the research and development, the firm would financially benefit twice. However, the end result of this policy has been to keep products from being developed as a result of the firm receiving government funding for research and development.

The last two stages of product development (demonstration and commercialization) are quite costly. If the invention is not patentable and a firm spends the time, effort, and financial investment to develop a product, the end result could easily be copied by competing firms at little or no cost. If the government is to continue supporting research and development for the reasons outlined above, then the government must find a way to allow the invention to move to an innovation. That is, the government must also support demonstration and commercialization of the invention so saleable products are the ultimate outcome and are completed within the United States. The role and strategy of the federal government in research and development will be revisited in chapter 10.

At the same time that major U.S. government research and development was going unused and undeveloped by U.S. companies, there was a bias against using research and development as an innovative tool by many firms in the United States. There was a widespread attitude that can only be described as business arrogance. There was a prevailing mindset among many firms that the consuming public did not require additional products. That is, there seemed to be an ample supply of choices for the American consumer, and no additional choices were required. Also, companies seemed to possess the attitude that their particular product or products could compete with other existing products from other firms. Therefore, additional new product development was not necessary for the commercial success of the firm.

Aligning with this business attitude of arrogance was the new and growing area of marketing and advertising. The conventional wisdom of many firms was that advertising could sell anything. The key to commercial success was no longer held in the understanding of production methodology, but rather was held in the future of advertising and marketing. This attitude was absorbed by not only U.S. companies, but also by the university students who aspired to be the next generation of corporate managers for U.S. firms. Many colleges and universities reduced offerings or even eliminated entire programs in production management. This prevailing attitude did little to bolster research and development activities and did even less to the development of new products and production processes.

Assuring the Success of Marketable Products

The end result of research, development, demonstration, and commercialization is marketable products. In other words, production was for the purpose of sales in the marketplace. This position requires the product to be appropriately priced in order for sales to take place. The entrepreneur must understand some economics of pricing and the demand for products if success from innovations is to be realized. The economic key to pricing products is the concept of elasticities. The three most important elasticities related to understanding demand for a product are price elasticity, income elasticity and cross elasticity of demand. Each of these will be discussed in turn.

Price Elasticity of Demand

Elasticity can be viewed as the responsiveness or change in the dependent variable when a change has occurred in the independent variable. In the case of price elasticity of demand, elasticity is the percentage change in the quantity demanded compared to some given percentage change in the price of the product. With any given change in the price of a product, an inelastic demand would have a very small change in the quantity demanded whereas an elastic demand would show a much larger change in the quan-

Figure 4.2 **Comparing Elastic and Inelastic Demand for a Product**

Elastic Demand	Inelastic Demand
$$\frac{\%\Delta QD}{\%\Delta P} < 1$$	$$\frac{\%\Delta QD}{\%\Delta P} > 1$$
Quantity demanded changes less relative to a change in price	Quantity demanded changes more relative to a change in price

tity demanded for the product. Figure 4.2 is used to help understand price elasticity of demand.

The significance of price elasticity of demand can be seen by relating price changes to total revenue. Because total revenue is simply the product of price and quantity, changes in any price will impact the price and quantity demanded relationship and therefore total revenue. Also, since price and quantity demanded are inversely related, an increase in price will result in some reduction in quantity demanded. Likewise, a decrease in price will result in an increase in quantity demanded. The conclusion is that if price increases relatively more than the quantity demanded decreases, total revenue will increase and if price increases relatively less than the quantity demanded decreases, total revenue will decrease. This end result of changes in total revenue is a direct result of whether the price elasticity of demand is elastic or inelastic. Table 4.1 categorizes this relationship.

The obvious objective from the view of maximizing total revenue would be to increase price if the demand is inelastic and find a way to lower price if the demand for the product is elastic. The price of a product could be lowered as long as the price remains above the average cost of production. It follows then that sometimes a price reduction might require the firm to make production changes in order to lower the average cost of production. As it can be seen from this description, the success of marketing a product can be greatly enhanced by determining the price elasticity of demand.

Table 4.1

Price Elasticity of Demand

For price increase	Result	For price decrease	Result
Inelastic demand $E_d < 1$		Inelastic demand $E_d < 1$	
Relative price increase is greater than the decrease in quantity demanded	Total revenue increases	Relative price increase is greater than the decrease in quantity demanded	Total revenue falls
Elastic demand $E_d > 1$		Elastic demand $E_d > 1$	
Relative price increase is less than the increase in quantity demanded	Total revenue falls	Relative price increase is less than the increase in quantity demanded	Total revenue increases

Income Elasticity of Demand

Income elasticity of demand is defined as the relative change in the demand for a product when there has been a change in the buyer's income. There are two classes of products with regard to income elasticities. Products that have a decrease in demand from an increase in buyers' incomes are considered inferior goods, and products that have an increase in demand from an increase in buyers' incomes are considered normal goods. Understanding this relationship between buyers' income and product demand could be useful in predicting changes in product demand from economic recessions as well as economic expansions where buyers' incomes can change rapidly. Goods that are considered inferior, a negative relationship between product demand and buyers income, will experience an increased demand during economic recessions but a decrease in demand during economic expansions. Likewise, if the good is considered a normal good, a positive relationship be-

Table 4.2

Income Elasticity of Demand

| Buyers' income | Inferior goods | Normal goods | |
		Necessities	Luxuries
Increases	Demand decreases	Small increase in product demand	Large increase in product demand
Decreases	Demand increases	Small decrease in product demand	Large decrease in product demand

tween product demand and buyers' income, product demand will increase during economic expansions and a decrease during economic recessions.

Another part of income elasticity of demand for a product is the differences in types of products that are classified as normal goods (ones that show a direct change in product demand from a change in buyers' income). Relative small changes in product demand from a change in buyers' incomes are considered to be necessity goods whereas large relative changes in product demand compared to changes in buyers' incomes are considered to be luxury goods. Understanding income elasticity of demand for a product can help assure its commercial success. Table 4.2 describes the relationship of product demand to income elasticity.

Cross Elasticity of Demand

Cross elasticity of demand involves products that are substitutes and products that are complements for one another. To determine this relationship, changes in the demand for a product are compared to changes to the price of an alternative product. If the demand for a product increases as a result of a price increase for another product, the goods are considered substitutes. Information about products being considered substitutes can be used to more appropriately price and advertise the product in the market. If, on the other hand, the demand for the product decreases as a

Table 4.3

Cross Elasticity of Demand

Price of alternative product	Complements	Substitutes
Increase in price of alternative product	↓ Demand for product	↑ Demand for product
Decrease in price of alternative product	↑ Demand for product	↓ Demand for product

result of a price increase for an alternate good, the goods are considered complementary goods. Complementary goods are products that are used together, similar to two goods used as one singular good. Examples might be gasoline and automobiles, salsa and taco chips, or bread and peanut butter. Table 4.3 demonstrates this relationship.

In the case of substitute goods, the goods will be in direct competition, and marketing strategies need to recognize the price competitiveness of a substitute. If product differentiation is not possible or advertising is not successful, the good will be marketed in a very price competitive market. In the case of complementary goods, the marketing strategy must take into account the complement. Sometimes no marketing will be required if there is rigorous demand for the complement. Also, joint advertising with the firm that produces the complementary good might enhance the demand for joint purchase of the two products. Again, understanding the relationship between the demand for the product and the price of alternative products can help ensure the successful marketing of that product.

Entrepreneurial Biography 4: Troy McWhinney

Name:	Troy McWhinney
Company:	McWhinney Enterprises
Number of Employees:	38
Annual Sales:	$30–60 million

What events and/or people were present in your youth or early adulthood that you now realize influenced your becoming an entrepreneur?

I'd have to say by far that it was my dad. As far back as I can remember, he put us on budgets by the time we were five or six years old. He'd give us enough money for a week and that was all we got. We couldn't go back and ask him for additional money if we wanted to buy candy or go to the movies. As we got older, he really made us work for everything whether it was school, paying for football, or paying for college, dances, dates and movies, car and auto insurance. We all had to work to pay our own bills. It was one of those things when we were young and growing up that if we didn't have a job, he would always make us work around the house, and usually we didn't get paid when we worked at the house. So when we were old enough, we realized that we were going to have to work anyway, either at the house or out at a job. We decided we'd rather work at a job and make money than work at the house and not get paid. So the whole family started working as soon as we could, usually around the age of thirteen or fourteen. We would work either at the local auto dealership washing cars or with the local boatyard where we waxed and painted boats.

What's your father's name?

Derek. He passed away several years ago.

Describe some of your early efforts at entrepreneurship.

Some of the real early ones would be to sell golf balls at the local golf course. I think we were about ten or eleven years old. We would actually go out at night and steal golf balls out of the lakes. I don't know if we were so much stealing them; we were probably taking ones back that we hit into the lake earlier that day. The golf course would sell them for about a dollar a ball, and we'd end up selling them for about fifty cents a ball. We'd sit at the holes and just ask golfers as they walked up. That was some of the real early stuff and then at the ages of fourteen, fifteen, or sixteen my brothers and I started a produce business. The family had some land in Orange County, and we leased the land to a farmer who grew strawberries. We would ask the farmer how much he sold the strawberries for to the grocery stores and find out what they sold for at the grocery store. Then we knew there was a lot of markup in the produce business. So we started with a strawberry stand on the side of a busy road in Orange County, California. We bought strawberries wholesale from the farmer at the same price that he would sell them to the grocery stores and basically sold them on the side of the road for about the same price as the grocery stores, if not just a little bit higher.

People would much rather buy fresh strawberries because we would only keep the strawberries for a day at a time while the grocery stores might keep them for five or six days. I remember the first day. I was fourteen years old, and I made $76, and I thought it was the best thing in the world. From there we decided each brother would work at one strawberry stand. We had four or five strawberry stands about a year later, and things were going well. We decided we could hire employees to work the stands, and there was enough money to pay the employees and make a profit. So we ran that business for several years and at our peak, we had thirty strawberry stands in Orange County. That business went from February to July. I remember being sixteen years old and walking into a bank Monday morning after Easter weekend with over $100,000 in cash, and it was pretty amazing.

Any other early efforts?

I did run a flower shop in Orange County. I did that for two or three years. I was presented with an opportunity to buy a flower shop at a pretty good price back in 1992 when things were in a recession. I owned and managed it for a couple years and ended up selling it and making a nice profit.

What were some events or projects that were not successful, but contributed to your success as an entrepreneur?

The strawberry business and the dirt business were successful in the early years, but we ended up losing money in the last year or two. Our second or third project in Colorado was a food court that we built next to a regional mall. I always say that the food court was my college education. We ended up building the food court and leasing it out to several smaller, less creditworthy tenants. When the food court started to do poorly, and the tenants started to leave, there was a snowball effect. Since the tenants were having financial difficulties, that led to poor management of the restaurants. We had several food court tenants vacate the space, and since they were not creditworthy tenants, we could not really enforce their contracts. It was very difficult to re-lease the space, and we had a substantial debt service to the bank as the tenants started to leave. That really cut into the income of the project. We ran a deficit for several years.

Recently, we sold the food court and converted it into an office building. I think that really opened up our eyes about how much more risky it is to do business with somebody that does not have a strong financial backing or good credit and how much more rent you need to charge someone to make up for that additional risk. I remember at the time we were leasing the food court we were offered several leases. One was by a credit tenant, and they were willing to pay 10 percent or 15 percent less than a noncredit tenant was and we saw the additional 10–15 percent as extra money. It ended up costing us a lot of money because we did not do business with the financially strong tenant.

What project stands out as one of your major entrepreneurial successes?

I'd have to say that would be the projects I'm currently working on now in Loveland, Colorado. We have assembled about 3,000 acres in one of the hottest growing areas in the nation. We had originally started out with 500 acres, and we saw the value that we were creating by taking agricultural land and turning it into development land. We put in the roads, the utilities, and infrastructure. When we first started, we thought 500 acres was enough to last us a lifetime, and we wouldn't need any more. We had seen the growth that happened in Orange County many years ago. We heard the stories that often you will increase the value of the property so much that the landowners around the developing area will become very wealthy just by holding onto their land. So we had the vision to look ten or fifteen years in the future and see that this area could be really prosperous.

We were able to tie up through options and purchases about another 2,500 acres of land while it was still trading at agricultural prices. One thing that became really successful is that we didn't even have to actually purchase the land. We could tie it up with an option and pay the current landowner, which may have been a farmer or family who had owned the property for a hundred years. Their income on several hundred acres might be $20,000–$30,000 a year in farming income. We would pay $10,000 or $15,000 a year for the right to buy property within the next five years. They saw that $10,000 or $15,000 as substantial income, and we saw it as a very easy and economical way for us to control large amounts of land. Sure enough, the value of the land increased and made it economical for us to buy the land at the agricultural price.

And the name of that project?

That is Centerra, located in Loveland, Colorado.

Anything else?

We were able to get some very favorable entitlements from the city of Loveland, and one thing I have learned in real estate is that entitlements are everything. If you own land that you can't develop, nobody wants to buy that land. If you have land that is zoned and titled for development activity, you'll have every homebuilder in the state wanting to purchase your land. We went into Loveland and got some very good vesting, which means they can't change their mind. That's one thing that a lot of the municipalities do is zone a property, and then in five years when there's a new council or a new mayor, they will change the zoning rules. We were able to get the city of Loveland to agree not to change the rules for twenty-five years. I think that was a pretty major feat accomplished here in Loveland.

But in addition to being very favorable for Loveland, you've also been very generous in terms of granting properties to them for various activities.

Yes, one thing that we pride ourselves on is long-term relationships. Before my dad passed away, he gave me a piece of advice. He said somebody could spend a lifetime building their reputation and lose it in about five minutes. We never do anything that will hinder our long-term reputation. We often make concessions that end up hurting us in the short run but pay off in the long run. We have recently agreed to donate to the city of Loveland 100 acres for a youth athletic complex. The land value that the city has placed on the property is somewhere between $3–6 million dollars. Several years ago we donated five acres to the city of Loveland for their Chamber of Commerce and Visitors' Center.

What event stands out as a major stumbling block that you needed to overcome as an entrepreneur?

One of them would be my age. I started doing business when I was thirteen or fourteen years old. But even now that I'm twenty-six years old, when somebody first meets me, they wonder if I understand what I'm doing and may not trust me as they would another person across the table that has been doing this for twenty, thirty, or forty years. That's probably one of the biggest stumbling blocks that I had to overcome. Finances early on were a problem. One of the reasons the project became so successful in northern Colorado is the 500 acres that we had originally owned had been in the family for 140 years. My grandmother passed away in the late 1980s and the IRS said we had inheritance taxes to pay on the land in Colorado that was producing very little income. At the time we considered selling all the property in Colorado just to pay the inheritance taxes. We realized that by developing real estate, and again turning that agricultural land into real estate development property, we could sell off just enough to pay the taxes. We ended up selling forty acres, just enough to pay the taxes, and kept everything else. So those financial stumbling blocks early on led to some success. The forty acres became the Prime Outlet Stores of Loveland, which is a 328,000-square-foot regional mall.

What advice could you give someone who has aspirations of becoming an entrepreneur?

That it is a lot of hard work. As your company grows and gets bigger and bigger, you find it hard to delegate some of the tasks that you enjoy. As an example, when I first moved back to Colorado six years ago, I think we skied forty days in the season, and the next year it went down to about thirty days, and the next year after that it was down to about twenty days. Then it got down to ten days, and last year I did not ski at all. This year it's the beginning of February right now, and I haven't skied this year either.

It's hard work, but I enjoy what's happening and what's going on. Again, you'll be surprised that people we used to do business with in the strawberries ten years ago are people that we can call right now. These are people who owned a lot of agricultural fields in Orange County, farmers, who opened a lot of doors and contacts for us to go back and start working with them on real estate development. Also, you have to stick with it; a lot of times you may fail on several projects, and you need to learn from your mistakes. One person told me that a mistake is a great moment because you've learned. We actually, in our company, encourage people to be open about their mistakes and not hide them so the rest of the company can learn from them as well.

Describe your current enterprise.

Our current enterprise is, again, named McWhinney Enterprises. It's a real estate development firm that focuses 75 percent of our time in northern Colorado and about 25 percent of our time in southern California. We pride ourselves on being a master land developer. We will take property that's currently used as agricultural and is in the path of growth, and it might be five or ten years until the growth gets there, but we get things ready. When the growth does come, the property is ready and properly planned for a long-term master plan. If you take that long-term approach, you can size the infrastructure, the roads, utilities, school sites, and libraries large enough so you don't run into growth problems and you can plan for expansion. When putting in a bridge, don't build right next to it so that you can never expand or widen the bridge. Those are some examples. We will take this property, title it, and then bring in very experienced partners in each field. We will team up with a residential developer that will come in and build homes, we will team up with a hotel developer that will own, operate, and manage a hotel, and we will do land leases for restaurants.

Originally, we had this vision of starting our own home building business and build[ing] all these homes ourselves. Then getting into the hotel managing business where we'd manage our own hotels and then get[ting] into our own restaurant business where we'd actually own a restaurant, gas stations, and all kinds of stuff. We realized there was a lot of learning needed when you have several hundred acres; now that it's several thousand acres, we can't do it all ourselves, and we can actually increase absorption by teaming up with very experienced people that are efficient in their own fields. It's worked out great so far.

Could you give two or three examples of those partnerships you've worked out?

We ended up forming a partnership with Hotel Company from Denver. This is a group that has somewhere between thirty and forty hotels nationwide. We had the choice of either selling them our land, and our land was probably worth $500,000, to build a hotel, or they asked us if we'd be interested in contributing our land to the partnership and own about 30 percent of the hotel. We did that and our first year cash-on-cash return for the hotel was about 40 percent. So if we sold the land we'd have to pay 40 percent in taxes and be left with maybe $300,000, maybe a little less. Instead, we were able to invest the $500,000 in the hotel and make 40 percent, which is close to $225,000 a year. We have been doing that every year since; it's been open for several years. That first hotel was a great partnership for us, and we ended up doing one more hotel here, and then we started to develop some property in southern California in Orange County back when it was in bankruptcy in about 1995. We were able to obtain some very good entitlements with the city of Garden Grove, which is about a half mile south of Disneyland and bring the hotel owners in as our hotel partners. We own three more hotels with them in Orange County. That's an example of a partnership ending up being a win-win situation for both of us. Instead of selling our first parcel of land to them, we did a joint venture.

Another example would be the homebuilding. We spent a lot of time interviewing multiple homebuilders from some really small homebuilders, to some of the largest in the nation. We teamed up with a company from Boulder, a family-owned company that's been in business for thirty-five years that really shared our vision of quality development projects. It's been going great for the last several years, and we hope to turn that into a relationship for the next twenty, thirty, or forty years for residential development.

Describe your feelings toward your enterprise. Would you sell your enterprise?

The only thing that we would ever do is to bring in a financial partner. We would never sell and not be active. We would consider bringing in a financial partner if we had to; right now we don't need one. We often say that if we sold, we would take the money and do the exact same thing somewhere else, maybe even next door, but we have no interest in selling.

Would you work for a new owner?

Probably not. I'm having some hard times even as the company grows to seventeen employees trying to delegate. I think the entrepreneur sometimes has problems following rules, and I don't think I could work for another owner that had a lot of strict rules. I need to be able to change every day and think outside of the box. I do not think that I could ever work for a new owner.

Would you take on a partner?

Yes, we would take on a partner, but I can say that it would be very difficult to do. We would have to make sure the partner is aligned and has the same goals and values we do. We have done a few partnerships in the past where our partner did not have the same values and goals, and we have been hesitant ever since. When it comes to being financially driven, they may burn some bridges in order to make the returns they need or want, and we are the opposite. So we would consider it, but be very, very, very cautious.

How do you stay competitive with other firms in your industry?

Right now the other firms in our industry are some pretty large firms, and I think by being small and quick moving, we can sit down with the landowner and have an offer back to them usually within a couple hours. We can meet with them; I can sit down at my PC and type a letter of intent and give them an offer and a check within several hours. With some of these larger companies, you have to wait for their weekly staff meeting to get approval; then that approval may need to go back to the corporate office in some other state, and it could take them several weeks to respond. So, I think that being small, quick moving, and aggressive is one of our big advantages.

Number two is to do what we know best. Don't get into trying to do everything yourself. We thought that by giving up some of the income, we could also increase some of our absorption. That is, we don't build all the homes ourselves, we don't build the hotels ourselves, but we bring in partners. And sure, we may have given up some income on the hotel side and the residential side, but that allowed us to do a lot more land development and also many more joint ventures.

And so one of those competitive advantages you realized is your expertise and you tried to excel in that area.

Right. Another thing is trying to keep your company financially strong. After seeing the experience in Orange County in the late 1980s, we actually would like to see some type of slowing in the economy where we could maybe use our financial strength to acquire some additional property. I'm not saying I hope that happens here in Colorado, but we're building up our balance sheets to be very strong financially so that when there is a downturn we can capitalize on everyone else's mistakes.

Do you try to keep your company from being leveraged?

Yes. And at times it's tough. It's tough when you're trying to purchase several thousand acres of land and keep money in the bank. But there's a balance where we may sell off some strategic pieces of land and take that equity and reinvest it.

Another thing that we do . . . is to try to get as much advice as possible. It's not uncommon for us to see an article in the paper or a magazine and actually call the person in the story and say, "Hey, I'm young; I'm in this business; I want to just pick your brain." You'll be amazed at how many people are delighted to sit down and give you their advice on what they've learned over the years. I think they think that's a way they can give back. So any time you can, sit down and pick someone's brain. You may not like everything they say, but there may be one or two things that you hear that may make a big difference.

What innovations have you implemented to improve your enterprise?

I think the biggest thing we have done is really getting the company to function as a team. This is a change that we have made in the last couple years. Before that we had different departments within the company; accounting was functioning great as a single department; and real estate sales was acting great as an individual part of the company, but the two weren't speaking the right language between them. We spent a lot of time with team building, having retreats where we brought in a professional business coach, and spent a lot of time having him facilitate some of the frustrations within the company. That really got the company to function as a team. Now when accounting says they need this, I understand why they say that and why they need it. Before I used to look at it as them just trying to make my life difficult; and I didn't understand why they needed the things they did. We got them to learn why we do things the way we do. Sometimes we can't move as fast as they can when it comes to a deal with banks, letters of credit, and lines of credit as well.

Also, another important thing that we have done is empowered our employees. We learned that a happy employee is a productive employee. Anytime you have employees that aren't happy, they're probably spending some of their time every day looking through the paper for a new job. By empowering the employees, making them feel wanted and needed—which they are—they will do wonders. We used to try and really push the company rather than pull it. We may have pushed them in a direction that they did not want to go. And now we try to get everyone within the company involved when we do something new. We want everyone to understand why we're doing something. I think you'll be amazed that employees' salary is not the number one thing that they're interested in: It's being respected and being in a workplace where they feel they're valued as well.

Any other innovations?

Another common innovation is technology. We spend a lot of money on our technology even though we're a pretty small company in relative terms with eighteen employees in the office. We're setting up something called Net Meeting. We can actually hold meetings over the Internet, and we'll have a big grease board on the wall where we can write and draw. Our architect in California will have a picture pop up in front of him real time and that really helps explain things to consultants that aren't there in the office.

How old is your current company, McWhinney Enterprises?

We started looking at this property when my grandmother died in the late 1980s. The first development did not break ground until 1992 or 1993.

So in roughly seven years you've grown, you and your brothers, into a company of maybe close to $40 million?

Yes. This includes land sales and construction activities combined. We actually want to slow the growth rate down and stay small and efficient and not grow too fast.

Notes

1. Bruce McDaniel, *Solar Energy and the American Social Economy*, Unpublished doctoral dissertation, Colorado State University, 1979, p. 180.
2. Eric Von Hippel, *The Sources of Innovation* (New York: Oxford University Press, 1988), pp. 9–10.
3. Kenneth J. Arrow, "Economic Welfare and the Allocation of Resources for Invention," in *The Rational Direction of Inventive Activity: A Conference*, National Bureau of Economic Research (Princeton, NJ: Princeton University Press, 1962), p. 612.

5

Innovations in Products

Temporary Monopoly Control

Innovation is the result of an entrepreneur converting ideas, concepts, and opportunities into marketable products and processes. Innovation is the means by which the entrepreneur implements change. If successful, this change will lead to economic advantages for the firm in which the entrepreneur implements the change. The two types of changes, product innovations and process innovations, create economic advantages for the firm in different ways. Product innovations are the focus of this chapter, and process innovations are the focus of the next chapter.

When a new, improved or different product is developed, the maker, entrepreneur, or innovator has created a product that is at least somewhat different from the rest of the market. This uniqueness in the product gives even a firm in heavy competition at least a temporary position as the sole producer or monopolist. This temporary monopoly control allows the firm to make at least temporary excess profit from the sale of this unique product.

Figure 5.1 helps explain the profits from this temporary market control. When a firm is producing homogenous or like products, the market is represented by a horizontal demand curve. There are many similar (or like) products, consumers have a wide variety of choices, and products compete through price, which over time is

Figure 5.1 **Products Sold in a Competitive Market**

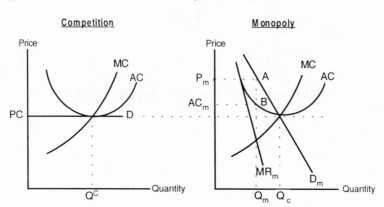

driven to the minimum point on the average cost curve. This position is represented in the figure by price P_c and a sales quantity of Q_c for the particular firm in the example. When an innovator develops a new, improved or different product, the entrepreneur has developed a product that has little or no competition. At least temporarily, the firm becomes a monopolist and, therefore, faces a downward-sloping demand curve. This monopoly position allows the firm freedom to set a price for the product different than under conditions of competition. Likewise, the firm, through adjusting the product price and production quantity, can establish a price and a quantity that renders a temporary excess profit for the firm. This position is represented in the figure by price P_m and a quantity of Q_m, which represents maximum profits for the firm. Note this monopoly price and monopoly quantity allows a per-unit profit of $P_m - AC_m$ or a total profit of $(P_m - AC_m) \times Q_m$ or area in the figure of $P_m \cdot A \cdot B \cdot AC_m$. This extra or above normal profit will continue so long as the firm can protect the uniqueness of the product. This profit is termed extra or above normal because in economics the average cost curve includes a normal rate of return as part of the opportunity cost of doing business.[1]

An example of this new product development in the U.S. economy before 1900 was the development of hard-grade steel often referred to as tool steel. Although the process of making steel as opposed to iron was already being used, innovators such as Andrew Carnegie transformed the steel industry and actually made a new product that allowed steel to be used in new and specialized areas. By using scientific discoveries of other inventors that added specific ingredients, such as vanadium and tungsten, the steel could be made much harder. In turn, this allowed new cutting tools and other machinery tools to be developed as a result of this new harder steel. This development of harder steel was aided by the refined use of electric furnaces and new processes such as the Bessemer process that strengthened the steel by burning out carbon and other impurities.[2]

Innovating and developing a new and improved product created a temporary monopoly market. Even though the product was still steel, it was a new, harder steel that allowed new uses of steel not before possible. This condition is described as temporary because as this new process and new ingredients become widely accepted and utilized by the industry, the product again becomes competitive and is produced in similar type by several firms. This competition drives the price downward toward an eventual price equal to the minimum of the average cost curve. The industry returns to a competitive market and the competing firms earn no excess (monopoly) profits.

Another example of an innovation leading to a new product is in the area of agriculture. Urea, $CO(NH_2)_2$, was developed in the early 1900s and found a waiting application as a nitrogen fertilizer used to increase yields in agricultural production. Although natural nitrogen fertilizer was available, it was quite expensive and sometimes cost-prohibitive in most agricultural applications. This new artificial nitrogen, urea, allowed farmers a lower-cost method of increasing crop yields. In this application, urea cost less than the existing natural nitrogen fertilizer. However, in this case the cost of producing urea was so low that the price of urea could be set below the natural fertilizer price and still render an excess profit for urea production. This product is heavily used today in agriculture, especially in the production of field corn, and has made major changes in U.S. agriculture as it has led to higher yields, larger machines to harvest those yields, and larger farms needed to pay for the increasing fixed costs of farming.

As the production of urea became more widespread, competition among firms resulted in the price of urea being driven downward toward the minimum of the average cost curve. The excess profits were reduced or eliminated through competition. The way in which firms gain the knowledge and expertise to compete with these unique products is the focus of the next section.

Competitors and Reverse Engineering

Once a new product has been developed and marketed by a firm, there is a continuous drive by other entrepreneurs to find a way to compete with the new product. Sometimes independent research and development leads to new innovations that allow the firm to develop similar products to compete with the existing product. This pattern of product development would follow the procedures outlined in chapter 4. A somewhat common alternative procedure to find a way to compete with this new product is through the process of reverse engineering.

As the term suggests, reverse engineering is the process by which a would-be competitor actually purchases the new product and works backward by taking the new product apart and analyzing each component. In this process of analyzing the components, attention is paid to potential product weakness from any component as well as areas that are excessively engineered to last beyond the useful life of the product. Since many new products are trademarked or patented, care must be taken to develop a slightly different product with sufficiently different components such that there are no trademark or patent infringements.

A recent classic example of reverse engineering occurred in the inline skate industry. This industry is often referred to as the roller blade industry because Roller Blades were the first inline skates and were trademarked. Originally, Roller Blades were developed as a skate to keep hockey players in shape during the off-season.

Obviously, these skates needed to be built ruggedly to withstand the abuse by fierce competitors in the professional hockey leagues. Wheels were made of very strong synthetic materials, soles were steel reinforced, rollers were made of steel ball bearings, and, in general, the construction was such that destruction of the skate was difficult if not nearly impossible. As competitors purchased the Roller Blade inline skates and participated in reverse engineering, the objective was not to produce inline skates for hockey players, but rather production for a growing demand by an amateur population of recreational inline skaters.

By producing a somewhat similar skate to the Roller Blade inline skates that were sufficiently altered, the competitors, such as Nike, Solomon-Adidas, K-2, and Roces, could produce a salable product to compete with Roller Blades. For the recreational skater, the inline skates did not require steel ball bearings, a full steel shaft in the sole, and likewise, heavy construction required by professional hockey players. By reducing the high-quality construction built into Roller Blades, competitors were able to offer the recreational inline skaters a cheaper product, but a satisfactory product, for less demanding use at a much less expensive price. Although the industry is often referred to as the roller blade industry, most recreational inline skaters do not skate on Roller Blades. As competing products are developed, there is an ongoing need for innovators to find new and different suppliers of inputs in the production process. This need originates from both a quality consideration as well as a constant push to lower the costs of production from new input supplies. This ongoing search by innovators for new input suppliers is the focus of the next section.

The Need to Discover New Input Suppliers

Once a product is being built with the assembled inputs, an ongoing need surfaces to search for new input suppliers. This need stems from four separate areas and each need will be discussed in turn. As Table 5.1 illustrates, first there is an ongoing need to continu-

Table 5.1

Four Areas of Needs to Discover a New Input Supplier

1. Change the inputs to improve, update, or better build the current product

2. Maintain or improve the quality of the inputs used in the product

3. Keep the input prices from escalating

4. Continually reduce the overall costs of inputs

ally change the inputs to improve the product for the end users that purchase the products. As the end purchasers use the products, there are ongoing changes to improve the serviceability of the product. Users often suggest weak points of the product, ideas about how the product could be made to last longer, and, in general, issues of product quality and product improvement. If the innovator takes these suggestions and ideas seriously, then there is an ongoing search for inputs that will meet the suggestions and ideas of the end users. If a product becomes broken or wears out and the same component part seems to be the reason, then the onus is on the entrepreneur to innovate to lengthen the useful life of the product. This solution is often found through new inputs that are stronger, more durable or otherwise help the product attain a longer use life.

The second need to discover a new input supplier comes from the area of trying to maintain or improve the quality of the input. As the increasing use of inputs places pressure on the input suppliers to provide ever-increasing quantities, this pressure often results in a decrease in the quality of the input. Also, as the entrepreneur attempts to improve the quality of the product, one way is to improve the quality of the inputs. Both of these reasons lead the entrepreneur to continually search for new input suppliers to maintain or improve the quality of the entrepreneur's product.

The third area requiring a need to search for new input suppliers results from upward price pressure from the input suppliers themselves. Once an input supplier gains the account for selling inputs to a producer, there is a tendency to increase the price of inputs slowly, but steadily, as the producer begins to rely more heavily rely on those inputs in the production process. Sometimes this is a result of the input supplier underbidding competitors to initially gain the business account and later making up for the initial low bid. Other times this upward price pressure comes from the input supplier believing that the producer is now forced into buying the input as it becomes required in the production process. Producers as well as entrepreneurs often take great pleasure in and boast about eliminating an input supplier who continually raised the price of the input being used in the production process. This escalation in input prices results in lower profits for the producer, higher costs in the production process, and/or product prices that no longer cover the costs of production. This, in turn, can result in economic losses for the firm. It gives entrepreneurs a real sense of satisfaction to reverse this profit squeeze position for the firm.

The last area to be described here for the need to find new input suppliers results from a need for the entrepreneur to continually reduce the overall costs of inputs in order to compete with lower-priced products. In the continuous drive of entrepreneurs to change to make the production process work better, one area of search is lowering costs. While overall cost reduction is part of process innovations to be discussed in the next chapter, input costs viewed separately are part of product innovations. As input suppliers vie for a production firm's business, one way to attain that business is through cheaper pricing of the inputs. As these input suppliers compete against each other for a production firm's business, the entrepreneur must evaluate the advantage of cheaper input prices with input quality as well as the possible need to change the production process with a new input. This is an ongoing evaluation and is part of the change that allows an entrepreneur to gain an economic advantage in marketing the product. Viewing this change as leading to temporary monopoly control and the economic arguments about which type of market best allows this change is the nucleus of the next section.

Attaining and Maintaining Temporary Monopoly Control

As was explained in an earlier section, temporary monopoly control resulting in economic profits can be attained and maintained through the discovery and utilization of new input suppliers. With new input suppliers, the desired result is a reduction in input prices and an increase in the quality of the finished product. The ultimate conclusion of this change is to allow the firm to innovate in order to attain temporary monopoly control in the industry. The type of market structure that best allows these innovations was much debated in the early part of the 1900s.

A great debate involving many economists, but championed by Joseph Schumpeter and Kenneth Arrow, revolved around whether monopoly markets or competitive markets would better serve the entrepreneur by bringing more innovations into the marketplace. Schumpeter viewed monopoly as best suited to allow entrepreneurs to bring forward innovations in the form of new products and new processes. This view stemmed from the fact that monopoly firms generally earned excess economic profits from the nature of the market and could support more research, investigation and product development, and would, therefore, successfully conclude the innovation process. The excess profits would be used to hire researchers and then employ entrepreneurs to innovate new products and processes from that research.

On the other side of the debate, Kenneth Arrow viewed competitive markets as better serving the entrepreneur because innovation was the only way for the competitor to make excess profits (albeit short-term excess profits). Professor Arrow saw monopolies as having the capacity for innovations, but lacking the initiative to develop them and bring them to the commercialization stage. Juxtaposed to the monopoly position was the position that the competitive firm was more aggressive in finding some path to economic profits. The obvious path was for the entrepreneur to innovate, creating at least temporary monopoly control of the change by bringing about new products or new processes.

There is much literature generated in this time period about whether large-scale industrial corporations or small competitive firms would, over the long term, best serve an economy by generating useful innovations. Indeed, the large corporations in the first half of the 1900s sponsored large amounts of funding for research and development. The electrical industry, comprising mainly Westinghouse, Edison Electric, and General Electric, is only one example of the large corporations in one industry that sponsored very large amounts of research and development.

However, Kenneth Arrow argued that while large monopolistic firms could and did provide major amounts of research and development, only a few of these inventions were transformed into innovations. On the contrary, innovations were often small in nature, but large in number; competitive firms continually sought ways to gain profits from a market model that allowed only short-run profits to those firms that could implement changes ahead of the majority of firms in the industry.

This debate about whether firms in competitive markets or monopoly markets are more innovative has never been conclusively resolved. However, it does appear that large corporations reduced their interest in innovations during the 1970s and 1980s. While these large companies focused on capital accumulation, expansion, and in general capitalist (but not entrepreneurial) efforts, the United States suffered from a lack of exports and increased imports of new innovative products from foreign countries. Downsizing, as it was often referred to, separated nonprofitable parts of these large firms that could no longer compete in domestic as well as international markets. However, these new smaller companies that were the product of downsizing, as well as new startup companies, seem to have generated many of the innovations that have led the United States to again be a major force in international trade.

Recent trends have had a major impact on product innovations. Two such trends are international competition among firms and technological advances in products and product development. Both of these trends have made it increasingly difficult for United States producers to gain and maintain a long-term competitive advantage. As a result, firms can usually only gain temporary monopoly control.

There are two market changes that have impacted this movement from a long-term competitive advantage to only a temporary monopoly control. First, because of the increased international competition, products have taken on a shorter product life cycle. For example, household appliances have had an 85 percent decline in life cycle over the past fifty years.[3] This trend is commonplace in many, if not most, consumer goods today. Secondly, in response to the trend in shorter product life cycles, firms are forced to introduce products into the marketplace more quickly as well as rapidly modify existing products to compete with these new products introduced into the marketplace. Short-term profits from temporary monopoly control are increasingly a result of new product introduction and product modifications. It has been estimated that new product innovations (new products and major product modifications) in the marketplace doubled in the five-year period of the early 1980s compared to the five-year period of the late 1970s.[4]

Entrepreneurial Biography 5: Gordon Hannaford

Name:	Gordon Hannaford
Company:	Point Five Windows
Number of Employees:	~60
Annual Sales:	$5 million

What events and/or people were present in your youth or early adulthood that you now realize influenced your becoming an entrepreneur?

When I was growing up, I really had no thoughts of becoming an entrepreneur. My dad was in the Air Force, so most of the kids I went to school with were Air Force children. Their parents were not entrepreneurs, and I didn't have a circle of friends really who had parents that were running their own businesses. So I really did not have many thoughts about entrepreneurship at all. When I went to college in Wisconsin, my horizons started to broaden a little bit, and my roommate's dad was a contractor, and another college fraternity brother's dad was a dentist. Most of the people in their circle of friends were entrepreneurs, and so I began to think in a broader spectrum. However, I didn't have any burning desire to launch into an enterprise.

My biggest exposure was my first job out of college at Dun and Bradstreet. As a business analyst, I would interview and rate hundreds, and over the course of thirteen years, even thousands, of different businesses from gas stations to department stores to whatever. I began to think about being more than just an employee somewhere because of the exposure to all the multiple businesses. The final jump into it was when my current partner, who I'd known for about ten years in Denver, went into business on his own making storm windows. After a year or two of doing that, he needed to expand and also look for outside capital. As a result, he decided to take on a partner. So until having an association with him, I really didn't have any master plan on getting into business myself.

Describe some of your early efforts at entrepreneurship.

Actually, I never had any entrepreneurial efforts other than starting Point Five. I had worked at Dun and Bradstreet for about thirteen years and thought that I'd probably work there for half my life and retire.

But was your partner involved in Point Five? Was that the start of Point Five with the storm windows?

Yes, he started in 1981, and I actually officially joined him in 1984. I knew he was operating with two or three employees.

And those were just storm windows?

Yes, just aluminum storm windows.

Just describe briefly that effort that you went through in that business. What were the buyer's products?

We manufactured storm windows, but we would sell, not direct retail just wholesale, to glass shops, remodeling contractors, that kind of buyer. If it were an individual that called up, we'd refer them to the dealer network that we had.

What were some events or projects that were not successful, but contributed to your success as an entrepreneur?

Like almost anything else, it's trial and error. You do something that sounds like a good idea, and when it doesn't work, you go to plan B. One time we were doing some windows for Bon Jovi in California, and instead of patina coloration, the architect wanted a shiny copper. They wanted us to lacquer the copper so that it would keep its shine. We thought whatever the customer wants, we'll do. So we accommodated the architect and shipped the windows to California. Over the course of sitting at the job site for two or three months before they were installed, they got scratched up and being on the saltwater oceanfront every scratch turned green. We had to go to California and strip them down and totally redo the finish. That was a definite mistake. Another instance came with a first request. A dress designer, who built a house in Aspen, wanted very dark tinted windows that faced the sun. We did that, but not ever having done it before, we didn't realize that in very intense, direct high-altitude sun on a very dark glass, the heat expansion causes the glass to fail. We replaced glass in her house for several years. Things like that made us a little older and wiser.

But most of it's trial and error?

Yes, I'd say much of it is trial and error.

Anything else?

Another example of trial and error would be developing a written contractual document through a long trial and error process. We started at first just having price and terms and delivery date, not really thinking of all the multitude of things that can occur when you didn't spell things out distinctly in the contract. Over the course of time we had a one-page contract, then a two and three and now it's about five, but we're much better protected from everybody saying. "Oh, I thought this." So the specifics of the contract were a serious learning period.

What project stands out as one of your major entrepreneurial successes?

One of the biggest ones was one of our first projects. We were doing pine historic restoration jobs and decided that we should consider some different custom wood species instead of the pine that most generic assembly-line manufacturers use. We thought that maybe once a year we'd find a big house that could afford some oak, teak, or mahogany. We had a salesman go to Aspen, and the first house he came across was the 55,000-square-foot home of Prince Bandar, the Saudi Arabian ambassador to the United States. It had 490 solid mahogany windows. We bid $600,000, thinking that no one could afford that. We were pretty naïve; on a scale of a $35 million house, that's not that much: He accepted our bid, and that was a pretty eye-opening experience. Our first $1.3 million contract just for windows was from a client in Lake Tahoe. That's been our record contract. We just signed our second $1 million plus windows-only contract for a house belonging to a software developer. Those are some of the larger contracts.

But you've done windows in houses for some very prominent people in the United States. Can you give us a brief list or drop a few names?

We've done work for Carol Burnett, Cindy Crawford, and Bon Jovi; however, not all the houses that we do belong to famous people. Some homes have belonged to investment bankers who have done exceptionally well and invested in large houses in the last ten years. Another job was for someone who had several Pizza Hut franchises, and when Pepsi bought them out, they cashed out with $5 million to put into a house.

So a lot of the people you deal with are rather affluent but are anonymous and want to stay that way.

They're not internationally known. They may be known in their town, their state, or in their industry, but not nationally.

What event stands out as a major stumbling block that you needed to overcome as an entrepreneur?

There were a couple near-killers, and many times we thought we should have hung it up instead of hanging in there. The biggest one was during the Iraq-Kuwait war in the early 1990s. We had just gotten the Prince Bandar job, and that had required us to go from forty to eighty employees in about a month, which was a huge mistake. In a custom environment you can't expand that fast, but we didn't know that. However, we didn't have much choice. We either had to turn the contract down, in which [case] we get the reputation that we couldn't do big jobs, or take the job and show people we could do a big job. In the middle of that project, the Iraq-Kuwait war hit. At that time we were doing about 50 percent of the high-end residential but still doing about 50 percent of the historic restoration projects. A lot of those were government projects of old courthouses, city hall buildings, or government entity types of situations. They are restoring a 100-year-old building to its original stature to be used as a functional government facility for the next hundred years.

Within days of the Iraq-Kuwait invasion, every government historic project got put on hold. Even the residential projects got pushed back because there was so much uncertainty. Until the U.S. coalition was formed, nobody knew if we'd be in World War III depending on how the Arab countries aligned. Our volume dropped

85 percent in thirty days and we'd just geared up to double our previous all-time record of employees, obligations, and overhead. We lost $300,000 in one year, and we had equity of about $40,000. That was a serious blow, and even though the Iraq-Kuwait war took about three months to settle down, government contracts stayed on hold in the historic area for about one year. We very nearly didn't recover from that and needed help from family, banks, and suppliers extending credit beyond our normal terms.

The second stumbling block was a historic project we did for East High School, which is one of the more prominent high schools of the old money in Denver. The school was restored using architecturally correct historic restoration. The general contractor on that project filed bankruptcy, and we lost about $200,000. Even though we had a performance bond, the project was strung out over such a long period of time that there was legal disagreement over when we could file the claim for damages to the bonding company. The bonding company ended up paying only a small percentage of the claim. Had we been older and wiser, we'd have shut down our production on it as soon as the contractor started delaying payment that would have limited our expenses. Since we had just suffered a $300,000 loss on the Saudi Arabian difficulty, we were so strapped financially that when the contractor threatened, "If you don't give me my next shipment, I'm not going to give you the last payment," we were between a rock and a hard place. We had to have some money coming in and so we continued to fund the project so we could get some money from it.

Those cumulative things were half a million dollars, and our investment in the company was now $50,000. Without begging and borrowing from about everyone we knew, we'd never have made it. Those were two stumbling blocks that to this day, I'm not sure how we got through either one of them.

Both of those relate to the capital versus cash flow problems that you see in a company. It was your cash flow that was your real stumbling block.

Yes. When we were a two- or three-man storm window business, our up-front money wasn't that big, but when we were fronting

$100,000 shipments on thirty-day terms like the contractor, we just didn't have the cash flow to cover our activities. If I had to do it all over again, I would change the initial capitalization as the first order of business. Even if I made the same mistakes, it was the capitalization that just about killed us.

What advice could you give someone who has aspirations of becoming an entrepreneur?

In my opinion, capitalization is probably the primary thing. You really should never stop looking for capital. You may be adequately capitalized for where you are now, but if you have any plans for expansion, you still need to continue looking. It doesn't necessarily have to be an outside investor. It could be an increasing bank line of credit or an outside investor. The existing principals need to put in more money or at least put themselves in a position to be able to put in more money so that you're able to fund the expansion. The bigger you get, the more up-front money you need. We were in a situation on those previous two loss periods where we had a negative half-a-million-dollar equity, and our interest in late charges to suppliers was six figures. If we'd been adequately capitalized, the six figures would have been profit, and we could have come out of that deficit a lot faster. As it was, it took us almost ten years to earn back that deficit. So capitalization is very serious.

What you're saying is that capitalization will allow the ease in cash flow for your day-to-day, week-to-week expenses, incomes and revenues. You have to have the capitalization before you can have the correct cash flow.

Correct. Everyone hears the story about someone starting with $200 in their garage, and four years later they're Microsoft or a company worth a billion dollars. That happens very rarely and is a one-in-a-million success story with an untold number of people who find this type of capitalization is unsuccessful for them. Starting on a shoestring and hitting the jackpot overnight is an incredible combination of picking the right place, right time, right product, right everything. There are thousands of bankruptcy cases in every state but you don't hear thousands of stories of overnight rags to riches.

Somewhat akin to the odds of winning the lottery?

Yes. Management is a serious component. You tend to think when you're starting out that you're willing to bleed for the company, you're willing to be there at 5 or 6 A.M. until 6, 7 or 8 P.M. and when you're there, it's your baby, and you're going to work hard all the time. You assume that everyone else is going to do that. Generally people are pretty good if properly directed, but if you don't have strong supervisory or management people and no structure, you might have a decent employee, a decent person with a decent work ethic, that might just casually stroll through the day and not do much else.

It's rather like having a coach in athletics. You may have a world-class athlete, but they won't do as well on their own compared to their success if they have a coach. You have to have a coach pushing you and directing you. Professional football has a strength coach, a speed coach, everything. They can work hard on their own, but they're not going to do as well without someone bringing out the best in them. Organizationally, you always have to have the combination of sales, finance, and management. You can have sales, but if you don't finance or manage well, they will not do you any good. You could have great financing and management, but if you have no sales, it doesn't work. You have to have those three things in place in their proper perspective.

Other advice includes the concept that you have to walk before you run. That was one of our problems when we accepted the Prince Bandar project. We thought we'd get a typical storm window order of $1,000; we thought we might get an entrance way to a house that might be a contract for $5,000 or $10,000 and that would have been better for us. We would have added one person, and then two people and gradually worked up. However, we got a monster job that gave us a reputation of being able to do that job, but it was too much too soon. We have a sign in our office that says, "Never give up." I think it's a commonly displayed poster. There's a stork or big bird that has a frog halfway down its throat, and the frog is just about to be swallowed. The frog's arms come out of the mouth of the bird with a chokehold on the bird's neck so it's not able to swallow the frog. We've had that sign in our office for twenty years. If you have something you believe in, then stick with it. However, sticking with it without everything in place may not be the smartest thing to do. We stuck with it without everything in its right place for a long time.

Describe your current enterprise.

We do strictly ultra custom wood windows and doors. We have no catalog; it's whatever the customer's architect can dream up in size, shape, and materials. If it's never been built in the history of the world, we tell the customer they can have it. We get blueprints from the architect with a conceptual drawing of the size, shape, and design of the window. Then it goes to our engineering department, and they discuss primarily with the architect joinery, what material options are, any kind of wood species, any kind of glass, every detail. Details including where they actually want the hardware placed, what spacing they want between the hinges, literally every detail possible. Mathematically, there are over ten million combinations in the computer of materials, size, shape, and design that we can offer someone in a window. It's about a two-month process once they sign a contract to just get the shop drawings okayed. Once they're okayed, it goes to the shop floor. We do everything in-house; we get our own lumber, do our own millwork, and make our own insulated glass units.

When we do the copper cladding, we bend our own copper to our own shape. When we do the milling, we cut our own knives for whatever profiles they want. We do our own patina on the copper, so really we don't sub anything out. We control the process all the way through to make sure we have a quality level that's above

what we could get from a normal supplier. Once the linear components have gone through the milling process, we cut to length and
process the joinery. Then it goes to an assembly process. Most
window companies just staple the components together; we glue
and screw everything together with solid brass or stainless steel
screws. After the basic sash and frames are assembled, we bend
the copper and the window gets the copper added. We hand fit
every piece; a mass-produced company would precut 500 or 1,000
of every length. We hand fit every piece so that there are no gaps
between the copper.

A mass-produced mentality would precut a lot of things and
then, if it didn't quite hit the corners, caulking it would be a solution. Our customer's looking for furniture and artwork rather than
caulked corners. After the copper is installed, the unit is complete
except for the hardware. It next goes into a finalizing stage where
hardware, weather stripping, locks, hinges, and handles are added.
These fixtures can be brass, pewter, cast iron, or whatever materials someone might want. The last stage is when the window goes
to the glazing area and gets the glass set. That's the last thing before
shipping because it adds the most weight. We've done bulletproof
glass in a house, tinted, stained, laminated, and tempered, whatever anyone wants. Then it goes out into the shipping process.

**You ship some pretty large windows. Can you give the reader
an idea of that?**

We've done sliding patio doors and screens that were probably
thirty feet wide and twelve feet tall. We've done picture windows
that are fifteen feet by twenty feet. We've done doors that were
fourteen feet tall, which are almost a story and a half. We had to
certify that they would hold up in a 140-mph hurricane and not
break. Those weighed about 400 pounds per door leaf. They had
to be pretty stout units. It wouldn't be uncommon for a door leaf
of 400 pounds to have a total weight of 1,000 pounds for one double
door unit. At the job site they have to be set with a crane almost
like a commercial installation.

You shipped a very large window to Montana that took some special permitting, a very large single A-frame window if I remember right?

Yes, it wouldn't fit inside a regular semi, so we had to get a flatbed and build an A-frame on the flatbed to put the window on and tie it down. Then we had to cover all that with a wood and canvas protected shell so that rocks on the highway wouldn't hit it on the long trip. The dimensions were about thirty feet by twelve feet.

You've done some fairly exotic woods in your windows. Do you want to tell us a little about that?

We've worked with African bubinga wood, which is a form of African rosewood, and we've done normal cherry teak mahogany. We had a request for long leaf pine, which is generic to the southeast United States, and the requirements were that the tree had to have been cut down over 100 years old. It was partially for ecological reasons. The owner wanted recycled wood but probably wanted just to tell the neighbor that it was 100-year-old wood. It couldn't be ninety-three-year-old wood. We found someone in Tennessee who dismantled old buildings and could verify from the real estate records that the building was built in 1872, so the beams and timbers would have been over 100 years old.

We also had a person who wanted cypress wood, and the source of the cypress had to be a dismantled Jim Beam whiskey vat. Jim Beam whiskey vats are about eighteen feet tall and as big around as most houses and last about seventy years. As whiskey vats have to be replaced, the customer bought the dismantled whiskey vat and shipped the eighteen-foot beams to us to use in making the windows. Again, this was probably just so he could tell his neighbor this used to be a whiskey vat because we could certainly have gotten cypress from a lumber mill. Iroka wood is in the teak family, and a lady in Aspen wanted that, but we couldn't just get a load of iroka wood. Instead, she flew to Italy to see a shipbuilder, picked out her boards, put them on a ship, and shipped them back to us.

We've probably had twenty or thirty different wood species over the years, and we still get jobs that have a wood species that is completely unknown to us. Someone will find a wood species in his or her travels abroad and decide that is the wood that they want for their windows.

Describe your feelings toward your enterprise. Would you sell your enterprise? Would you work for a new owner? Would you take on a partner?

Now that it's been twenty years I probably would sell my share of the enterprise. As you approach sixty, your willingness to risk being $0.5 million dollars negative equity is far different than when you were thirty-five or forty. Even though we're not in that situation anymore, the risk of that happening is less palatable, especially since we've been through it before. We have entertained the idea of selling and will probably do that in the next two years. We probably would sell if we had an arrangement that would make us financially independent. If it were just trading a job for something else, then we would probably not sell. I would sell even if my partner did not sell. I think I could work for a new owner if there was a two- to three-year transition period without any trouble.

Since you have a partner, would you take on a different partner than your current partner?

Probably. I would want it to be some reasonable personality and philosophy match. If you're basically a conservative person or your partner is a riverboat gambler, the two extremes would be salt and pepper, oil and vinegar, and probably not match up. When we needed financial help before we turned the corner and pulled our way out through profits, we had a number of discussions with additional investors. Even though we were in a little more desperate situation at that time, there's still concern about the compatibility of how somebody else would want to do business. But yes, I would consider a new partner pending some degree of compatibility.

How do you stay competitive with other firms in your industry?

There are probably three things. At least in our market, number one is your integrity and reputation. Somebody with a lot of money is accustomed to having people try to gouge them and say, "Oh, they've got big bucks; I'll just pad my bid and make a big score." They didn't get to be wealthy by not paying attention to that kind of thing. So we are really conscientious about being straight shooters. A lot of the construction industry has a bad reputation for bidding something at cost and then making it up on change orders. They are hoping there will be change orders and that they can double the change order costs and make a profit that way. They'll bid the project at no cost just to get the job. We're real conscious about making sure that nobody has any questions about whether we're shooting straight or not. One of the ways we do that is when we bid a job, we give a copy of the bid disk with the bid. If they cancel two windows and replace it with one bigger one, they can go in to the computer and subtract those two smaller windows, or they can enter the bigger one. It will give them a pricing change, and they'll know that we're making that change order at exactly the same pricing structure as when we bid it. No other window company we've dealt with has ever done that.

One of the older companies in New York that's been doing custom work for about 100 years has a terrible reputation of increasing prices on change order requests. They'll bid a job and leave out $30,000 worth of a certain kind of glass. When the project is in the final stages and ready for delivery, they'll call up the customer and say, "Oh, we forgot something; we have to add $30,000 to your contract." It's too late, and the customer usually ends up paying the increased cost. Because of the size of the house, standard openings are not available, and the owner can't just go down to the lumberyard and say, "I want your windows." They've already built the house, they've framed it out, and they've got bizarre window sizes and shapes. They could select another window company and get those sizes and shapes, but they'd have to stop production on a $5 or $10 million house for four months and that's going to cost them more than $30,000. Therefore, they are forced to pay a ransom. We've had several bidding competitions with this particular company where, before we got our reputation, we lost the bid to this company. Later, additional work was given to our company because the owner felt taken advantage of and wouldn't deal with the other company for the rest of the project. If your reputation is such that the customer can trust you to give them honest value, then you will gain business volume. In the long run your repeat business is going to be a lot greater.

The other competitive area is software. My partner has written the software for both the programming and the bidding, and we're able to bid those 10 million combinations in a very responsive time. We can bid a project that's several hundred windows and a several-hundred-thousand-dollar window job. If we bid it out of oak, we can get them a bid in about one day; most companies take about two to three weeks. Then if there's any change in the bid such as "what if I had this same job out of mahogany," "what if I had the same job, but different glass," we can get a return bid to them in a matter of hours. Other companies say they need weeks to figure out what would result from that change. Responsiveness of our software, as well as being able to let the customer bid it without even asking us, is essential.

The last thing is service and that's probably generic to most companies. When you're doing one-of-a-kind items, no matter how you engineer and plan it, there can always be something that doesn't operate quite right. However, as long as you correct it, the customer will be satisfied. They want to know even if something needs adjustment; they want to know if it will work in the long run. We'll go to great lengths to make sure they end up with what they want. For instance, with the tinted glass on the Aspen house, the architect did the specs and approved the tint for the glass. We warrant the glass for five years, sometimes longer if it's in the contract, but we probably wouldn't have had to warrant it at all because of the expansion in the glass. We replaced glass units for almost eight years. We had no legal obligation to do that. However, we wanted to make sure if anybody ever asked our customer, they could never tell anyone that we'd left them high and dry. We did it for several years beyond any legal requirement. Our important success factors are service, integrity, and the responsiveness in our software.

What innovations have you implemented to improve your enterprise?

The unlimited wood species is one of the primary innovations. There are about 2,500 window manufacturers, and probably only about half a dozen of them would do different wood species. Some of them just do mahogany and cherry. I don't know if there are any other firms that will do any wood species in the world or the dismantled whiskey vat. Usually it's too much organizational trouble to use those wood species in the plant. We're the first company to put copper on the exterior of a window to make it maintenance free; most mass-produced companies use vinyl and aluminum. We do a patina finish on the copper like a sculptor would use; a couple of the mass-produced companies have tried to copy us, but they don't do the patina, only shiny copper. Therefore, we were the first to do copper cladding work, which was an idea of one of our salesmen so we could do something different from everyone else. The patina on the copper is pretty unique. Outside of a casting foundry, probably no one does patina on anything.

Most companies have a catalog with size limitations. The houses we bid on are usually on a lot that cost $1 million or more, and it overlooks the lake or the ocean or a ski slope, and the owner may want to maximize that view. They don't want a bunch of little windows strung together to make a view; they want huge windows. We've not had any size or design limitations where most other companies have limits. Basically, if someone comes to us and says "We want this," and nobody else will do it, we try to be the candy store for the person who wants something that nobody else can provide. We try to have ourselves organizationally placed so we can actually put that idea through to a plan. Other companies are just not geared to do anything other than cookie cutter sizes and shapes.

Notes

1. Robert W. Clower and John F. Due, *Microeconomics* (Homewood, IL: Irwin, 1972), p. 345.

2. Chris Freeman and Luc Soete, *The Economics of Industrial Innovation*, 3d ed. (Cambridge, MA: MIT Press, 1997), pp. 58–61.

3. Hamid Noori, *Managing the Dynamics of New Technology* (Englewood Cliffs, NJ: Prentice-Hall, 1990), p. 76.

4. S. Fraker, "High-Speed Management for the High-Tech Age," *Fortune*, March 5, 1984, pp. 62–68.

6

Innovations in Process

Standardizing the Product and Streamlining the Production Process

As new products are first developed, as was explained in chapter 5, they are first-hand built or custom made in the development and demonstration stages of product development. As the product becomes accepted by increasing numbers of consumers, a need rapidly arises to produce the product in ever-increasing numbers. Two events occur simultaneously allowing this increased production to occur. The first event is standardizing the product and the second event is the development of a more rapid assembly-line process. Although these events often happen simultaneously, each will be discussed separately.

Before a product can be produced in a rapid assembly-line process, often referred to as "mass production," the product must go through changes and adjustments allowing it to be standardized. This is sometimes referred to as "product uniformity." As a product begins going through the demonstration stage of product development, the product may be custom built much like products in a machine shop or fabricating plant. The product is described to the fabricator by the user in terms of the use that is needed, and the fabricator attempts to build a product that is functionally acceptable to the user.

Once the product fulfills the intended use, it may be duplicated by the fabricator for other potential users. Likewise, the product may be altered to better fit the use or changed to better fit additional uses. As this process continues, a more standardized product develops. Possibly some of the components can be purchased from another manufacturer, and this becomes a standard component of the new product. These standard components begin to make assembly quicker, easier, and more efficient.

Whether additional components are steel, wood, plastic, etc., once increased production occurs, these components can be ordered from input suppliers in specified dimensions. This ordering process eliminates wasted input supplies that are left over after custom cutting or custom shaping specific input pieces for the new product. Also, this cutting and shaping process is costly in time and effort, as it is not directly part of the desired product development. Again, by ordering inputs in specific dimensions, wasted excess inputs are eliminated, as well as the custom labor for cutting and shaping.

In order to allow this standardization of inputs and preassembled parts, the final product needs to become even more standardized. In order for this to be acceptable to the user of the product, a "one size fits all" uniform product must be developed. Continued innovations will likely be needed in order to develop the product into a standardized unit that meets the requirements of many, if not most, of the users. During this stage of product development, prototype innovation is high and the entrepreneur rapidly modifies, changes, and upgrades the product in an effort to establish a dominant design that best fits the various needs of most potential users.

This standardization of the product was first made possible by Eli Whitney's development of interchanging parts, as described in chapter 3, and military firearms and the automobile industry are obvious examples. As military firearms became standardized for many different divisions of the military, a more uniform firearm could utilize interchangeable parts. These parts could be preassembled, manufactured by many different firms, and assembled into a final product in different locations. This standardizing process allowed mass production to occur.

Likewise, Henry Ford developed an automobile that had many parts that were replaceable through purchases from local hardware stores. Parts that were specific to the Model T were at least standardized and interchangeable so that replacement parts could be ordered and retrofitted, which in turn allowed the continuation of the serviceability of the automobile. Before the Model T, most automobile makers offered several different sized engines requiring job shop type assembly. Henry Ford left no options for the Model T, but produced millions of autos with a single basic engine and design.[1]

The standardization of the product is a necessary prerequisite of process innovations in order to streamline the production process. However, once the process innovations begin, continued product innovations may be required to continue improvements in process innovations. These process innovations are required to speed the production process and increase the volume of products generated.

The two main results of process innovations are cost reductions and increased quantity. Also, less important but a usual result of process innovations, is enhanced uniform quality. This mass produced product with substantially reduced cost of production does leave the firm in a highly inflexible state, but if the product innovations have been properly developed, the consumer needs have been properly met. Figure 6.1 summarizes the flow from product need to the mass produced product.

Input Changes in the Production Process

In an attempt to understand fully the production process, as well as the push to make the production process more efficient, it is important to understand the economic relationship between inputs and the product (output) generated from this production process. Because of the two-dimensional restriction of a figure, it is common to discuss the economic concepts of production by allowing only one input to vary at a time and observing this variance on the changes to production. This analysis could use any

Figure 6.1 **Flow Progression of Product Development and Refinement for Process Innovation**

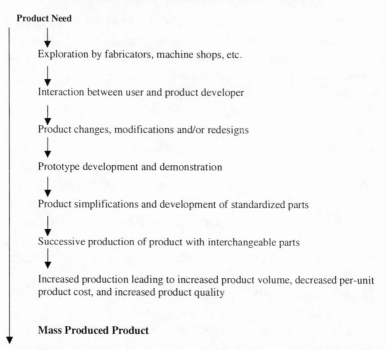

Product Need

↓

Exploration by fabricators, machine shops, etc.

↓

Interaction between user and product developer

↓

Product changes, modifications and/or redesigns

↓

Prototype development and demonstration

↓

Product simplifications and development of standardized parts

↓

Successive production of product with interchangeable parts

↓

Increased production leading to increased product volume, decreased per-unit product cost, and increased product quality

Mass Produced Product

variable input and be repeated for each variable input, but the theoretical relationship between the variable input and production will always remain the same. That is, the theoretical relationships between total product, average product, and marginal product will always remain unchanged and only the numbers for inputs and the amount of production will vary as different inputs are substituted into the graphical model. Figure 6.2 will be used to show the relationships that always exist between a variable input and the resulting production.

Total product is simply the sum total of the units of output being produced with differing quantities of the variable input. Average product is the result of dividing total units being produced by the amount of variable input required to attain that particular level of production. Likewise, marginal product is the additional or extra production attained by a particular unit of input. That is, mar-

Figure 6.2 **Production: The Relationship Between Total Product (TP), Average Product (AP), and Marginal Product (MP)**

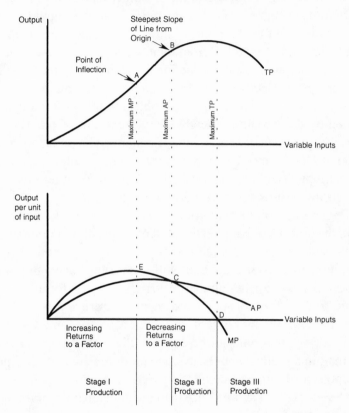

ginal product is the additional production from an additional unit of input. The first significant point on the total product curve is the point of inflection (point *A*). This point represents the change in slope of the total product curve from increasing to decreasing.

Although the slope of the total product is positive to the left of the point of inflection, the slope of the total product curve is increasing at an increasing rate. To the right of the point of inflection, the slope of the curve is still increasing, but at a decreasing rate. This point is significant because it identifies the maximum of the marginal product curve—that is, the point where additional variable inputs will increase total production, but by a lesser amount than the previous unit of variable input. For example, the variable input just to the left of the point of inflection might have added thirty units of output, whereas the unit of variable input immediately to the right of the point of inflection would have increased total product, but by a lesser amount, possibly twenty-four units. Although output or total production is continuing to increase, it is increasing by successively lesser amounts with the addition of another unit of variable input. Graphically, this point is demonstrated by the maximum height (output per unit of input) of the marginal product curve or point E. Economically, points to the left of point E are referred to as increasing returns to a factor (variable unit of input), and points to the right of point E are referred to as decreasing returns to a factor (variable unit of input).

The second point of significance is the steepest slope of a line from the origin to a point on the total product curve (point B). This point represents the maximum height of the average product curve. Adding a unit of variable input will increase the average product (output divided by the number of variable inputs) for all units of inputs to the left of this point and decrease average product for all input quantities to the right of this point. Also, for some very technical reasons that will not be explained here, this point is where the marginal product and the average product are equal. This point is represented by point C in the figure.

The last point of significance in this discussion is the point where marginal product (additional production resulting from an additional unit of variable input) becomes zero. The level of production is represented by the point where another unit of variable input will not increase the total amount of product. This point is represented by point D in the figure. Although total production remains large, it decreases and marginal product becomes negative to the right of point D.

The purpose of this detailed analysis of production and variable inputs can now be revealed. In every efficient production process, no matter what kind of product, firm, or industry, maximum efficiency will always occur in stage II level of production. This area of production will always occur between points C and D in the

figure and is appropriately labeled in the figure as stage II production. Maximum profits, production efficiency, and correct input utilization for the firm will always occur in this narrow region of the total
product (*TP*), average product (*AP*), and marginal product (*MP*) curves.
With this limited amount of knowledge of economic theory, the entrepreneur can move easily and quickly to the region of production
that is required to maximize profits as well as production efficiencies
for the firm. The question then quickly becomes, "How does the entrepreneur find stage II production"? Some quick examples will illustrate the ease with which this stage can be located.

Using labor as an example of a variable input in a production
process, the entrepreneur can quickly determine if the firm is still
in stage I production and thus is in need of adding more labor or in
stage III and needs to reduce labor input in the production process.
In stage I production, the marginal product is always greater than
the average product. Therefore, if an additional unit of labor (possibly the output from adding one additional worker for one day)
adds more production than the average product (total production
divided by the total number of all workers), marginal product is
greater than average product and the firm is still in stage I production. Therefore, adding the additional worker (unit of variable input) by the entrepreneur will lead the firm toward stage II
production. Thus, adding variable units of input (labor) should be
added until the marginal product falls below the average product.
This area is determined by the fact that the marginal product (additional production from adding an additional worker) will be less
than the average product (the value of total production divided by
the total number of workers). It should be noted here that while
returns to a factor (increasing and decreasing) are significant in
economic theory, they do not have a part in determining production efficiencies or maximum profits for the firm. The importance
of returns to a factor are that maximum profits will occur (1) after
decreasing returns to a factor have occurred, and (most impor-
tantly) (2) after marginal product has fallen below average product.

Stage III can also quickly be determined using labor as the example of the variable unit in the production process. If an addi-

tional worker is added and the level of total production decreases, stage III production has been attained. Obviously this position is detrimental for the firm because the worker is increasing costs at the same time revenues from the production process are reduced as a result of the decreasing production level. Production process efficiencies will quickly increase with a reduction in the amount of labor (variable input) used in the production process if a firm is in stage III production.

The economic reasoning behind why profits for the firm will be maximized and highest efficiencies will be attained in stage II production will not be detailed in this brief analysis of production and production curves. However, the entrepreneur will be assured that somewhere in stage II production both maximum profit and maximum production efficiency will occur. Stated another way, if the entrepreneur does not adjust inputs to move production to stage II, it can be guaranteed that the firm will neither attain maximum profits nor maximum production efficiency.

Moving from the Batch to the Flow Process

Over the past century many industries, including steel, oil, and chemical industries, have enjoyed a high rate of productivity advance from innovations in the production process. However, many industries, including the three examples above, experienced major changes in process innovations as changes in techniques of each industry allowed the movement from batch to flow processes of production. This change from a batch to a flow process allows three major economic changes to occur. First, this change allows major economies of scale to be captured. Second, new plant construction for flow processes will drastically reduce per-unit cost of production. And third, major reductions in labor costs and resulting large increases in labor productivity will occur.

The transition from a batch to a flow process is an important and usually essential step to both lowering the cost per unit of production and speeding the production process in the movement toward mass production. The flow process of production is sometimes referred to as "continuous process manufacturing." In continuous process manufacturing the plant is arranged so that production is done from inputs to the ultimate output product in as nearly a continuous, routine order as possible. That is, a continuous flow process occurs from the first and most basic ingredient to the next required ingredient or part until the final finished product is complete.

This transition from a batch to a flow process was probably first achieved by Oliver Evans in the textile industry in the very late 1700s. This transition in the textile industry, however, did not require assembly of input parts in the production process. As mentioned earlier, the first flow process of assembly of input parts into a finished product was accomplished by Eli Whitney to fulfill government contracts for military firearms in the 1800s. This flow process was duplicated by agricultural machinery companies with the use of conveyor belts, and later by Henry Ford in the moving assembly of automobile production, in the early 1900s.

When Henry Ford originally began assembling automobiles, he used a stationary system of subassemblies where a batch process was used to assemble one automobile at a time. This early process could not utilize a continuous movement assembly-line process. Beginning in the early 1900s, the Ford plant adopted a moving assembly concept that began the movement toward the flow process of more complex manufacturing. The success of Henry Ford, Andrew Carnegie, the DuPont Company, and other entrepreneurs was made possible as they envisioned their products being manufactured in methods that allowed a transition from the batch to the flow (continuous movement) process.

Flow processes in production are far more efficient than the discontinuous batch processes for most industries and a flow process allows a more uniform product through facilitation of a monitoring and control system for the product. This monitoring process often leads to a higher-quality product from a flow process. An example using the oil industry might help the understanding of the economic benefits of moving from a batch process to a flow process of production.

Although the refining of crude oil was successfully demonstrated in the mid-1800s, little was done with the "cracked" oil for several decades. The original (batch) process consisted of heating a vat of crude oil and through a series of different elevations and tubes for liquid and gases, different types of products were captured from the crude oil. This batch process could capture petrol (gasoline), a light product known as kerosene, and a heavier product that became known as fuel oil. Demand for these products eventually started increasing as a result of the growth in the automobile industry and as a result of fuel oil replacing coal for home heating. This resulted in a need to increase the refining capacity for ever-increasing amounts of refined petroleum.

The batch process of oil refining production had two problems. First, this process was slow and the start and stop process to change batches restricted available supplies and was quite costly per unit of product. Second, this batch process of oil production used methods that gave a very low yield of the lighter products that were increasing in demand. As a large number of smaller refineries continued the batch process, the product demand neared production capacity and exploration began on new and improved processes to extract lighter fuels in greater volume.

Over several decades, the development of a catalytic cracking process allowed for a continuous flow of crude oil processed into ever-increasing volumes of lighter fuels for the rapidly increasing automobile market. This process allowed a continuous flow of crude oil to flow into the refinery and a continuous flow of different qualities of fuels to be processed without interruption. The estimated total research and development cost to develop this original flow process of fuel products was historically recouped each year in royalties. In addition, per-unit cost of refining fuel in real dollars has been drastically reduced. Likewise, labor efficiency has drastically increased.

The transition from a batch process to a flow process has occurred with similar results in other industries such as steel and the chemical industry. The basic transition is to stop the one unit process where ingredients are placed and mixed in a vat or container and to move to a continuous operation where inputs are added continuously at the beginning of the process and the final product is continually supplied at the end of the flow process.

The early batch process plants at the turn of the century were producing refined petroleum at a capacity of 500 barrels per day. By the mid-1950s with a flow process for producing refined petroleum, the capacity of an average refining plant had reached 100,000 barrels per day.[2] The plant size had not grown drastically, but the process had allowed an enormous increase in productive capacity. The innovations in the transition from batch to flow process are some of the most impressive and successful developments in the general area of process innovations.

Entrepreneurial Biography 6: Tim Galloway

Name:	Tim Galloway
Company:	Summit Restaurant and Summit Limousine
Number of Employees:	27 in the restaurant and 9 in the limousine service
Annual Sales:	The restaurant makes $800,000; the limousine service, $180,000.

What events and/or people were present in your youth or early adulthood that you now realize influenced your becoming an entrepreneur?

I have two that I can think of. One is a relative, and the other is a very close friend of mine. My relative is a great uncle of mine who was dean of the business school at the University of Colorado and was very influential in my rearing as a child, just talking to him and the great knowledge that he had. And he put a challenge, I guess, in my heart that you don't have to do things just the way they say they are sometimes. Another is a good friend of mine also in Boulder that I grew up with. He was about three years older than I was. I saw him go through some successes with businesses that he started from nothing and the fact that he could succeed really intrigued me. Everything he touches still seems to turn to gold, so he really does have that golden touch. I realized early on that I wasn't the type of person that would be well suited behind a desk and having the same office space every day. I'm just much more energetic than that and feel that it's just not suited to my brain waves and the way I like to think.

Describe some of your early efforts at entrepreneurship.

In my early efforts I had a paper route. One thing that I did as a child was to turn my backyard into an amusement park. We had putt-putt golf, slides, and all sorts of different things, and I charged the entire neighborhood to come in and play. I turned the garage into a maze that was completely dark, and we had a scare house and that sort of stuff. I think early on I kind of saw that I could use my own little intuitions to make something out of nothing. That was probably my earliest recollection that I could really succeed in something.

In college or just out of college, what were your entrepreneurial interests?

All through college I worked for people. I just wanted to absorb the knowledge. I did that out of college also. In my mind's eye I knew that I wanted my own restaurant, but I knew I didn't have the means or the expertise. So I battened down and put together a ten-year game plan of what I needed to accomplish and what I needed to learn. I received training with some large corporations, very successful corporations that showed me how to run a restaurant both in front of the house and in the back of the house. I also went to work for a food brokerage firm—the people that sell food to institutions and restaurants. I wanted to learn the book of the salesman. I wanted to learn the attitude of what a salesman is thinking when he walks in the back door. So I did that for a year and a half. Then when I was twenty-seven years old, I had an opportunity to finally get involved in a business, and the carrot was dangling in front of my face, and I was challenged. I got burned on that deal, though; it never turned out the way I really wanted it to. However, it certainly gave me the knowledge of what I could sustain and what I could achieve.

What were some events or projects that were not successful, but contributed to your success as an entrepreneur?

One was what I just mentioned. I was working for a gentleman who was one of my early child acquaintances and really influenced my life. He challenged me while working for him at his restaurant that if I did this and I did that that, I could achieve ownership. The bigger the hoops, the higher I had to jump. That really didn't work well for me. It really was a failure in my life and almost cost me my marriage. The fact that it was a nightclub with all the influences that go with that just weren't conducive to family life. So when this restaurant became available in 1988, that's when we fantasized and massaged the ideas of what we could achieve. However, my biggest failure would have to be the involvement with the nightclub and not being able to buy it.

What project stands out as one of your major entrepreneurial successes?

It has to be the limousine service and the fact that I actually started it from nothing. There were no services available in Loveland and at the time my partner and I, Tim Veldhuizen, realized that all the limousines would pull up to the restaurant. We did a little research and found it's an unregulated business, and only the strong survive in that industry, but we decided we'd take a chance. To get into that industry, you first have to purchase a limousine, and then you can get your licenses through the state and through the Public

Utility Commission (PUC). So it's a backward situation, but we took a leap of faith that maybe we could make this work and purchased a car. The first year and a half we did all the driving ourselves. I mean, we did everything. We worked here full time, we did that full time, and had to dedicate ourselves to make it work. We couldn't afford to hire anybody, had no advertising, and it was just a word-of-mouth business. That was eight years ago, and every year since then has been an incredible success.

And the restaurant?

I became involved in the restaurant in 1988. In 1994, I bought out the stock of my partners. That's also when I bought out my partner in the limousine service, and now it's just my wife and I in the restaurant and myself in the limousine company.

What event stands out as a major stumbling block that you need to overcome as an entrepreneur?

For me it was financing. The time had come for me to step up to the plate with the bat and buy out my partners. Six months previously, we'd had our stockholders' meeting and had developed a good value of the stock. I knew what amount of financing I needed, and I put together a really strong performer. The restaurant was performing well, but financing depended on my personal assets. Having a successful corporation, having a successful business, wasn't good enough. I had to find some private financing because the institutional lenders just wouldn't do it.

How many banks did you approach?

Nine.

Nine banks?

Yes, and I got turned down by nine banks. I worked together with the Loveland Economic Business Development Council, and they helped me put together some strong ideas on how to approach a banker. What I got from my father was an insurance policy that could be cashed out, and I used that as collateral. So for every dollar that I borrowed I had to put up a dollar in collateral. So really getting in and being an entrepreneur was an awakening for me on how hard it can be when you try to do it on your own. The stumbling blocks are huge.

What advice could you give someone who has aspirations of becoming an entrepreneur?

I would recommend that they do their homework. They really need to learn as much as they can about the particular industry that they want to get into. Try to find a mentor that would be able to guide you over some of the stumbling blocks, one perhaps that has been through it in the past. I would recommend possibly getting into the industry and working for an individual; trying to find the ups and downs of the whole thing. I think partnerships work great because instead of trying to do it all by yourself, you can bounce things back and forth. But you have to make sure that things are mapped out exactly in your partnership and that you know what your responsibilities are, what your partner's are, and then you won't trudge over each other's ideas or responsibilities. You share them and you grow together.

Describe your current enterprise.

I currently run the restaurant. My title is general manager, and my wife is office manager. She is actually president of the corporation, and I am vice president. We work in tandem running the operation, and I have some key employees that help me run the restaurant when I'm not there. The enterprise is a dining house that's been quite successful in the twenty-four years that it's been here; but it's always challenged me by being an independent, and all the corporate restaurants wanting my slice of the pie. I've not only built the restaurant on its own merits, but I've built it on my own personality. A lot of people who come to the restaurant not only want the quality of the food, the atmosphere, and the ambience, but they want to see Tim and that's something the corporations can't do. You've got to find a niche, something that works for you, and something you can build around. You really have to believe 100 percent in that and can't have any kind of negative thoughts. You've really got to believe in yourself and what you can do and what you can sustain and not let the stumbling blocks burst your bubble. You can get sidetracked quite easily.

The limousine service enterprise is running five vehicles right now—four stretches, one sedan—and nine employees. I am constantly working hard to build the client base, the corporate base that really increases the volume of the business. Then we build around the blue collar, average Joe that just wants to go out and have a good time with the limousine. Many times these people are spending a good week's wages for one evening in a limousine, so you must make sure their experience in the car is at the highest level and that you treat them like gold. They're a rare commodity that wants to go out and really have some fun, and it's your job to make sure that happens. It's your job to be very subservient to the clients in the car and succeed in surpassing their expectations of what they thought it would be like. That's how you succeed in that industry. Anybody can get into that industry; it's very unregulated, but only the ones that are smart and understand customer service can really succeed.

Give a couple of examples of the kinds of limousine service that you would provide. What would you do?

We do a lot of evenings on the town; going to theaters where they will go to dinner and then go to the theater. We do a lot of sporting events: Nuggets games, Avalanche games, Bronco games. They're just looking for specific luxury transportation so they can spend an evening with their friends. Basically, the back of the limousine is a small living room so you provide all the accoutrements and make sure they're as comfortable as possible. You make them feel as safe as possible, and you make them feel that they are just like gold. Then they will have a good time. When you get into traffic, you can make a client very nervous, and it's your job to make them feel very at ease, that you have total control over the vehicle, that you have total understanding of that vehicle. Training is crucial with my drivers. Each driver goes through a fifteen-hour course on what each vehicle is like because no two limousines are the same. Internally with each vehicle they have to know exactly what to do with the car, and then they have to learn customer service skills and how to treat people correctly.

We do a lot of birthday parties with kids; we're very kid oriented. We do a total birthday party in the back of the limousine and go around to all the kids' friends' houses and drive around town and do whatever they want to do and that's been quite successful. You don't shy away from children because of the inventiveness and the creativeness that kids have in an atmosphere like that. Kids love that sort of stuff. They're so drawn to limousines that just to see the sparks in their eyes is worth it when you pull up to their house.

We also provide a lot of corporate transportation to the airport and we're transporting important men and women that are responsible for thousands and thousands of employees, and it is important to give them a little peace of mind. We allow them an hour break in the back of the car while we're transporting them, and this is sometimes crucial to their day because that's the only time they get some downtime. You must be there on time—it's crucial—and you must have the temperature of the car just right and the music just right. You must set the atmosphere for the client however they want and make them comfortable. Then they can sit back, relax, and concentrate on what they need to do next, and we have been quite successful at that. I have ConAgra as my largest corporate client, and I do a lot of smaller corporations. I'm constantly trying to sway the other corporations to take our limousines instead of using our competition. It's a very competitive market and one that I'm constantly challenged to succeed in.

Describe your feelings toward your enterprise. Would you work for a new owner? Would you take on a partner?

I've built two companies, and I've groomed two companies around my personality. I love being a host; I love being subservient to people; I love taking care of people; I love taking care of their needs. Having a restaurant and building a staff around me with quality food and quality environment has really been a blessing for me, and I have a lot of fun here. I enjoy coming to work every single day; no two days are the same. I deal with a lot of friends and meet a lot of new people. It's really been a fun twelve years just getting to know this community; getting to know this restaurant; getting to know my staff. The staff is one that's constantly changing. The only ones that are really here to do this for a lifetime are my chefs and myself. The rest of the staff, the wait staff, the bus, the bartenders, are all in a transition time looking for what they want to do for the rest of their lives. You must constantly train and persuade your staff that every day is like being on a stage, and you're giving the performance of your life. The staff must leave all their personal problems behind them at the back door and walk in and be fresh, be sharp, and really go out of their way to take care of the guests.

I don't have customers here. I have guests. Every day we have a new guest that comes in, and we get to try to get them to relax and forget about what's going on outside that door. I try to get them to have a good time and be able to let their stresses flow away and sometimes it's a real struggle. Some people come in and have a chip on their shoulders. If I can get through that, if I can chisel through that, I feel that's a success. That's always a goal of mine, too: to really make people feel at ease and relaxed and have a good time when they come here.

Would you sell your enterprise?

I think being an entrepreneur makes one realize that everything is for sale. It would certainly need to be a pretty serious price for me to go away. I would rather bring on a partner than sell. That's some-thing we're going to do at next week's meeting with my chefs: to see if they would be interested in buying stock in the company. I would like to bring in people that I could mentor more than I'd like to sell. There are other things that I'd like to do, some other ideas that I'd like to be involved with, but right now I'm totally consumed by these. If I could find someone as a partner, I could pursue additional interests. I would rather do that than completely sell out. If I would sell, I'd probably work in that venture where I'd take on a partner and then just sell more and more of my stock.

I actually did put the restaurant up for sale two years ago just for a six-month commitment. I wanted to get the feel for potential buyers or partners. The people that are interested don't have a lot of money. They want you to carry them and for me to do that, I've got to work with the individual. For a total stranger to walk in and ask for me to carry them is just not going to happen, especially in the restaurant business. It's really hard to find the financing, so you must get a break in a business like this one. If the right person comes along, I'd be willing to give that break to them. If a new owner did come along, I would work for a new owner.

I've worked for people before and have had a good working relationship. I have a good solid work ethic, and I understand and can see the whole picture. Working for someone else doesn't bother me. It might be a relief to think that they have to deal with all the stresses of how to run the business. Taking on a partner is something I'm trying to do right now. I think I'd like to bring on several partners. I've found that since I bought out my partners in 1994, it's really stressful to do everything yourself. I take it home all the time, and that's not good on a marriage. To have partners, they must all have the same financial interest. You just can't have an interest and be an employee. When it's coming out of your wallet, and you have the responsibility of paying a bank back, paying a relative back, or buying stock, when you've actu-ally got stock in something, then it changes your perspective. It changes your outlook on how you do your job and how you want to perform.

How do you stay competitive with other firms in your industry?

With the restaurant industry, competition is really tough. That's why I've built this restaurant around myself, and I built the personality. I think it is great that I can build a business around a business. I have this one gentleman who is a waiter who has worked for me off and on for nine years. He has certain clients that come in every single week to see him, and I think it is great that with an opportunity he can succeed. Basically, it's a business within a business. He succeeds with his clients; they treat him really well, and they come here and buy food and drinks. It's a win-win situation for both of us. To build your business around yourself and your personality is the way you can compete against corporations, and I'm competing against all the corporations that are moving into this area.

You're talking about Applebees?

I'm talking about Applebees. I'm talking about Johnny Carino's, Carrabas, Olive Garden, and Lone Star Steak House. In 1998 my wife and I counted twenty-one restaurants that opened up in this area in just one year.

And most of those are corporate?

And all of those are corporate that I just mentioned, not franchised. They're all corporately owned, and they want my slice of the pie. Granted, if I had to do this over today, I don't think this could be accomplished. Money's too precious, and it would be too expensive to do this sort of enterprise all over again. I was lucky enough to get into it twelve years ago at a very reasonable price, and I've been able to succeed. But with all the competition out there, I'm not sure that it could be done again.

What innovations have you implemented to improve your enterprise?

Empowerment to my employees has been crucial. I give them a lot of latitude.

That's not typical in a corporate restaurant.

That's not typical in a corporate restaurant at all. They want every decision to be made from a textbook; they've got to have every restaurant run the same, and that's the only way they can succeed. I understand that philosophy, and when you can understand someone else's philosophy that's how you can succeed at your own. I've empowered my employees to succeed in their own way, and I challenge them to excel and work past their own inadequacies. I really try to encourage them so they can help in their own successes, and that's been crucial.

Notes

1. Hamid Noori, *Managing the Dynamics of New Technology* (Englewood Cliffs, NJ: Prentice-Hall, 1990), p. 106.

2. Chris Freeman and Luc Soete, *The Economics of Industrial Innovation*, 3d ed. (Cambridge, MA: MIT Press, 1997), p. 98.

7

Integration of Product and
Process Innovations

Stages of Integration

As was explained in chapter 4, the development stage of a product may include making a prototype. This is usually a "one of a kind" product to show that the product actually exists. The prototype is most often very expensive and will normally only partially resemble the eventual product that will be produced in volume. Once it appears that the prototype has commercialization potential, the product moves to the demonstration stage. This stage is a life-sized, real-world example of the product that is put into actual practice or use. It is during this stage that user feedback starts to change the product to make it better able to meet the user's purpose. Changes in design, fabrication, and components can alter the product substantially from the image of the prototype, and the end result will be a more functional product. Once a dominant design and form have been demonstrated, the product is ready for commercialization.

Commercialization can be stated most simply as production of the product for sale in the marketplace. The beginning of the commercialization stage of the product can still be quite rudimentary, with products being handmade from standard inputs with general-purpose tools and machinery. During this process of custom mak-

Table 7.1

Three Stages of Integrating Product and Process Innovations

Facilitating factor	Initial stage (product)	Conversion stage (from product to process)	Maturity stage (process)
Competition	Field testing for most functional product	Changing product for better production	Decreasing average cost of production
Source of innovation	User feedback	Production feedback at plant	Market presssure to reduce cost
Type of innovation	Changing product to meet user needs	Product changes allowing increased production	Improved production techniques
Production-line assembly	Diverse products customized design	Change to one dominant product with increased volume	Standardized product with high-volume production
Equipment	Standardized equipment with skill required to produce product	Standardizing parts of product; subareas of automation	Specialized equipment with unskilled operators
Materials	Off-the-shelf materials	Specialized materials in parts of production (subassembly specialization)	Mostly specialized materials and vertical integration of process inputs

ing the product, many product changes usually occur. In an attempt to expedite production, there is movement toward more specialized tools, custom inputs, and an assembly-line process of production. Changes occur in both the product as well as the production process.

As can be seen in Table 7.1, there are some common changes that occur in any product and process as the item moves from demonstration of a prototype to a mature stage of production. During the initial stage of product development, competition drives field-testing of the product to find the most functional product for users who find an application for the product. The source of innovations at this point generally comes from the user as feedback to the manufacturer about how to make the product more functional or useful. These innovations usually require changing part of or the entire product to better facilitate the end user. This change often requires the product to be customized to meet the diverse specifications of the particular end user or customer. The equipment used in the manufacturing process is generally much more standardized, and the manufacturing skill is generally highly skilled in order to turn the shelf materials into the customized product.

Table 7.1 shows that the product and process innovations soon move to an intermediate stage where the manufacturing emphasis begins to change from the product itself to the process by which it is made. This intermediate stage where the emphasis begins changing from product to process can be referred to as "the conversion stage." During this stage, competition pushes the manufacturers to find a better, cheaper, faster way to produce the product. Demand for more products, demand for a lower price, demand for a more uniform product are all part of the overall demand that requires a more standardized product that is produced in increasing quantities. The source of innovations now springs from the production facility or plant and, in general, the question changes from "what kind" of product to produce the question of "how" to produce the accepted product. These innovations allow the product to be produced in increasing volume. In order to increase volume, production changes to more of an assembly-line process that in turn requires one dominant form of the product to evolve from the initial stage of product innovations.

It is important to recognize that in this second or conversion stage both product and process innovations are simultaneously occurring. As product innovations lead to one dominant product, the process innovations are leading to streamlined production methods in an assembly-line process to increase production volume. The production process requires the product to become more standardized so areas of the production process can be more automated. Sometimes this goal is accomplished by jobbing or subcontracting component parts of the final product. These subparts, then, become more specialized to the particular product, but speed final production.

The final stage of the integration of product and process innovations is referred to as the maturity stage and focuses almost exclusively on process innovations. Competition pushes the firm to lower the price of the product, and that in turn necessitates innovations that will decrease the average cost (per-unit cost) of production. Substitute products and/or attempts to gain new buyers and/or keep existing buyers for the increased production sustain the pressure to reduce the average costs of production. There is continuing pressure to spread the fixed costs required to purchase specialized assembly-line equipment over larger and larger production volumes in order to lower the per-unit cost of production. The push for specialized equipment is somewhat offset by the ability to hire less skilled assembly-line workers.

The materials used in production during this stage of innovations become much more specialized and if it becomes difficult to purchase these specialized materials, the firm may be forced to vertically integrate the production of these specialized inputs in the production process of the final good. That is, the firm may develop its own production of the specialized inputs for the production of the final product. This maturity stage of process innovations continues until full and complete production factors have been utilized. This product will continue to be produced until a newly innovated product is introduced and starts to develop through these stages anew. The integration of product and process innovations through these three stages is outlined in Table 7.1.

Timeline for Product and Process Innovations

In the life cycle of a product, the timeline for product and process innovations occur in a somewhat predictable time path for most products. Figure 7.1 depicts the timeline from the commercial introduction of a product through the end of the product's marketability. The three stages of integrating product and process innovations were introduced in section II but are discussed using a timeline figure in this section. For any particular product, the graphical representation of the life cycle of the product might be

Figure 7.1 **Integrating Product and Process Innovations over the Life Cycle of the Product**

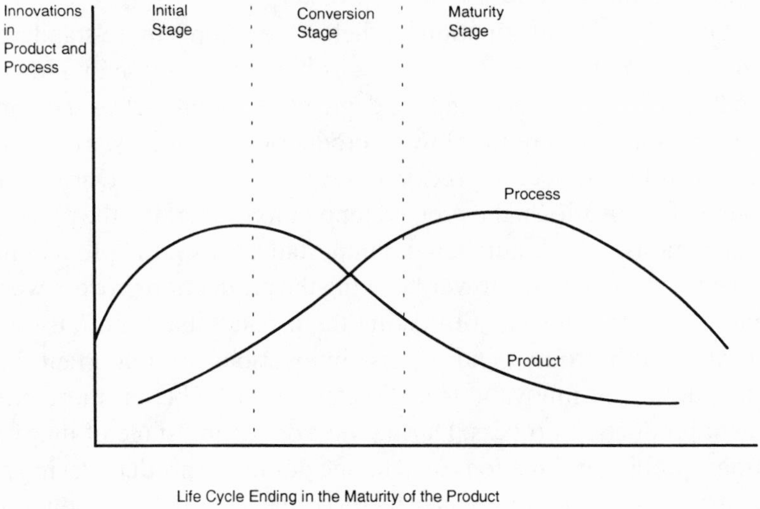

Life Cycle Ending in the Maturity of the Product

compressed or elongated, but innovations over the timeline still occur in a somewhat consistent manner.

From Figure 7.1 it can be seen that at the early stage of innovations, the initial stage, product innovations increase with a somewhat consistent pattern. Process innovations may occur, but are very limited compared to product innovations.[1] Exploration leading to the right product of the correct size and shape is focused on the product to make it more useful to the end user. Again, the user of the product often helps with the innovation by telling the producer what would make the product more beneficial or useful. Also, this exploration can lead to new uses of the product that may not have been envisioned by the producer at the development stage of the product.

Most interaction between the producer of the product and the user of the product occurs at this initial stage of innovations. Sometimes producers will place products with users on an experimental basis to check the functional performance of the product. This action is an attempt to further refine the product so it becomes more useful. It also leads to a more streamlined production process. This practice obviously leads to frequent product changes and modifications in the search for a better product.

Once the user information has helped develop a more standardized product, the process innovations begin to increase in number and importance. This change is depicted in Figure 7.1 as the conversion stage, where the flow of product innovations starts to decrease as the number of process innovations increases. During this stage of innovations, the process innovations overtake the product innovations in both number and importance. Also, the product innovations are directed toward making the production process work more smoothly instead of making the product itself more useful. That is, both product and process innovations are important, but the purpose of innovations is directed toward a better, more efficient production process. During this conversion stage of innovations, product innovations lead to one dominant product design so that process innovations can increase the volume of production through process automation. Process innovations lead to standardized parts and components of the product, which further speed the production process.

Once the process innovations have gained dominance, the life cycle of the product enters the third and final stage of product and process integration. This stage is referred to as the maturity stage and is dominated by process innovations, with very few additional product innovations occurring. The driving force in this stage is toward automated, high-volume production; efficient, specialized production techniques and equipment; and a lowering of per-unit cost of production. Standardizing the product leads to two results. First, the product innovations become less frequent and less important, and therefore, they are of less interest to the producer. Second, the standardized product allows process innovations to increase production volume, decrease per-unit costs of production, and bring about specialized equipment for faster methods of production.

After the product and process innovations have decreased in number and importance, the maturity stage of integrating innovations fades. The product can still be produced in sufficient volume to meet consumer demand, but there are few, if any changes to either product or process. The product will continue to be produced so long as there are consumers who demand the product and profit exists for the producer. Sooner or later this product will meet increasing pressure from a new, improved product or some other innovation will render the product useless. At this point, profit from production disappears and the product will no longer be produced. However, this process starts anew with a new product that repeats this product and process integration of innovations over its life cycle from introduction to maturity.

Economies of Scale, Economies of Scope, and Economies of Integration

In discussing economies of scale, it is common to start with an explanation of increasing, decreasing and constant returns to scale. However, since scale is a long-run concept and production is a short-run phenomenon, returns to scale are normally shown graphically using long-run average cost curves instead of short-run production curves. If all inputs are increased and output increases more than proportionately, the result demonstrates increasing returns to scale and is shown graphically with the decreasing (left) portion of the long-run average cost curve (*LRAC*). If all inputs are increased and output increases but by less than a proportional amount, the result demonstrates decreasing returns to scale. Graphically, this decreasing return to scale is depicted by the increasing (right) portion of the long-run average cost curve. Also, there exists, at least theoretically, a condition where an increase in all inputs would lead to an exactly proportional increase in output and this condition would be represented by the flat (middle) portion at the bottom of the long run average cost curve. Again, increasing economies of scale are graphically represented by the decreasing portion of the long-run average cost curve and are often referred to as economies of scale. Decreasing economies of scale are graphically represented by the increasing portion of the long-run aver-

Figure 7.2 **Relationship Between Short-Run Average Costs and Long-Run Average Costs**

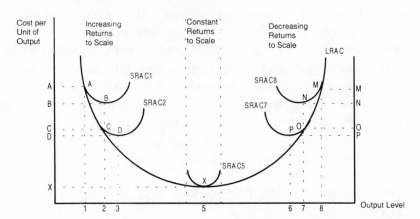

age cost curve and are often referred to as diseconomies of scale.

The long run, and thus long-run average cost curve, refers to the planning stages, and long-run decisions are made by a firm's owners, its board of directors, and/or its president. These planning sessions are used to determine the size of the firm, the size of the production facilities, and other long-run planning decisions. The short-run, or production decisions, are carried out by the production manager and the goal of the production manager is normally to find and operate at a production level that will minimize the short-run or production costs. The goal of the planners (long-run) would be to establish the optimal size of the firm and thus the size of the production facility that would result in the lowest long-run average cost for the firm.

Figure 7.2 shows the relationship between decisions made by the production manager and decisions made by the long-range planners for the firm. At the outset of a firm's existence, the planners (*LR*) establish what they feel is the appropriate production size. This could be represented by point *A* on the *LRAC* curve and would be represented by level 1 output. This point is always a tangency point between the long-run average cost curve and a short-run cost curve. However, once production is started and the production manager takes charge of day-to-day (*SR*) production levels, the manager quickly seizes the opportunity to lower *SRAC* represented by point *B* in Figure 7.2. This lowering of the average cost of production is accomplished by expanding production past the level of the planned operating capacity. The common phrase for this activity is the overutilization of plant. Examples of this procedure would be to turn storage into production areas, placing an additional production machine on an existing production floor, etc.

Once the planners (*LR*) realize that the plant is operating above capacity, they quickly realize that average costs (per-unit cost of production) could be further reduced by building a larger production facility and making additional reductions in the average cost again (point *C* on Figure 7.2 at level 2 output). The procedure is repeated as the production manager takes charge of day-to-day production operations and moves to lower the cost per unit production (*SRAC*) to point *D* at output level 3 on the figure. Tracing the movement from points *A* to *B* to *C* to *D* forms a decreasing ratchet and is thus referred to as a ratchet effect of decreasing costs per unit production. This decreasing ratchet effect will continue so long as the firm experiences increasing returns to scale.

On the right side of Figure 7.2, the opposite impact is encountered in efforts to lower the cost per unit production. Assume for the moment that the planners mistakenly overestimated the appropriate size of the production facility and choose output level 8 at *M* long-run cost per unit of production. In this case, once the production manager takes charge of day-to-day production, the level of output could be lowered to decrease the short-run per-unit costs to level *N* at the level of output 7. This lower short-run per-unit cost of production could be achieved by using less than all available plant size and available equipment. Using less than all available plant and equipment is commonly referred to as underutilizing capacity. Once this lower cost and underutilized capacity is viewed by the planners (*LR*), it is quickly observed that by decreasing the capacity of the production unit, the long-run cost per unit production level could be lowered to cost level 0 at level 7 output. Again, once this size plant is established by the planners of the firm and day-to-day production is relinquished to the production manager, short-run costs are further reduced to level P at output level 6 on Figure 7.2. This process of cost reduction creates a ratchet effect in the opposite direction, as depicted in Figure 7.2 by moving from points M to N to O to P. The ratchet effect of decreasing per-unit costs by decreasing the level of output will continue so long as the firm is operating on the right side of the *LRAC* curve or, in other words, in the decreasing returns to scale area of production.

This movement of increasing or decreasing the output level will continue until the firm finds the minimum region of the *LRAC* curve. Once the constant returns to scale portion of the *LRAC* curve is located or accidentally found by the planners and day-to-day production decisions are surrendered to the production manager, there is no ability for the manager to lower the per-unit cost of production (*SRAC*). Technically this results because, at this level of output, the minimum of the *SRAC* curve coincides with the minimum of the *LRAC* curve. This point is illustrated in Figure 7.2 by output level 5 and cost per unit level X. Once this constant returns to scale region is utilized by the firm, there is no method available to lower the cost per unit of production and the planned cost per unit production, level X, is the same minimum level of average cost observed by the production manager. At this output level 5, there are no economic reasons for the firm to expand or contract the existing output level or plant size.

After the issues of economies of scale have been appropriately explored by the firm's planners and operations managers, the issue of economies of scope can be addressed. Economies of scope can be addressed differently for large firms and small firms. Economies of scope for large firms usually entail lowering the cost per unit of production by jointly producing two products in the same production process. By producing two products in combination rather than separately, the fixed costs of plant and equipment can be spread between both products with possibly a higher volume of total production and thus, a lower cost per unit of production for each single unit.

In the case of smaller firms with smaller production facilities, economies of scope generally refer to the niche marketing of different qualities being demanded by different customers or different customized products that could be jointly produced by the smaller firm. This economies of scope concept in smaller firms revolves around the production flexibility of being able to produce somewhat different products jointly in the production process. In this case. the joint production will again spread the fixed costs of plant and equipment over a greater number of products and lower per-unit cost of production.

The third and last of the economies to be discussed here are the economies of integration. Economies of integration occur when a firm has the capability of implementing economies of scale at the same time as economies of scope. This integration generally results from innovations using technology in the production process, which greatly speeds the changing of a production line from one product to another or from changing color, type, size, and so forth of a group of products. The advent of robotics, CAD design process, and computerized equipment in the production process greatly increased the ability and speed with which to change the production line from one product to another or from one group of products to another. This ability to produce multiple products almost simultaneously on one production line in one production plant can greatly speed production with no interruption in the production flow. Switching from one product to another with a flip of a switch or a single entry into a computer at virtually no additional cost and no assembly-line downtime, integrates the economies of scale with the economies of scope.

Entrepreneurial Biography 7: Tom O'Gorman

Name:	Tom O'Gorman
Company:	Bronze Services of Loveland, Inc.
Number of Employees:	27
Annual Sales:	$1.4 million

What events and/or people were present in your youth or early adulthood that you now realize influenced your becoming an entrepreneur?

I think that would be my father. He had his own drywall business when I was a kid. I worked with him, and I would spot nails and wash buckets for him. I saw all the struggles that he had with the management of his business. His idea was to "work like hell" and he worked seven days a week. He went bankrupt, but it wasn't entirely his fault. I don't think he managed the business; I think he tried to work the business. Another person who influenced me was Don Ober. Don was a Boy Scout leader and lived in Virginia. He had a business called Holly and Honey, and I used to work for him. He had twenty acres of holly trees and he would sell them. He also had about sixty or eighty beehives, and we'd harvest honey. He was an eccentric kind of guy and a good influence. Bob Zimmerman was the first person that exposed me to foundries at Art Castings. I worked for Bob for four or five years and then I also worked for an artist, George Lundeen. George taught me a lot, too. He taught me how to be human and how to treat people. George is a really good craftsman. Whatever he does, he does well. There are also numerous artists that have influenced my becoming an entrepreneur. They are great craftsmen and have a drive that's different from other people.

So part of the events were the attitude and professional philosophy that those people carry with them?

Yes, because they want something different. They don't want something that can be bought off the shelf. They have a vision of what they want and how they want their product to look.

Describe some of your early efforts at entrepreneurship.

I opened a seafood store in 1979 called The Flying Fish Brothers here in Loveland. The problem was getting fresh fish flown in from the coast, but I stayed in business for nine months, lost about

$1,500, and learned how to do bookkeeping. That really helped me when I went to work for George Lundeen because his idea of bookkeeping was two brown paper bags and a suitcase full of receipts. I learned bookkeeping and also ate a lot of fish. I did residential drywall work and also worked with my brother doing a lot of odd jobs.

What were some events or projects that were not successful, but contributed to your success as an entrepreneur?

I think that would be The Flying Fish Brothers. Our supplier wasn't that good because we were too far from the ocean.

What did you take away from that experience that was positive?

That would have to be bookkeeping. I learned process control, inventory control, and learning how to control the cash flow of a business. We had to pay bills and rent, and we had to make payroll for one or two employees. That was my first dealing with employees. In 1979 there was only one Safeway and one King Soopers in town. Within two weeks after I opened my doors, both stores tripled their deli space in seafood. Also, the drywall work gave me a good work ethic, but I learned that it was not what I wanted to do forever.

What project stands out as one of your major entrepreneurial successes?

That would be the current business that I've operated for eleven years. I have a foundry that I opened in 1987 with a partner. A year later we brought in another partner, and a year after that, they both approached me and said, "Either we want out, or we want you out." After looking at the numbers and the amount of money it would have taken me to buy them out, the purchase would have allowed me to buy everything brand new and start my own business. I literally moved next door and opened up another shop and worked by myself. I then hired two employees, and those two people are still with me, and now we have twenty-seven. At that time the economy was pretty good around here in 1988–1990, and I got a good deal on buying a 4,500-square-foot building. It was more room than I was going to need, but I added on to it and actually had two tenants in two 1,500-square-foot bay areas. Eventually, though, we took that area over, too. Now I'm thinking of adding on another 4,500 square feet because of my expanding business.

What event stands out as a major stumbling block that you need to overcome as an entrepreneur?

One of the real stumbling blocks occurred in 1987 when I was with Loveland Sculpture Works. We would do wax work and send it to a foundry. They would actually give us weld castings to bring back, reweld, and grind the pieces together. The management at Art Castings at that time would not deal with me. They called it third-party casting, and they would cast for artists, but they wouldn't cast for another shop. I had to deal with someone in Fort Collins who really wasn't highly qualified. Then I got into casting with a place called International Art Castings in Denver. They were doing a big project for me two weeks before Christmas, and I had already given him a big down payment. He let his slurry freeze in the shelfroom and that ruined a lot of the process. At the time I had fourteen or fifteen employees. He called me one day and told me they were closing the doors. The damage cost me about $17,000. I had only been in the business six months, and I couldn't financially afford the loss. I couldn't give my employees any Christmas bonuses or a party. My welder at the time told me, "I just want you to know we're in this business for the long run with you. We're going to have a potluck and a party." We did, and we all pulled together to overcome that large financial loss.

So the stumbling block was the inability to get quality work, which financially put your company in straits?

It did. It also set in motion the process for us to actually put in a foundry. We brought in a third partner, and his money was the investment for the foundry.

What advice could you give someone who has aspirations of becoming an entrepreneur?

Do it. Otherwise you're always going to wonder. Some people are made to do it, and some are not. You must be able to roll with the punches. You can't just do it your way, especially if you're doing work for someone else. You must be able to listen and grow with what you're doing. It also helps to have a good, understanding banker.

Describe your current enterprise.

We are a full-service, bronze sculpture art foundry. We do bronze castings of anything from a little belt buckle up to a twenty-one-foot-tall elk and anything in between. Lately we've been doing a tremendous volume of life-size kids. The artist will do an original in clay or sometimes in wood or stone carving. Then they take the original to a mold maker to make a worker mold. The next step is to pour wax into the rubber mold and then the sculpture is actually cast from wax.

What happens once you have the cast?

Once it's cast, then the patina is applied. Patina is the color on the metal. Then it's either shipped or, since a lot of the artists are local, they will come and pick up their work. Big pieces are sometimes delivered and installed by us.

But once you have those casting parts, you must put them together?

Well, once the piece is actually cast, we have to weld them together. For instance, the big elk in Steamboat Springs is twenty-one feet tall. I believe it was 180 pieces that were welded together. You take grinders and smooth it down and make it look like it was never welded. If you can see any welds, then the job is not satisfactory.

So you do everything from the concept of the artist through the bronze that comes out as a finished product?

Yes, we give them in metal what they originally sculpted in clay. It's a very time consuming, labor-intensive project.

How many large pieces would you do in a year ranging in size from life-size children on up?

We probably do fifty life-size kids and a couple life-size Arabian horses, 150 to 200 smaller busts, and a lot of other small things. For instance, we're doing 140 Arabian horse belt buckles. I think that big pieces are notoriety; small pieces are cash flow.

Describe your feelings toward your enterprise. Would you sell your enterprise? Would you work for a new owner? Would you take on a partner?

Sure, anything's for sale. If someone would give me what I think it's worth, I can do something else. In fact, if I could sell my enterprise, I'd like to start sculpting myself.

So if you sold your enterprise, you might do the artistic work that would go to a foundry?

Yes, and play a lot of golf and fly airplanes. I don't think that the new owner, though, would want me to work for him. For a short length of time I probably would, but I think anytime you have a new ownership, they're going to have different ideas on how things are going to be run. I think it would be too much like butting heads. For too long I have been used to doing things the way I want them done, and no one questions it. I'm always open to suggestions, but the final decision is mine. That's one of the things that frustrate me. When I tell someone how I want something done and they do it another way that fails, the cost comes out of my pocket, not theirs. On the other hand, if they do it a different way and it comes out better, I can't hamper that creative energy. Communication is essential, and I must know what's going on. For example, I took on a partner once, and at the time he was a very good friend. After our partnership, though, it took a long time to be friends again. He was in the business for nine months and had a business philosophy, more like a corporate machine. He had worked at Hewlett-Packard for thirteen years, and I think their financing was much different from our enterprise. I think I could sell my enterprise, but I could not take on another partner unless he could come in and invest as much money as it would take to buy it. I don't think there's enough cash flow in the business right now to support a partner.

How do you stay competitive with other firms in your industry?

First, by doing a project with the best possible quality. We have time constraints with people bringing things in the door and wanting them done now. It's not always possible. There's a line of reasoning that says you can have three things: price, quality, and timeliness. Which two do you want? Quality to me is the biggest issue. I don't want to put anything out the door that over time someone will have to fix. I've had to fix a lot of pieces brought in to my shop that were cast other places. Also, casting prices must be competitive. Second, production deadlines for casting must be competitive. If you give a customer a deadline, you have to meet it. Sometimes that means people have to work overtime, which requires employee dedication. I don't set deadlines. I leave that to my production manager. The quickest way to run people off is to give them a job description and then, without telling them, change it and make them powerless to do anything about it.

Virtually, though, you've done every part of the sculpting and foundry work. You've done every part that an employee would be hired to do.

That's correct. I know what to expect and the problems that may arise. I know what it takes to operate and maintain the equipment.

I can tell if someone is neglecting it or if they're abusing it. Understanding the entire process is what has kept me in business.

What innovations have you implemented to improve your enterprise?

We've made quite a bit of our own equipment that can't be purchased. For instance at a bankruptcy sale, I bought a different furnace. Right now we use a gas-fired furnace, but the new furnace is an induction furnace which heats with electricity. It cuts the heating time in half. The longer you have metal in a molten state, the more impurities it can pick up. Hopefully, when it is installed, this furnace will cut down on defects.

Part of your innovation has to do with your customer relationship that you develop, maintain, and work to improve. Can you explain that?

There are two kinds of people that I deal with. Some people are very loyal. When they find someone that will do the work they want done, they form a trust. You can count on that being a good relationship because they're not going to go anywhere else.

They have faith in the work being done like they want it done. The other kind of person is the one who goes from foundry to foundry looking at bids to see who offers the cheapest product even if they know that business doesn't have the best reputation. With this second type of person there's going to be frustration on both sides.

You can attract the first kind of person with the quality of your work; how do you deal with the second kind of person?

You must figure your bid on quality work and be firm. Sometimes I've let people hammer my bid down, but it ends up that I don't make any money, and the people aren't happy. So the end result is not favorable for either party.

So by setting the standard and explaining that quality comes at a price, those people either accept your position or go elsewhere?

Yes, and I don't advertise. My best advertising happens when people get together at sculpture shows here in Loveland and all over the country. These people talk among themselves, and some of my best advertisers are my clients. I probably should be giving them a commission.

Note

1. Adapted from Hamid Noori, *Managing the Dynamics of New Technology* (Englewood Cliffs, NJ: Prentice-Hall, 1990), p. 105.

8

Technology and Economics: A Multidisciplinary Approach to Innovations

Implementing Technology into Innovations Using Management and Economics

Technology has virtually changed some facet of production of every product that reaches today's markets. Not all products have had profound changes, but all products have been impacted. Three very radical changes from technology are: (1) in 1960 it took several thousand telephone operators to handle one million calls; in 1998, one dozen telephone operators could handle the same one million calls; (2) the number of circuit components per microprocessor chip has doubled every year since 1959; and (3) one pound of glass fiber optic cable (made from sand) can carry as much information as one ton of copper wire.[1] Again not all products have had radical changes from the advances in technology, but all products have been affected.

The approach developed here is an interdisciplinary approach using science/technology, management, and economics, as fields that aid and guide an invention through the process of becoming an innovation and finally into a marketable product. Through product and process innovations, there is an ongoing transition of improvements to both the product as well as the production process as the marketable product becomes fully developed. This transition was explained in detail in chapters 5, 6, and 7. To better understand these rapid changes in the technology for the production of goods, an interdisciplinary approach to technology seems most appropriate. The approach utilized here makes use of a minimum of three fields: science/technology, management, and economics. In addition, to begin the interdisciplinary approach, the concepts of technology and innovation must be separated and defined. Managing the process by which an idea or concept finally constitutes a marketable product involves four stages.

As was developed in chapter 4, these stages include research, development, demonstration, and commercialization. The first two of these stages are usually associated with the term "invention," and the last two stages are generally referred to as "innovation." In addition, the first two stages are generally associated with exploratory science and technology, while the latter two stages are generally associated with applied science and technology in the refinement of a salable product. However, all four stages are interlinked in an ongoing effort to develop and improve products and production processes through innovations.

Another way of looking at this process of transforming an idea or concept into a marketable product is to separate the economics and management of technology and the economics and management of innovations. The economics and management of technology revolves around the complex process of turning ideas and concepts into inventions. This process includes blueprints, testable prototypes, and the creation of a tangible product and is the result of scientifically applying technology to an idea or concept. On the other hand, the economics and management of innovations involves making this invention marketable. The concepts of cost cutting, production management, and product marketing are all part of the innovation process.

The implementation of technology for innovations bridges at least three separate disciplines—management, economics, and science—and to be successful in the implementation of the innovation these fields must be integrated as the innovation is adapted

Table 8.1

Implementation of Technology for Innovations

	Science	Management	Economics
Stage I	Technology	Organization for implementation	Analysis of cost reductions from technology
Stage II	Feasibility: prototype, blueprint, testing model	Relationship between inputs and products	Analysis of demand for product
Stage III	Demonstration: refinement of product for consumer satisfaction	Relationship between products and consumers	Relationship of costs and product revenues

by a particular firm. Table 8.1 illustrates the different tasks required for the technology to be utilized by a particular firm.

Once these three fields are bridged and the innovation begins to be implemented in the particular firm, these three fields blend into one unit as the product is developed and improved, costs are reduced and the product is produced in increasing volume.

Invention is normally brought about through science and is some form of technology. As is shown in Table 8.1, the scientific application of technology in the first step leads to the feasibility in step two. This feasibility usually presents itself in a prototype, blueprint, or model that is presented for testing. The process continues through the demonstration where the product is refined for improvements in consumer acceptance and satisfaction.

Occurring either simultaneously or at a second stage, the management of a new product or process begins to take place. The first stage in the organization of a plan is to lead the technology into the implementation of a new product or process. Next, stage two begins the development of relationships between the inputs and the products that will result. At this stage, product and process innovations improve and simplify this input-product relationship, which was developed in chapters 5, 6, and 7. Connected to this second stage is the third stage of the management of innovations from the implementation of technology. This third stage develops the relationship between the product and the potential consumers. This stage includes product changes, product refinements, and further product developments that are directed toward consumer acceptance and willingness to purchase the product in the marketplace.

The third area of implementation of technology for innovations is addressed by the field of economics. The first stage is the ongoing analysis of technology to explore areas of cost reductions. This stage would include cost reductions for both product and process changes in an ongoing application of technology. A technologically improved product or a technologically advanced machine used in the production process that brings about cost reductions are examples of a stage one application of economics. Stage two of the application of economics is an analysis of the potential demand for the product or process being innovated. This stage could be as simple as a quick survey or as complicated as an econometric estimation of demand using variables such as price, buyers' incomes, price of related goods, economic growth in national production, and changes brought about through advertising and product awareness.

The third stage of the application of economics to the implementation of technology for product and process innovation encompasses the relationship between costs of producing the product and the revenues generated through sales of the product. This relationship will determine profits from product sales and will typically move through a product life cycle, as described in chapter 7. However, in this stage, technology can be utilized to explore ways to further lower production costs, increase consumer demand for the product, and increase the life cycle of both the product and the process through applications of technology used for innovations.

Technology and Innovations Used to Reduce Time Lags in the Development of Marketable Products

The transition from scientific discovery to a marketable product is fraught with time lags and dead end avenues that impede or delay

Figure 8.1 **Invention-Innovation-Production Process Showing Time Lags**

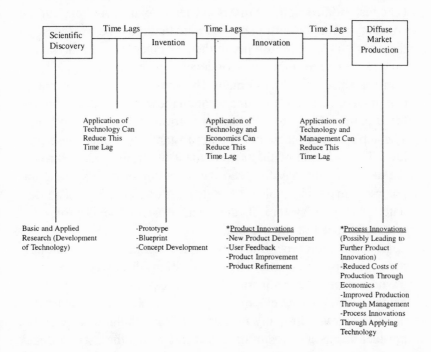

the final product development. The application of various types of technology can decrease or eliminate some of the time lags that prevent final product development. Figure 8.1 depicts these time lags and demonstrates the application of technology at various stages to reduce delays in the development of final products.[2]

Scientific discovery involves both basic and applied research, although most products are developed as a result of applied research. Very often this applied research involves the development of technology as a part of the process toward product development. That is, the final product might be a technology or alternatively involve the use of a developed technology.

As the research moves from the scientific discovery stage to the development of an invention, there are often time lags created by the discovery process. Some research avenues will lead to concepts that are simply not feasible. The development of the infamous perpetual motion machine would be an obvious example. Likewise, some scientific discovery leads to an invention, but the concept is fraught with complications that must be overcome in the creation of the prototype. In the movement toward the invention, the outcome at this stage of development is a prototype, blueprint, or concept for development. This movement toward invention can involve considerable time through these delays, dead ends, or blind paths leading toward progress from research to invention. The application of technology can substantially reduce these time lags. The example of the development of circuit boards through the use of technology to speed the invention of high-speed computers is an example of this application of technology. The outdated electronic system of tubes and resistors simply prohibited increased speed of the machines.

Once the prototype, blueprint, or concept has been developed, the next step is innovation. The innovations discussed here are in the area of product innovations, and these product innovations include new product developments, product improvements, and product refinements. In many product innovations the change in the product occurs as a result of field trials where the user feedback leads to the product change.

The transition from prototype or blueprint to products and product changes can also be mired in time lags preventing the new or improved product. These delays can be costly not only in research time and costs but also in opportunity costs associated with lost sales, advances by competitors, and less time the new or improved product will be in demand in an ever-changing world. The application of technology and economics can reduce this area of time lags. The application of technology and economics in product innovations include substitute materials in the product, product redesign for improved product use and combining product components for less problems during product use. As described in an earlier chapter, product innovation makes the product better. This is contrasted with process innovations where changes in the product have the purpose of improving the production of the product.

As the product moves from a new improved, refined, or other-wise changed product in the innovation stage to the last stage of diffused market production, the transition can again be plagued with time lags and time delays. At this stage of product and pro-cess development, the application of technology and production management can reduce these delays. As stated earlier, process innovations may involve product innovations, but the alteration in the product is for the purpose of process innovations. The applica-tion of technology and management leading to process innova-tions include per-unit cost reductions through production efficiencies, improved production process through managing the various production stages, and process innovations through ap-plying technology to the actual production machinery.

The path from scientific discovery to diffuse market production is rarely smooth and can incur major setbacks from time lags slow-ing the progress of this path. The application of technology through science, economics, and management can shorten the time lags and thus speed the occurrence of high levels of production for market.

Examples of Technology Used to Develop Better and Cheaper Products

Entrepreneurs are on a never-ending search through innovations for different products that better perform the consumer task at hand. Table 8.2 illustrates a few examples of the use of technology re-sulting in better and cheaper products. Genetic engineering has drastically increased agricultural crop production and thus de-creased the cost of food in most areas of the world. Examples of this technology include increased resistance to frost and drought, decreased time cycles for growing and maturing, and increased volume of harvest. Developments in cell and tissue culture have helped the health care industry cure and prevent diseases as well as reduce infant mortality around the world.

The technological development of robotics has drastically in-creased the speed and efficiency of a wide variety of manufactur-

Table 8.2

Examples of Technologies and Their Resulting in Better and Cheaper Products

Technology	Products
Genetic engineering	Increased agricultural products
Cell and tissue culture	Health care and pharmaceuticals
Robotics	Manufacturing
Composite materials	Home, auto, and aircraft manufacturing
Remote sensing	Security, defense, U.S. forestry management
Fiber optics	Communications
Lasers	Medical instruments for surgery
Speech recognition	Voice-activated products

ing from automobiles to mining. It is difficult to find an industry that has not applied robotics in some facet of product development. Composite materials include plastic and metal framing materials for homes, metal alloys for safer, faster, more fuel efficient airplanes; as well as safer and more comfortable automobiles.

Remote sensing has increased home security, decreased the severity and size of forest fires, and increased national defense information for security. Fiber optics has drastically improved communications through increased volume and decreased use of materials as well as reduced the cost of communications worldwide.

Lasers and their use have drastically changed surgery procedures and instruments in most areas of the medical profession from eye surgery to plastic surgery. The laser has changed the length of the operation as well as the required recovery period. Computerized speech recognition has allowed authors to compose a text without either writing or typing. It has allowed increased security for buildings and homes and also been used as an identification procedure.

These eight examples of technologies resulting in better and cheaper products are but a glimpse at the multitude of applications of technology for product development. In addition, one of the most widespread applications of technology for product development has been in the area of computer-aided design (CAD). This widespread application of CAD includes product design, product development, direct control and monitoring the manufacturing process as well as simulation of the new product production processes to decrease the time involved with the learning curve for increased efficiency in the production process. Obvious applications of CAD include architectural drawings for buildings. Before CAD, architects would draw a set of plans, mark corrections and changes, and then redraft a new, updated set of drawings at considerable time and cost. With the application of CAD, the architect can change plans and prints with the touch of a computer mouse. Rooms and/or entire buildings can be changed left to right, increased or decreased in size or any myriad of changes can be incorporated with instantaneous results.

A variation of CAD is computer-aided manufacturing (CAM). There are various aspects and applications of CAM, but each aspect assists the efficient flow of marketable products to the eventual consumer. An example of the application of CAM is to assist in the direct control of the production operation. This application directs the manufacturing machinery for speed, stages of production, as well as instructions about what to do and how to do it. A second application of CAM is in the area of product control for quality. Product acceptance based on function, size tolerances, and complete units are examples of some of the applications for quality control.

A third application of CAM exists in the area of materials handling. Bringing material inputs to the production floor, moving partially completed products to various stages of production as well as moving and storing the finished product are all examples of CAM-assisted materials handling. A fourth application of CAM is in the area of linking the production and supervisory components of production to the higher level, corporate decision-makers through instantaneous information systems. These four applica-

Table 8.3

Technology Used for Product Improvement

Area of change	Product improvement
Product flexibility	Faster product development
Conversion flexibility	Product modification
Design alteration	Input modifications
Performance testing	Quality improvements
Product design	Lower-cost products

tions of CAM connect technology to the development of better and less expensive products.

CAD and CAM are but simple examples of technology being applied to the production process to provide products to consumers. This application of technology to production can be viewed as segments of the course of action needed to continually improve the product as well as the production process. This improvement can be seen in five areas of change as Table 8.3 illustrates. The first area of improvement is in the area of product flexibility. Products can be improved, new products can be developed, and components can be altered in a more rapid time frame with the application of technology.

The second area of product improvement is in the area of conversion flexibility. Production as well as product design can be modified to meet production demands or consumer needs with the described application of technology. The third area of product improvement is in the area of design alteration. Technology and its application through CAD and CAM can actually redesign and alter a product to meet input specifications as product demand changes.

The fourth area of product improvement brought about through technology is in the area of quality and performance testing. A new, existing or improved product can be tested for performance or quality before actual production of the product in fact takes place. Varying consumer requirements can be met before products are actually produced and tested. This obviously saves time and money in the production process.

The last area of product improvement brought about by the application of technology is in the area of machine design for production. CAD and CAM can be used to design the machinery used to produce the final product. This application of technology can obviously reduce production costs, increase production volume efficiencies and save valuable time in choosing the correct production machinery for the desired results.

Entrepreneurial Biography 8: George Lundeen

Name:	George Lundeen
Company:	Lundeen Sculpture, Ltd.
Number of Employees:	8–15
Annual Sales:	$1–2 million

What events and/or people were present in your youth or early adulthood that you now realize influenced your becoming an entrepreneur?

First of all my parents influenced me as much as anybody. My grandfather was a farmer and a terrific draftsman and great penman. My father was an inventor and an entrepreneur. He also sold real estate and insurance and did whatever he could to raise six kids. The best thing he ever taught me was that if you really needed something, you could go out in your backyard and build it. So he invented and built everything from scaffolding to boat trailers. I can't even think of all the things he invented.

How about your college experience?

Well, I had a great high school art teacher. She was a wonderful teacher. I went off to college and was blessed to go to a small college where I got to know the faculty members. I wasn't what you'd consider an intelligent student at the time, probably border-line stupid. However, I had some great college professors. One in particular was a terrific sculptor. So that's when I took up sculpt-ing. I went to graduate school and studied with another great sculp-tor at the University of Illinois. From there I got lucky and had a Fulbright scholarship and studied in Italy for a year. When I came back, I couldn't find a job to save my soul, so I was a bartender for about a year and a half. Finally, I got a job teaching at the Univer-sity of Nebraska-Kearney and then found this little foundry in Loveland, Colorado, and moved out here a year after that. So I really didn't teach very long.

You had some negative experiences with the people in the uni-versity who opposed your going out on your own, did you not?

Well, I don't know if they opposed it. They all thought, however, that you couldn't make any money as an artist. Most of the profes-sors in the university think that if you do make money at it, then you're kind of prostituting yourself because you're doing some-thing for someone else. All the time that I was in school I either was a sign painter or sold the artwork that I made in school. Of course, that didn't always set well with them. However, I didn't care; I needed to get the cash so I made it and I sold it and I loved it.

And you were an entrepreneur?

From the time I was fourteen I was a sign painter and always had a job doing something in the arts and trying to sell it.

Anyone else that you can think of that impacted you becoming an entrepreneur?

I suppose a lot of people. Even when I was a bartender, I had a couple great bosses that had made their way through life just work-ing hard. I think every time I had a good boss that worked hard, I really enjoyed it whether it was driving a wheat truck in the summertime on a harvest crew or learning how to paint signs from the local sign painter. They weren't always people you looked up to from a personal standpoint, but they knew how to survive in this world, and that's what you learned from them.

Describe some of your early efforts at entrepreneurship.

The first thing I did while in high school was to start a sign painting company in my garage. My dad built me a big desk and stool, and I painted a lot of signs for the local feed yard and cattle company and also painted names and numbers on hot rods. I learned a lot about brushes and paint back then.

What else did you do in your efforts to be an entrepreneur?

When I got to college, I took a ceramics course. I found that people really liked hand-thrown cups and saucers and teapots, and I made a lot of them. The first thing they always tell you in a ceramics course is don't make any ashtrays, but I made a whole bunch of them and sold every one of them. I was terrible in English courses and always had to make a deal with my professor and paint him a picture for Christmas or throw him a couple of pots as a little extra credit on the side. It worked out great.

Anything else in describing your early efforts?

I came from a farm family. My father was the first generation off the farm, and I always helped the cousins irrigating the corn, and I helped with the harvest crews. I think when you're from the Midwest and you grow up in that environment, you learn to wake up every morning and go to work. When you go to work, you try to figure out the best way to work. You're not working for somebody. No one in my family until this generation ever worked for anybody except themselves. With the exception of teaching, I never thought of working for somebody, and I just hated that part of it.

What were some events or projects that were not successful, but contributed to your success as an entrepreneur?

I'm sure I had a lot of them, but I don't try to think about those. Most people in the first ten years out of college would probably think I wasn't very successful because I didn't make a lot of money at what I was doing. As a sculptor, I knew that maybe I would never make a lot of money doing what I was doing, but I sure loved to do it. Anytime you can take a piece of mud and make it into something that someone buys, it's just an incredible thing for me and still is. I've just been very fortunate, some would say lucky, to be able to do as well as I have in the business.

Was there a way that those jobs helped you become a better sculptor?

Well, I suppose. A lot of times you think you're your own genius, but I've done a lot of pieces for people who probably had better ideas than I did. They knew my style and what kind of work I did and would bring in a subject that I maybe never would have thought about. It gave me an opportunity to work with them on a new idea and to open up my vision a little bit more.

What project stands out as one of your major entrepreneurial successes?

A very good success was after I had been in business here in Loveland about five years. My hometown called me and wanted me to make a portrait bust of the namesake of my hometown in Nebraska. Well, I don't know if the fellow the town was named after ever really set foot in the hometown. He was a railroad magnate and vice president. Nobody knew who he was, and so I suggested we do the farmers and people that built this area. I did a small model of a farm family, and the town agreed. We agreed to make it ten feet tall, but they didn't know how they would ever pay for it. However, I made some small models for sale to people interested in the project. We took a model to one meeting, and they sold enough of them in five weeks to more than pay for the whole project. That project got me on my feet financially as much as anything. Also finding a couple of really good art galleries at different points in my career really helped. Almost 100 percent of the gallery people are self-supporting entrepreneurs and start their own businesses relying on their own wits for their survival. It's a lot of fun working with those kinds of people, too.

Name a few of the pieces of art you've placed in the United States or out of the country of which you are particularly proud.

I did Promise of the Prairie for my hometown, which was the quint-essential farm family. I did Ben Franklin for the University of Penn-sylvania, Robert Frost for Dartmouth University, and my brother and I teamed up to do Jack Swaggart for the Capitol Building in Washington, DC. I did Elray B. Jefferson for the new Denver Air-port. I also worked with an elderly lady here in Loveland that al-ways wanted to put a couple musicians in public, and I worked with her on a piece called "the Joy of Music." A lot of these pieces are done in limited editions, and Ben Franklin is everywhere from Mexico to France to England, and quite a number of them are around the United States as are most of the pieces. I just did Thomas Jefferson on my own, and one of the first ones we made went to Williamsburg.

What event stands out as a major stumbling block that you needed to overcome as an entrepreneur?

The biggest stumbling block that I had upon moving to Loveland was when I went to buy a house. It wasn't a very expensive house, but when you walk into a bank and tell the loan officer that you're a sculptor, they tend to wonder what the heck this guy is doing here? You have no income that you can really rely on and not much money to use as a down payment. Fortunately for me, I had grown up in a small town. After the age of sixteen and since I knew the local bank president, no matter where I was, I could call him up and ask for his help backing me. The wonderful thing about him was he never said no. The nice thing about Loveland was nobody ever said yes. I never got too far indebted, but it has worked out great. I can't say I've had many stumbling blocks in my career. I've always looked at all of those things as more of a jumping- off place than a block.

What advice could you give someone who has aspirations of becoming an entrepreneur?

I'd say, "Go for it." There's no greater feeling in the world than having success at something that you enjoy doing. It may be something that keeps you awake at night. You may wake up at 2:00 in the morning thinking how can I do this better? It's just terrific. There's nothing better in the world. I've traveled throughout the world, and there's no place like the United States when it comes to entrepreneurs. The last place I visited was Cuba. There are a lot of entrepreneurs in Cuba, but the government does not allow them to follow through on their ideas—whereas here, hopefully as long as the government stays out of our way, we're in good shape. When they start to decide that they're a little smarter than we are, then we're going to have a tough time.

So you would see basically that the biggest drawback for an entrepreneur is their uneasiness at striking out to do something on their own?

You can't be afraid of failure. You only fail when you quit. All the rest of it is learning. So unless you finally quit, throw up your hands and say, "That's it; I'm done," that's the only failure there is. I've read lots of biographies about people who have all these stumbling blocks, but those are the ones that really hit it big in the end.

Describe your current enterprise.

I'm still taking a piece of clay and making it into something. Right now I've got a piece of clay of a lady who was a terrific writer from Nebraska. The State of Nebraska called me up over a year ago and asked me if I'd do a portrait of her and I said yes. The State of Nebraska has just been wonderful to me as a sculptor because whenever they've needed something, I'll get a call from the governor's office with a request. The nice thing is that they think I'm doing something wonderful for them. So I never turn them down.

I have a couple other commissions; the biggest one is a contract to do Ronald Reagan. When the final contract comes back after they sign a contract with the people at the Reagan Building in Washington, DC, then we'll have about eighteen months to produce a piece a little over life size of Ronald Reagan. I also have lots of new work to do for a gallery and have a couple other portraits to do for different people.

Your lead-time is now stretched fair into the future in terms of new projects, isn't it?

Yes. If Ronald Reagan goes through, then we probably won't be able to take on another commission for another two and a half years.

Do you have other people help you with the artwork or are the people in the office entirely support staff for you?

I have a couple girls that come up and warm my clay up in the morning before I get here. They start work about 6:00 A.M. I'm the only one that actually moves the clay around and does what you consider the creative work, but I do have a number of people plus the foundries that work for us and do a lot of the craftsmanship work. We're lucky in Loveland because we have the greatest foundry in the country, maybe in the world, right here and, in fact, we now have two foundries. It's been a great place to live.

Could you explain a little bit of that process from your creativity to the point that it actually becomes a bronze piece of artwork?

The first thing you have to start with is an idea, and hopefully it's a good one. You might make a sketch of it on a piece of paper or with clay. From there you take that clay piece, and get your models together and get it in the right shape. Then I'll make the whole piece out of clay. From there we make a mold of the piece so we have a negative of that piece when it's pulled off the clay shape. Then we pour hot wax into it and make a wax copy. We then take the wax copy to the foundry, and it's put through the lost wax casting process. This is the step where they attach a cup to the piece, cover it again with a mold compound that is very solid, put it in an oven, and melt the wax out of that mold. Next it's turned upside down, the foundry gets the bronze very hot, and they pour the hot metal into the mold. When that's cool, they knock the mold off that piece, and you will have a bronze piece that looked like the wax piece that looked like the clay original. Then the work starts. You have to start to file down and finish the bronze piece, probably weld it together because it's been cut apart through the different processes, until finally you get to the end when you sandblast the piece after it is finished and put on the final coating or patina. Then you get it out, and the hardest part can sometimes be selling it.

Describe your feelings toward your enterprise. Would you sell your enterprise? Would you work for a new owner? Would you take on a partner?

Lundeen Sculptures is basically me since it not only has my name on it, but because I'm the artist and the only designer. All the work comes from me, and ends up with me. Yes, I'd sell my business if anyone were crazy enough to buy it! I'd walk across the street and start all over again.

But if you sold your business it would be a temporary move to another location?

Well, yes. Of course, all my good employees would move across the street with me, and I'd get sued for fraud. What I have is myself, and I can't sell myself.

I also couldn't work for a new owner. No, that's also impossible because an artist just can't do that. My wife's a sculptor and has her own studio. My brother's a sculptor and has his own studio. We partner up on pieces, but we never consider ourselves what we'd call partners in the business. We are, however, all partners in this area of creating artwork.

So you would do individual parts of a much bigger piece?

Absolutely. I have a lot of friends in the business, and anytime anyone comes into town, I invite them up to look at the piece I'm working on and ask them their opinion. A lot of times they'll take out a tool and start working on it with me. I'll do the same for them. I go down to Santa Fe a couple times a year and work with Glenna Goodacre on whatever she's working with or Jerry Balsiar in Denver. It's a great business and the kind of business you can't be successful in unless you have some sort of character to start with. You have to be a hard worker and be able to work with people, and you have to have some talent.

And you have to be able to work on your own.

Absolutely. You have to be able to go to work early in the morning and work until late at night. I don't work half as hard as I used to now that I have a family. Thank God I don't have to.

How do you stay competitive with other firms in your industry?

I just still outwork them. There aren't very many people that like to work as hard as I like to work or take as many chances as I do when it comes to hiring people. In my line of work, very few artists have employees, and for the last twenty years I've had upwards of twenty employees at a time. I probably employ more than that because we sometimes get so busy that we have to farm things out. I've always got a good core of people that work for me and have had a great secretary and office manager, and they do a part of the work that I completely dislike—paying bills, writing checks, dealing with banks. I enjoy all the physical parts of the job and hire the right people to do the rest of it.

Are there some things in your line of work that you wouldn't want to do as a sculptor because you don't particularly like that form versus other things that you really want to do?

We turn down many more commissions than we ever take. We turn down a lot of ideas that would probably be financially good, but if it's not interesting to me, I don't see any reason to spend my time doing it. We get a lot of people that want us to come and speak at different places and do slide shows. If it looks like it's going to be a nice setting or if it's some people that I want to talk to, I'll do it in a heartbeat. However, if it's the local flower club wanting to talk about putting sculpture in the garden, I usually haven't got the time.

What innovations have you implemented to improve your enterprise?

A lot of things have changed in the sculpture industry and the art business. We've got much better tools now than when I started and much better foundries. We've got more people that know how to make the things that we want to make and that helps. We also use the computer to access the Internet in order to find people and resources. I told people for years that my pencil and Big Chief tablet was just fine, but five years ago we put up a Web page thinking it was going to be a big waste of money. It was going to cost between $40 and $50 a month. The first month it was up we sold a $100,000 piece of sculpture. So we update it and try to work as hard and smart as we can. We've helped develop several different ways to produce sculpture that have helped the industry. We try to keep professional organizations active. We started a couple of big sculpture shows that have turned out to be the biggest sculpture shows in the world right here in Loveland. One is Sculpture in the

Park and the other is the Sculpture Invitational. They're both held the first weekend in August. They're getting so big now they will probably split up someday because we don't have enough parking.

Artists are invited worldwide?

We get artists from throughout the world coming to Loveland. This year we will have over 500 sculptors each bringing between five and twelve pieces of every different kind of sculpture that you could imagine. We've also tried to work with some of the local charitable nonprofit people like the Rotary to start a couple sculpture shows. We started the Artist's Charitable Fund in which we try to help local sculptors and also artists all over the country. We also help people, and it's basically the artists that fund the organization through the sale of Christmas ornaments and a big auction every year. So that's been a lot of fun. We get to work with a lot of people throughout the country.

Any other innovations you can think of as you've moved through twenty years or so in the art profession and sculpture industry?

I suppose there have been minor innovations, but the world of sculpture and art hasn't changed a whole lot in the last thousand years. You make something out of paint, canvas, wood, or bronze and try to make it attractive enough that somebody else wants to put it in their house. It's pretty basic.

You have some very definite ideas about the government attempting to hamper entrepreneurs as they go out and try to do something innovative or something that hasn't been done before.

Sure. The government tries to get their hooks into you about everywhere they can. The basic thing is, I guess, that if you're successful, they're trying to take what you have and pass it around and put it in the hands of somebody else. I don't always know what they do with all their cash, but I do know that when they take half your money every time and you look forward to giving them the other half later, it doesn't create a great deal of enterprise within you. If you don't have that carrot in front of you, you don't work as hard.

For instance, we had the government decide that the artist always got shortchanged on resale of their pieces. If I sold you a piece and you bought it early in my career and paid me $500 for it, twenty years later you might sell it for $500,000. The government wants to come in and get 10 to 20 percent of that amount from you and give it back to me saying the artist did it and deserves it because he didn't get enough money for it in the first place. That's crazy. Number one, all the government wants to do is tax you on that money. Number two, they get into your business, and who would want to buy a piece if later on you had to give a percentage back to somebody else? Does that mean that if I sold a piece to you for $500 (and this was the point I made to a couple senators one day when I talked to them) and that piece sold for only $5 twenty years later, that I would owe you 10 percent of the $500 that you just lost? That was inconceivable to them, but more often than not, that's what could happen. I would just as soon they do what they do best, which I'm not sure what that is, and leave the rest to us.

I think the entrepreneurs in this world, the business people and the people who take care of themselves, are the real strength of the American economy. You can look throughout the world at the rest of the economy and see a bunch of struggling people that have a hard time succeeding simply because of all the rules and regulations and things by which they are limited. But given the liberty and freedom to do what we think we need to do, that's what makes it; that's the biggest opportunity there is.

Notes

1. Hamid Noori, *Managing the Dynamics of New Technology* (Englewood Cliffs, NJ: Prentice-Hall, 1990), Chapter 1.
2. Bruce A. McDaniel, Paper presented at the Sixth Annual Conference of the American Society of Business and Behavioral Sciences, Las Vegas, Nevada, 1999.

9

Microeconomics and Innovations

Changing the Production Function

The nucleus of the connection between microeconomic theory and innovations is embedded in production theory. Production theory will again be reviewed, and then the area of entrepreneurship and innovations will be addressed as they apply to this theory. It needs to be stated at this outset that neoclassical microeconomics has provided little room for the entrepreneur in the equilibrium analysis of production theory.

Production theory is quite universal, and the precise nature of the decision unit that directs the production process is of little concern in production analysis. The inventories of raw materials, variable and fixed inputs, machinery, labor, buildings, and types of finished goods are all standardized into a universal production function that demonstrates a rigid link between the variable input and the output from the production activity. With one input allowed to be variable all other inputs are held constant. Generally, the plant (building), equipment, and other raw materials are held constant, and labor input is allowed to vary in an effort to show the universal relationships between a variable input and the changing nature of the quantity of output produced.

With varying quantities of labor being measured on the hori-

Figure 9.1   **The Product Curve Using Labor as the Variable Input**

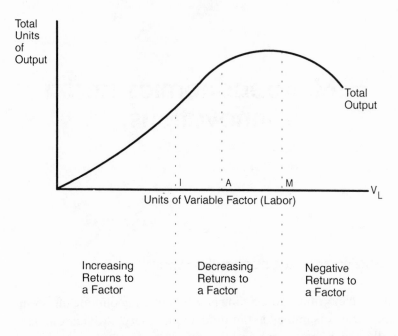

zontal axis and the level of produced output being measured on the vertical axis, Figure 9.1 depicts a typical production function. This should be both a review and an extension of the production theory discussed in chapter 6. From Figure 9.1 it can be readily observed that as variable units of labor input are added to the production process, the total amount of production rises rapidly (up to point I), slows in its amount of increase (from point I to point M) and then starts decreasing in volume (past point M). Using microeconomic theory and geometry, it can be concluded that point I is the point of inflection. Point I represents the level of inputs where total output continues to increase but at a decreasing rate. Likewise, Point A is the maximum of the average variable input (output per unit of variable input-labor), and point M is the maximum attainable level of output regardless of the changing amounts of the variable input-labor. In other words, beyond point M, additional units of the variable input-labor will only decrease the total amount of output produced. Almost any principles of economics text will supply additional detail if more explanation of these points is desired.

These three points from Figure 9.1 translate into returns to a factor. The beginning of production to point I demonstrates increasing returns to a factor. That is, each additional unit of labor that is added to the production process will add more units of output than the previous unit of labor. The output level between points I and M represent decreasing returns. That is, each unit of labor added to the production process will add some positive amount to total output, but it will add less additional output than the previous unit of labor. In other words, between points I and M, additional labor adds units of output but in decreasing additional amounts as more units of labor are added to the production process. Finally, beyond point M, additional units of labor added to the production process actually are detrimental and reduce the overall total amount of output.

To this very cursory explanation of the total product curve, it is important to add a general description of the marginal and average products that visually expand the analysis of the total product curve. Figure 9.2 depicts the average product curve and the marginal product curve. Points I, A, and M in each figure represent the same levels of the variable input—labor. However, the vertical axis has changed in order to measure output per unit of variable input associated with both the marginal and average curves. Point I, the end point of increasing returns to a factor in Figure 9.1 is actually identical to the maximum level of the marginal product curve as can be seen in Figure 9.2. Point A in Figure 9.1 is the maximum of the average product curve as can be seen in Figure 9.2. Also, point A is the only part of either figure where average product and marginal product are equal. Finally, point M in Figure 9.1 where total product reaches a maximum is identical to point M in Figure 9.2 where marginal product is equal to zero.

In addition to the above analysis of production, Figure 9.2 shows the three stages of production that theoretically occur in any production process. Stage I production occurs where average product

Figure 9.2 **Average and Marginal Product Curves**

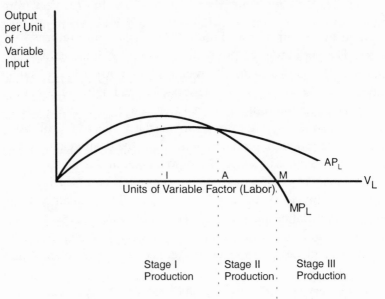

is increasing. This increase in average product occurs because marginal product is greater than average product and, therefore, an additional unit of variable input will add more to the total product than the previous unit of labor and thus the average product will increase. In Stage II production, the average product starts to decrease. Likewise, the result occurs because marginal product is less than average product. That is, an additional unit of labor will add less to the average product than the previous unit of labor, and thus the average product will decrease. In Stage III production, the marginal product becomes negative. An additional unit of the variable input, labor, will actually reduce total product. It must be noted that production theory states that if a firm is to achieve maximum efficiency in production (as well as maximum profits), it must produce somewhere in Stage II production. Any firm in any industry producing any product will not be achieving maximum efficiency unless that firm is producing in the area of Stage II production. The theoretical point of maximum efficiency cannot be determined with the limited amount of above information from Figures 9.1 and 9.2, but it will always occur somewhere in Stage II production.

With this brief review of neoclassical microeconomic production theory, the assumptions can now be viewed in terms of the entrepreneur and innovations. In order to describe the production function, either graphically or otherwise, a specific production process must be chosen and strictly adhered to. That is, the relationship between fixed and variable inputs cannot be changed. The specific combinations of fixed and variable inputs needed for production cannot change. The technology used in the production process cannot be altered without requiring the development of a whole new production function. Furthermore, with strict adherence to a specific production function, the entrepreneur and the resulting innovations have virtually no mission to be accomplished once the production process is set in motion. The static nature of the production function requires that each time an entrepreneur creates an innovation (better technology, a more efficient input combination, a different sequence of the steps for assembly, etc.) a whole new production function must be developed, and this changes the theoretical analysis specific to each production function. Likewise, the total production that results from four units of labor and ten units of other inputs will be changed each time the entrepreneur affects the production function. The level of production will change, as will the boundaries for the stages of production and returns to a factor. This has led many professionals to conclude that while the entrepreneur and the resulting innovations are extremely important in the ongoing process of production, they cannot be accommodated in the current existing static microeconomic theory of production. The challenge for current economists studying microeconomic theory is to incorporate the important contributions to the production process of the entrepreneur into a more complete economic theory.

It seems clear that if the objective of the entrepreneur is to innovate by changing the product and/or the production process, there is little room for the entrepreneur in neoclassical microeconomic theory. It would follow then that there is no established economic production theory of the entrepreneur. Other social sciences, such as sociology, psychology, and political science, do address different aspects of the entrepreneur, but in production economics, the analysis is devoid of entrepreneurship.

Within economics, the theory reduces decision making to a mechanical application of mathematical rules for optimization within a rigid set of assumptions. Therefore, there is no place for the creative innovation of the entrepreneur where change is the means to the objective of altered products and production processes. Each new innovation leading to change would require a new production function with accompanying changes in marginal product, average product, and the resulting changes in points for stages of production and returns to each factor of production.

One should quickly question why microeconomic theory is still used in light of such a serious shortcoming. The answer lies mainly in the fact that critics of the neoclassical theory have offered little in the way of a complete theory to replace the existing analysis. Therefore, neoclassical microeconomic theory remains influential in both theory and practice. It becomes incumbent on the critic of microeconomic theory not only to summarize the criticism but also to offer a new analysis to meet this criticism. Criticism has come from many different schools for many different reasons, but to date no new comprehensive theory has been suggested to replace the existing theory. Notwithstanding this lack of a comprehensive replacement theory, it must be recognized that today's entrepreneur is operating largely outside mainstream neoclassical production theory.

Bringing About New Products and New Markets

It should be made very clear that each time an entrepreneur innovates by making a change to bring about a new or improved product or a different production process or develops a new market for an existing product, the production function has been changed.

This must result in a new production function to accommodate the change that has taken place. According to Joseph A. Schumpeter, when the concept of innovations are introduced into the capitalist process, these innovations will be identified with the development of new products, the founding of new firms, and the opening of new markets.[1] Each of these occurrences will in fact require a new production function to be developed in the process. If these changes occur rapidly, the neoclassical theory of the production function becomes only theoretical in nature and loses its practical application and usefulness in production analysis.

Once the entrepreneur introduces change in products, markets, or processes, the innovation leads to a decreased usefulness of the old product or process and emphasizes the advantages of the new product or process. This transition from the old to the new was referred to by Schumpeter as creative destruction.[2] These changes to new products or processes lead to the potential profits that are sought by capitalists. In turn, the widespread use of the innovations by producers determines the size and length of time that profits will endure for the firm. These varying degrees of profits for the firm can be associated with the speed with which the innovation is incorporated into the product and production process. There are three levels of profitability determined by the quickness of the firm to adapt.

In the first case, the firm will be the origin of the innovation. In this case the firm can take full advantage of the innovation leading to a new product or process. In the case of a new product, the firm can operate as a monopolist and receive a monopoly price and above-normal profits as long as the innovation is in the sole possession of the innovating firm. The examples of successful innovations leading firms to experience high levels of profits are a prime example of why firms seek out entrepreneurs and their innovations. In the matter of the innovation leading to a change in the production process, the activity leads to excess profits through decreases in per-unit costs of production. In the former innovation it is the demand curve that represents the change and potential for excess profits and in the latter innovation it is the supply side of economics that offers opportunities for expanding profits.

In the second case of firms seeking to expand profits, firms that do not have the entrepreneurial effort to create the innovation can quickly become copycats or imitators of the new product or production process. Once the product has been marketed, other firms are free to analyze the new product and attempt to find ways to produce similar copies without violating patent or copyright laws. Or, if the innovation has occurred in the production process, similar production machinery, techniques, and/or production schemes can be duplicated by the firms wishing to imitate the successful innovations of the original firm that utilized the change. In this case, the imitating firm will experience some level of economic profits, but these profits will be at a lesser level than the original innovating firm will. In the case of the new product, competition from similar products will reduce the monopoly price for all firms, and fewer profits will be available for each firm. In the case of the innovation leading to a decreased per-unit cost of production, competition will again force a reduction in product prices, and per-unit profit will be reduced.

In the last model of firms in an industry experiencing innovations are examples of firms that are resistant to the change. There are two types of firms in this last model. The first type of firm will eventually make the change and incorporate the innovation in order to survive in an industry where prices are falling and excess profits are disappearing. These firms continue producing but experience only normal profits sufficient to keep the firm operating in the industry. The second type of firm steadfastly refuses to incorporate the innovation into the product or production process. In this case the firm experiences decreased product prices and has no reductions in the costs of production to compensate for the lowered revenues. These firms eventually exit the industry and become casualties of a changing industry because they experience economic losses.

This process of creative destruction is an ongoing change, with new firms entering an industry with new products and new production processes and existing firms leaving the industry as their products and processes do not include the necessary changes required for sufficient profits to remain productive. This selection process may seem harsh on those firms that do not adapt to new innovations, but the end result is better products at lower prices for consumers who purchase products in this industry. This transition over time in an industry is duplicated over and over from industry to industry as entrepreneurs innovate, and these innovations are implemented by firms seeking to expand profits.

The analysis of these innovations brought about by the entrepreneur and implemented at different levels and times by firms within an industry is not captured by the static nature of the neoclassical microeconomic production analysis. However, these changes are an important driving force of firms seeking to expand profits. The inability of production analysis to address and incorporate the entrepreneur and the resulting innovations does not diminish the importance of either the entrepreneur or microeconomic production theory. The inability to make economic theory and the reality of the entrepreneur compatible does, however, draw attention to the ever-increasing need to modify existing theories to better explain occurrences in the real world of entrepreneurs and innovations.

Changing Economic Theory to Incorporate the Entrepreneur and Innovations

Contrary to what some people believe, economic theories change. Economic theory used within western capitalistic economies has existed for a mere two hundred years. The two most notable changes were major upheavals in the theoretical explanations of capitalism. The first was the development, implementation, and use of neoclassical economics about one hundred years ago. Among the notable economists attempting to modify the classical view of economics were Alfred Marshall, Carl Menger, John Bates Clark, and John Maurice Clark. The concepts of marginal analysis, diminishing returns, analysis of supply and demand, and a view of behavior of the firm were slowly integrated into an accepted theoretical base that became known as neoclassical microeconomic analysis. A second major theoretical economic change is attributed to John Maynard Keynes, in the area of macroeconomic analysis. This major upheaval in economic theory started almost sixty years ago and became commonplace approximately thirty years ago when Richard M. Nixon, then president of the United States proclaimed, "We're all Keynesians now."

To better understand how these changes in economic theory occur, it is important first to look at how scientific theories change over time. In his book, *The Structure of Scientific Revolutions*, Thomas S. Kuhn attempts to explain how changes in accepted theories can be accomplished and how new theories can be developed and widely accepted.[3] After a theory is established and depicts what a part of the world is like, that theory becomes widely accepted. This theoretical basis, once widely accepted, becomes known as "normal science." The theory encompasses an accepted set of assumptions with logical consequences predicted by the theoretical model. This set of assumptions and predictions (or model) becomes the accepted and shared paradigm by which professionals further explore their discipline. This paradigm then is the accepted set of rules and standards used in professional scientific investigation.

Sooner or later in scientific investigation a phenomenon occurs that does not fit the accepted paradigm for explanation. A project or experiment whose outcome does not fit the accepted paradigm is generally referred to as a research failure. That is, the inability to fit the accepted paradigm is blamed on the researcher or scientist and not viewed as an actual natural phenomenon. These occurrences are referred to as an anomaly. Likewise, for whatever reason, the results are seen as being outside the accepted paradigm. Two results might develop from the occurrence of an anomaly. The first is the notion that something went wrong in the experiment or investigation and the problem lies outside the paradigm. The occurrence is therefore outside the boundaries of investigation of that particular scientific field. The second result, if the anomaly is repeated several times over time by many different professionals, is that the anomaly has exposed a gap or flaw in the accepted para-

Table 9.1

Stages of Scientific Change

Preparadigm—Several competing schools of thought.

Normal science—One school of thought gains complete or near-universal acceptance (normal science is puzzle solving with accepted direction for research and methods for doing research).

Anomaly—Results of scientific research that are not explained by the normal science paradigm.

Crisis—Widespread acceptance that the anomaly is important and violates the rules of the normal science. There is failure of the paradigm to account for the results of experiment.

Period of extraordinary science—Widespread search for a new paradigm.

Resolution: Either

A. Anomaly is resolved by the normal science (existing paradigm).
B. Normal science resists the anomaly, and it becomes accepted as insolvable (anomaly is outside the area of normal science).
C. A new paradigm emerges and starts the battle for acceptance.

digm. The mainstream scientific community will resist this view because most professionals have spent many years within the comfort of the well-known accepted paradigm.

Once the anomaly gains credibility through widespread scientific investigation, one of two choices remains. First, the anomaly can be accepted as not being an explainable part of the paradigm. In this situation science recognizes that there is a flaw in the paradigm, but the existing paradigm continues to be accepted and used and dominates in the profession. The second choice is to continue to modify the paradigm so that the anomaly creates a new, more explanatory paradigm. This change is sometimes referred to as "scientific revolution" and results in a stronger, more complete theory by which professionals base their discipline. Table 9.1 depicts these stages of scientific change.

Within the field of economics, anomalies created the two major changes in economic theory mentioned above. The new paradigms of neoclassical microeconomic theory and Keynesian macroeconomic theory resulted in a stronger, more complete theory by which economists could explain economic events. However, the entrepreneur and the innovations within the economic system present a present-day anomaly that is yet to be resolved. The innovations of the entrepreneur are not captured by the static economic analysis of production theory, yet they are a common occurrence in the development of products and production processes.

To date this anomaly of the entrepreneur and innovations has not gained the widespread recognition of the economics profession and is seen as largely outside economic theory. However, it is the entrepreneur and the driving force of innovations that make market capitalism so appealing to world populations. The challenge to the economics profession is to find a way to integrate the entrepreneur and resulting innovations into a new theory of production that encompasses the current anomaly. This way, the economic theory of production will be better able to describe and predict daily economic activity. The new paradigm may then be accepted as normal science in the economics profession. Entrepreneurship, innovations, and economics will then be a more explanatory part of the ever-changing production processes and products.

Entrepreneurial Biography 9: Linda Ligon

Name:	Linda Ligon
Company:	Interweave Press
Number of Employees:	53
Annual Sales:	$6 million

What events and/or people were present in your youth or early adulthood that you now realize influenced your becoming an entrepreneur?

I didn't enter into entrepreneurship through any conventional influences. My father was a civil servant, my mother was a housewife, and my brothers went into the military or held conventional jobs. As a child, I was pretty timid. I never had a lemonade stand; I couldn't even sell Girl Scout cookies. My teachers encouraged me to pursue careers in art or science; my parents thought teaching would be suitable. I studied for a master's degree in English with the idea of teaching, which I did, both at the university level and later in public schools. Nobody who knew me growing up in small-town Oklahoma would have thought I would have my own business, or that it would be successful.

Describe some of your early efforts at entrepreneurship.

My early effort would be those Girl Scout cookies. My mother bought them all!

What were some events or projects that were not successful, but contributed to your success as an entrepreneur?

I'm going to stray from the pattern here because I don't fit very well. I taught school until I was thirty-two, and I really enjoyed that career. Although I had children, it was important for me to work outside the home and pursue my own interests. Then unexpectedly I got pregnant for the third time, and our youngest son was born with enough medical problems that it was out of the question for me to go back to work. I knew I needed something to do while I stayed home with him and his brother and sister who were in primary school. I hit upon the idea of publishing a small regional magazine for hand-weavers. This idea developed from the fact that weaving was my hobby, and I knew a lot of other people who were engaged in the craft. At the same time, as a high school English teacher, I had sponsored the student publications and had become familiar with all the processes—journalistic writing, photography, typesetting, layout, and printing. It was a lot of fun!

When my son was born, I took my teacher's retirement fund ($1,500!) and cobbled together a twenty-four-page, black and white, slick little magazine and gave it away free to a couple of thousand hand-weavers. It was a very low-key way to launch a magazine, but enough people sent in subscription checks that I could afford to put out the next issue, and the next, and so on. It was a part-time effort for about five years and actually more of a serious hobby than a job. But aside from not paying myself much, it was profitable, and I was able to hire part-time help for the parts I didn't or couldn't do, such as advertising sales, accounting, and so forth.

What project stands out as one of your major entrepreneurial successes?

After five years, my one magazine had grown into two, and I was publishing the occasional little book as well—vertical marketing! My husband came home from work one day and surprised me with the news that he had quit his job. He wanted to spend some time pursuing personal interests that weren't likely to earn income for quite a while. This was highly motivating for me—the sudden need to support a family of five with two kids in high school and college looming ahead. I suddenly found myself taking the business side of my business very seriously. Revenues started growing anywhere from 30 percent to 50 percent a year; I published more books, started a third magazine in a more mainstream subject matter area, hired more people, and so it went.

For twenty years my business style was to take one step at a time, to mine the markets I understood and had ready access to, to bootstrap every new effort so that if it failed, I wouldn't be putting the business at risk. Every year I was blessed with both growth and profit. After twenty years in business, I had about forty employees, sales volumes of $5 million, and money in the bank. However, five years ago, because of stresses in my personal life (death of parents, temporary disability of my husband, the last child leaving home), I reached a crisis of confidence and brought a partner into the business, someone with a much more sophisticated business background than I had. Together we pushed the business out—doubled our revenues, launched new products, and entered a joint venture with a major publishing house in the East. It was fun, exciting, and risky, and it got me in trouble.

What event stands out as a major stumbling block that you needed to overcome as an entrepreneur?

The joint venture became a nightmare; my partner and I began to have divergent personal and business goals, we incurred substantial debt, and morale problems abounded. I have spent the past year unraveling all this and building a new company vision and a new management team. Today we're poised for new growth. The debt is under control, cash flow is healthy, and I have strong people in place who I feel can take the company forward when I no longer want to be so fully engaged.

What advice could you give someone who has aspirations of becoming an entrepreneur?

My advice to a budding entrepreneur is to trust yourself and believe you can do anything. It's not always necessary to go "by the book." It's more important to listen to your instincts. Always ask yourself, "What's the worst thing that can happen?" and let that be the limit to your risk taking. Never stop learning. Care about the people who help you succeed and keep your ego in check. Be clear about your personal goals and values and let them drive your business. Try to maintain a balanced life.

Describe your current enterprise.

Interweave Press publishes five nationally distributed special interest magazines and a line of books in the same subject matter areas (traditional crafts). It is also majority owner and sole manager of a separate company, Natural Home LLC, that publishes a shelter/lifestyle magazine with strong newsstand distribution; this is an important growth area. Together the two companies, which are housed under the same roof, have about fifty-five employees and sales volumes of $8 million.

Describe your feelings toward your enterprise. Would you sell your enterprise? Would you work for a new owner? Would you take on a partner?

Occasionally companies approach me with an interest in buying Interweave. My dream, though, is to sell it to my employees, and I'm working on that possibility at this time. Natural Home, on the other hand, is being positioned to sell eventually. But I couldn't possibly work for a new owner after twenty-six years of being able to call my own shots! The joint venture I was in for almost three years was as close as I'd ever care to come to having to answer to someone else. Having had one highly educational experience with a partner, I feel prepared to do it differently next time. Ideally, that would be with some of my key employees whom I've chosen, developed, and feel in sync with.

How do you stay competitive with other firms in your industry?

I don't worry too much about the competition. I try to go into markets where I can build a clear, dominant position quickly. When there are competitive challenges, I try to remind myself and my staff of that old motto, "Always try to exceed yourself, not the competition." It seems to work for us.

What innovations have you implemented to improve your enterprise?

Change and innovation are daily facts of life. I've always tried to stay on or ahead of the curve with technology, outsourcing, and product development. Helping employees feel comfortable with change is a big challenge, one that requires constant communication and encouragement. The one area I've held back in, and am not sorry, is e-commerce. We have a commercial website, and it generates incremental income, but I have been reluctant to invest a great deal there. I'm comfortable thinking about the Internet as another way to deliver product, but I don't think the future is clear enough yet to leap too far ahead.

Notes

1. Joseph A. Schumpeter, *The Theory of Economic Development: An Inquiry into Profits, Capital Credit, Interest and the Business Cycle* (Cambridge, MA: Harvard University Press, 1936), p. 66.

2. Joseph A. Schumpeter, *Capitalism, Socialism and Democracy* (New York: Harper and Row, reprinted 1962), p. 83.

3. Thomas S. Kuhn, *The Structure of Scientific Revolutions,* 2d ed. (Chicago: University of Chicago Press, 1970).

10

Economic Sources of Innovations

User-Led Innovations

As explained in several areas in previous parts of this book, there is a clear distinction between capitalists and entrepreneurs. The distinction is important because the driving forces behind the actions of the entrepreneur are quite different from those of the capitalist. Entrepreneurs set about making changes through innovations and are motivated by objectives other than profits. That is not to say that entrepreneurs are not interested in profits, but profits are not the main factor encouraging entrepreneurs to innovate. Innovations come from entrepreneurs, not capitalists. However, once an entrepreneur innovates and profits are generated, most entrepreneurs become capitalists and certainly desire to benefit through profits from the innovation. Many entrepreneurs become capitalists, but far fewer capitalists ever become entrepreneurs.

The above analysis is reinforced when observation is made about where innovations originate. There are many industries in which the user of the product originates the actual innovation. According to Eric von Hippel in his book *The Sources of Innovation,*[1] there are three sources of innovations in a market economy. Initial innovations in products are made by users of the product, suppliers (wholesalers) of the product, or manufacturers of the product. The origin of the innovation is referred to as the functional source of the innovation. Although the functional source of the innovation varies from industry to industry, most innovations in the U.S. economy originate with the user of the product. Some industries have innovations dominated by manufacturers and some industries have innovations dominated by suppliers, but most industries have innovations dominated by users of the product.

Since a user-led innovation is not common knowledge, the manufacturer often takes the credit for the new product or improvement in the existing product. The reason this phenomenon is not common knowledge is rather simple. Once a user becomes the functional source of the innovation, that innovation is often shared with the manufacturer in an attempt to get a better product. The manufacturer then takes the innovation, makes changes, redesigns the product, places the manufacturer's name on the product, and advertises the new and improved product. Buyers generally assume that if a manufacturer's name is on the product, then the manufacturer innovated the product or improvement.

Many manufacturers give experimental prototype products to special customers in order for those users to make innovations and give beneficial feedback on the product so that it can be improved. This joint effort between the manufacturer and the user does not nullify the fact that users are still making the innovations. The user is the source of the innovation, and the manufacturer makes the changes and accepts by default or by deception the recognition for the innovation. The user benefits by receiving an improved product after the innovation has been incorporated into the prototype, even though the manufacturer profits from the sale of the innovated product.

The functional source of innovation can usually be traced to who benefits from the innovation. The profit motive is one source of motivation for manufacturers. However, an example of benefits from innovations can help explain why users would also want to innovate even though they may not financially profit from the innovation. Suppose that a user bought a piece of machinery used in the production of a product that the user sold in a very competitive market. If the user is able to innovate and make the machinery more functional, the user now has a better production process. The user can benefit from the innovation as long as the innovation can be kept secret from other competitors. This option is seldom available to manufacturers because they can profit only from making the innovation available for sale to a large number of users.

It must be reemphasized that entrepreneurs are driven to make changes in order to make things work better. This driving force of innovations may result in profits, but is most often not the rationale for attempting to innovate. However, once the innovation has occurred and there exists a profit potential, the entrepreneur often takes advantage of this potential. Table 10.1 attempts to clarify this chronology.

Knowing that profits may follow a successful innovation does not make the entrepreneur a capitalist. Profits may be a reward, but not the motivation for innovations. The motivation for the entrepreneur is a more efficient, smoother operation as a result of making changes. The entrepreneur does not seek profits as a motivation and thus looks for an innovation to provide those profits. Rather, the nature of the entrepreneur is a never-ending search to make changes in order to make the process work better and if successful can often profit from those efforts as a reward.

The source of innovations and the motivating forces that stimulate the entrepreneur to create innovations has enormous economic impacts on efficiency and economic growth as well as firm creation and expansion. However, as great as these economic impacts are, economic literature or analysis of the entrepreneur is scarce. The entrepreneur and the resulting innovations has by far a greater economic impact than does economies of scale or even returns to a factor yet little economic analysis has led to its inquiry.

In chapter 7 an analysis of short-run average cost and long-run average cost demonstrated that the entrepreneur often innovated and moved the production firm to a lower point on the short-run average cost curve. This movement is almost without exception attributed to the production manager inducing efficiency into the production process. No mention of the entrepreneurship or inno-

Table 10.1

Chronology for User Innovations

Stage	Motivation →	Creative vision →	Innovation →	Results →	Retrospection
Rationale	1. Improving the production process 2. Entrepreneurial drive to make something work better	1. Exploring ways to change the process	1. Trial and error experiments to find a better way	1. Efficiency 2. Lower costs of production 3. Improved product 4. Simplified	1. Compensatory measure of success 2. Profits-reward not a motivation for innovation 3. Returns from a successful innovation process

vation is used to introduce reality into the cost analysis of production. As has been stated several times in this book, the economics profession must find a way to expand the economic paradigm to include the entrepreneur as a viable working component of the economic system.

Producer-Led Innovations

In his book, *Capitalism, Socialism and Democracy*, Joseph A. Schumpeter[2] discusses producer-led innovations and how the successful innovations allow the firm to gain temporary monopoly control over what the firm has created. This temporary monopoly control in turn allows the firm an enhanced position in the industry that allows monopoly profits as a reward for their efforts. As long as the firm can control the innovation by secret production process, controlled inputs, or other means, the firm can maintain this monopoly control and the resulting monopoly profits.

Firms that seek these monopoly profits, however, are likely not the innovators directly, but rather they employ a staff that includes entrepreneurs who create the innovations used by these firms. Again there is a strong distinction between a capitalist attempting to risk finances with the possibility of gaining monopoly control with its resulting profits and the entrepreneur who has a driving passion to create changes to make things work better. Furthermore, the entrepreneur attempting to make a successful innovation may or may not share directly in the profits of successful innovations. Firms are motivated by profits; entrepreneurs are motivated by a sociologically distinct drive to make improvements in products and/or production processes.

In small firms where the entrepreneur is also the owner of the firm (the capitalist), the distinction between entrepreneurial behavior and the behavior of the capitalist may be clouded, but its basis is still perceptible. The same individual must take command of two separate tasks for the firm. First, the individual as entrepreneur is motivated by the drive to make creative changes to better the product or production process at hand. Secondly, once a successful innovation has occurred, the entrepreneur takes on the additional role of a capitalist. Now the same individual accepts the responsibility to generate the appropriate profits from the newly created innovation. Without this distinction, the entrepreneur is defined as a capitalist, and little if any credit is given to the creative process of innovations. If innovations are to remain and be recognized as an important driving force of economic activity, then a special distinct domain needs to be identified for the entrepreneur separate from the capitalist.

Once the entrepreneur successfully innovates new products and production processes, the role of the capitalist often enters the decision-making process of the entrepreneur. This usually creates a problem for the entrepreneur. Some of the driving motivation for innovations and time spent being creative are now replaced with the need to generate and maintain profits. This time requirement and change in motivation now starts detracting from the entrepreneurial ability to create innovations. The entrepreneur now becomes less of a creative innovator and more of a police protector of the organization that generates and maintains the monopoly profits.

Examples abound about the hard-working entrepreneur who creates a major innovation in a garage, basement, or small shop, then expands to a national firm and generates millions of dollars in profits. That individual now takes on an administrative role to protect those profits, and the creative efforts of the entrepreneur are diminished. Computer hardware and software, publishing, pharmaceuticals, and electronics are but a glimpse at the industries that have seen entrepreneurs create celebrated innovations, build empires, and then lose that creative process of innovation once success forces the individual to become a protector of the capital empire that has been built.

In addition to the problems created when an economic system loses the creative innovations of the entrepreneur once success changes the individual into a protective manager of the capital assets, many larger firms stumble onto innovations quite by accident. These innovations sometimes go unnoticed and unused for decades because of a lack of understanding of their potential use-fulness as products or processes. An excellent example of an ex-traordinary innovative discovery is in the photovoltaic process of creating electric current from light. In 1954, Bell Laboratories was involved with the testing of conductors for uniform transforma-tion of electric current. The experiment attempted to establish a consistent current flow over time that was not impacted by differ-ences in temperatures. The electrical experiment was consistently monitored day and night. However, when the nighttime lights were turned on to more accurately check the metering of the flows of electrical current, the current increased dramatically. The experi-ment was halted as a failure, and only many years later did an innovator attempt to use the same conductor to actually create electrical current with the use of light. Today the use of solar pho-tovoltaic electric power has widespread use in remote areas and holds the prospect of long-term electrical generation with a re-newable energy source.

Producers who create innovations also have the possibility of patenting or licensing the innovation if certain criteria are met. However, the number of patents and licenses applied for or issued compared to the vast number of innovations is dramatically small. There are several reasons for this small fraction of innovations getting patents or licenses. First, many entrepreneurs are impa-tient in attempts to get their innovation turned into functional prod-ucts and production processes. Patents and licenses take time and effort that most entrepreneurs do not want to expend.

Second, many innovations have questionable qualities that might not qualify as patentable or have the ability to hold a license. Many innovations are merely a different, better way or a different, better product that is not original in the sense of a patent. The uniqueness of most innovations would quite likely lack the qualities of a pat-entable product.

The third reason for the lack of patents and licenses for innova-tions revolves around small firms compared to large firms. If a small firm with limited capital creates an innovation that is pat-ented and then copied by a large firm, the only recourse for the small firm is litigation. This process is very costly and most often very time consuming. By the time the legal system would force a large company to halt use of the small firm's innovation, that innovation might be outdated and the small firm might be financially bankrupt from the litigation.

A final reason for the lack of patents and licenses for innovations rests with the lack of royalty incomes to cover the legal cost and efforts to secure the patent or license. With the ability of competitors to create very close imitations without violating the patent or license, the income or royalty from a patent or license might be extremely low. Therefore, most innovators have a reluctance to go to the trouble to secure patents and licenses. Rather, they prefer to push ahead, move the innovation to commercialization, and secure temporary monopoly profits while their innovation is in public demand.

Government Research and Development for Innovations

In the 1950s and 1960s, renowned economist Kenneth Arrow steadfastly and sometimes almost single-handedly demonstrated the economic importance of the need for the federal government to support research and development in the U.S. economy.[3] There are several economic justifications for government-sponsored research and development. These justifications include the social value of the benefits of the results of the research and development of new advanced products; the national benefits of a strong economy from international trade as a result of new and improved products; a national defense need to be able to produce products domestically in times of international war or military conflict; and the environmental benefits of cleaner, safer products.

In many instances the invention, innovation, product, or process that is developed from successful research and development has benefits that are received by society at large and they occur outside the market structure. That is, benefits occur outside the framework of the buyer and seller. These social benefits cannot be recouped by producers through the marketplace, and thus producers are less willing to invest in research and development if they cannot recoup the profits from product development. In these instances, there is a defined role for government support of research and development since private investors will underinvest in such activities.[4]

In addition to products that have social benefits that are not redeemable by private producers, there are products that can very easily be duplicated by competitors in the marketplace. Again, the benefits from research and development of a marketable product will be underfunded in the private sector, and this often presents a role for federally funded research and development if the social benefits warrant such investments.

A second large economic rationale for federal support of research and development is in the area of international competition in the production and sale of products. Many foreign governments support most of the research and development for the goods and services of their country that eventually get sold in the international marketplace. These goods are sold to the United States, as well as to countries to which U.S. companies attempt to sell their products. When these foreign producers receive subsidies in the form of government-supported research and development, they have an unfair competitive advantage over the U.S. firms that are expected to carry out their own expensive and time-consuming research and development. For international fair trading reasons, a case can be made for the U.S. government to support some level of research and development.

National security is a third area often set forth as a rationale for federal support of research and development. Aviation, military weapons, armored carriers from the automobile industry, and computerized surveillance are a few examples of areas often espoused as needing federal research and development support. The argument states that if the military relied on foreign production of such products and components used in defense and trade channels were cut off or countries refused trade during a military conflict, then the military would not be able to adequately defend the United

States. In these cases research and development, as well as sources of domestic production, are most often supported by the federal government.

The fourth area of economic rationale for government support of research and development to be mentioned here is in its area of growing concern for the environment. The two broad areas in this argument are nonrenewable resources and pollution. Often the market does not adequately reflect the nature of nonrenewable resources in the price of the product. If, for example, there are many decades of petroleum available for the production of gasoline, then the product price will not be reflected in the fact that the source of gasoline is nonrenewable. However, the more farsighted planning ability of the federal government can easily support the research and development of alternative new energy sources such as solar, geothermal, and wind energy sources. Likewise, for pollution problems the federal government could support the research and development of the same alternative energy sources and make the results available to firms that want to use the results of the research and development in an effort to produce products from this new technology that are more environmentally sound.

An historic role has been well developed for the economic importance of federal government support for research and development of new products and processes for U.S. firms to utilize and market. However, the research and development policy of the federal government has not had the economic impact that has been experienced in other countries. There are two major reasons for this lack of economic success from federal-sponsored research and development in the U.S. economy. The first reason revolves around a no-profit policy from successful research and development, and the second is that producers alone have been the almost exclusive recipients of research and development funds.

For some obviously good reasons, the federal government has historically barred companies from profiting from products developed as a result of receiving funds from federally sponsored research and development. The rationale suggests that if a company is paid by the government to do research and development, then the same company should not benefit again through profits from using that research and development in the marketplace. The rationale seems appropriate, but the results have been disastrous.

The result of the no-profit policy imposed by the federal government has led to very successful research and development of processes and technologies that never get developed into products. The firm that completes the research and development has the most knowledge about product development, but instead of taking the next logical innovation step and developing a marketable product, the research and development results often get placed on a shelf and no product is ever developed. Oftentimes very high quality research and development never finds its way into quality, marketable products. This seemingly very rational policy of not profiting twice—once from federal funds for research and development and again from profits from the sale of the new product or process—has weakened the ability of U.S. firms to successfully innovate.

The second major shortcoming of federal support for research and development is in the placement of the funds. As mentioned in an earlier section, many if not most innovations are brought about by the users of products instead of the commonly accepted view of producer-led innovations. Yet the federal government has almost exclusively channeled research and development funds to the producers of products and not the user (innovators) of the products. As a direct result of this bias toward funding producers, the federal government has wasted huge sums of money by not supporting the actual innovators in product development.

It seems obvious that there needs to be some major shifts and realignments in the policies directing the allocation of federal funds for research and development. First, the federal government must focus on the innovation and not just research and development. Therefore, some allowance must be made so that firms successfully completing research and development can also profit from the development of the marketable product. Special taxes on products developed from federally funded research and development would be one example of how firms could profit, but partially repay the government for research and development funding.

Second, the federal policy regulating research and development funding must recognize the source of innovations and support those sources with research and development funds. If that source of innovations is the user of the product, then users should be supported with research and development funding. Federal government understanding of users as a source of innovations would be a start to redefining research and development policy. The ultimate goal should be to get the greatest innovation impact from research and development regardless of whether the funds go to producers or users of products. Developed new products and processes should be the ultimate objective of any research and development policy and the source of the innovation should be the recipient of research and development funding.

Entrepreneurial Biography 10: Chuck Freitag

Name:	Chuck Freitag
Company:	American Armored Transport, Inc.
Number of Employees:	125
Annual Sales:	$15 million

What events and/or people were present in your youth or early adulthood that you now realize influenced your becoming an entrepreneur?

There's probably as much influence on the negative side of entrepreneurship as there is on the positive side. My father was a hardworking blue-collar guy who went drinking after work. This specific group of people became immersed in disdaining life, and they lost their vision about what's out there. I saw how to spend your life that way, and I knew I did not want to become as narrow or confined as that group of people.

In my younger days I worked for independents in the construction business, never really working for a bigger company. I saw how they worked and lived, they all had nice pickup trucks, and that's important to a young man. They all had a really good local status. They were hard working and men of their word with good integrity. They could borrow $250 from another guy, and that guy would know he was going to get paid back. They couldn't borrow too much money from a bank, but when money was needed to buy a tool or just get to the end of the week before you got a paycheck, you could find money from this group of independent people that took care of each other.

The independent guys also take care of their people and depend on their people much more than a larger corporation. I liked being treated as if I was important by the independent guys. I always worked hard and was a good employee so I was always treated well. That gave me a very positive attitude about the independent companies. I like to treat people well, and I like to be liked. So I saw how that would fit in my life. I did not see monetary success other than the short-term tangible things like the new pickup. I liked the fact that there were a group of people like me that I could count on and would take care of me. I just tried to be a positive member of that group.

Was there a particular person that you recognized who was the entrepreneurial image of what you wanted to do?

When I was in my late teens or early twenties, I met Gerald Cochran. I saw how solid he was and how he believed in what he was going to do. He had a coachlike attitude to him, and I learned more from him about life and business than anybody. He was a big influence on me.

Describe some of your early efforts at entrepreneurship.

When I was eighteen, I decided I had good enough skills to go into business as a remodeler or carpenter. Everyone with a hammer thinks he is a carpenter, but a carpenter in real life is so hard to find. A real carpenter is a craftsman and knows how to use his tools and be able to envision and build from an idea. It's a dying art. I had my fancy pickup and tools and thought I knew what I was doing, but I starved. One thing about being on your own is that you don't get a weekly paycheck, and nothing is consistent. You have to make tomorrow happen. If you don't go to work and make it happen, then the next day's not going to come. You learn that you have to dig pretty deep into your character. You may be hung over or sick, but if you have payments due, you get up and go to work, and that's hard to do at times. After a short period of time I got to the point where I couldn't make my apartment payment or feed myself, so I had to go to work for someone else.

I went back to work in construction. During the winter, business slowed down and I knew a guy with a snowplow business and parking lot sweeper business. Since I had a four-wheel-drive pickup that would let me hook a plow onto it, I talked to him about the snowplow business. He said I would need about $1,400 to buy the plow. I didn't have the money, but I borrowed the money from him. He drew up a promissory note so I could pay him monthly on a two-year term loan. I bought the plow in October, and I finished hooking it up one night at 1:00 A.M. because a snowstorm was coming. I used a garage I had borrowed from someone and put the plow together myself to save $250. That was a nightmare, but I got it working. I pushed some snow and made sure it worked. By 6:00 A.M. I was out patrolling the streets like a piranha looking for anyone's driveway or lot that wasn't plowed. If I saw a person, I would go talk to them. I started plowing snow in the winter of 1978 with one truck and plow, and in 1992 I sold the business. During all that time I never enjoyed the serenity of a snowstorm, a walk in the park, cross-country skiing or anything like that because from October through April, I had to be on call.

By the time I sold the business, I had sixty commercial accounts in Loveland. I found out that you don't plow snow at four inches, you plow snow at half inch. You talk to all the companies that are worried about slip and fall liability insurance, and I promoted my snowplow company through the aspect of minimizing liability claims of men wearing fancy shoes and women wearing high heels and slipping in the snow. So when it snowed half inch, my company of all five trucks and several sidewalk maintainers were all out while everyone else was in the coffee shop waiting for four inches of snow. That was my first successful business, and it provided me income that almost exceeded my construction income. In five or six months of plowing snow, I made more money than I did pounding nails all year long. It ended up being a pretty good crutch and pretty good side business. But remember, I failed the first time I went out on my own in the construction business, and I failed the second time, but the third time it stuck, and I was quite successful.

What were some events or projects that were not successful, but contributed to your success as an entrepreneur?

Money was never the driving factor; money just complicates everything. You need a vision of what you want to do because that's what is going to get you up in the morning. If it's just purely money, someone can always take that away from you. There are so many factors that are out of your control. But if you really have a vision of something you want to do, you will have something internally that gets you out of bed each day. The first time I tried, I was neither mature enough nor ready skill-wise to be successful.

The second time I took a job and worked for a guy for a year and a half. But I'm not good at working for someone else. However I worked for an excellent guy, Dick Johnston, who showed me how to build my first house with $500 in my pocket when I was just newly married. He showed me how to get it done without money. That was the first time I realized you didn't have to have money to achieve something. However, my next effort didn't work, so I took another little break. Being married also gave me more of the responsibility factor; you grow up and mature. The third time I tried being an entrepreneur, it stuck and all came together with Debbie helping me and giving me moral support.

Another thing I did was go to a bank because I wanted to be an

apartment maintenance manager. You take care of all the maintenance, construction, landscaping, remodeling, and outside repairs
to the apartment complex. I went to the bank in the late 1970s with
that idea and wanted to borrow $2,500. I thought I had a good
plan, but without collateral I was turned down. I found the only
way I could get money was from private individuals.

**What project stands out as one of your major entrepreneurial
successes?**

My first success was the snow removal business. That was a long-
term thing and gave me a good reputation that helped my construction business also. I painted my phone number and name on
the side of all my equipment and that was my first advertising
experience. I used it for the snow removal business, but since my
business name was Freitag Construction, I'd get calls for the construction business too. The snow removal business helped build
the construction business. They both worked together really well.

After that I had a company that I had built with my father and I
ended up owning 100 percent of it. A bigger corporation approached
me about buying my company and wanted me to blend that company into the organization. At that time the name of their company
was United States Armored Corporation. They began contacting
me in November 1991 with issues such as health insurance, paid
vacation, weekly paychecks, and job security, and they were going to let me manage my company internally in their corporation.
They offered me the best of both worlds. After six months my
wife and I decided it might not be a bad idea to finally have some
stability, and we sold the business in 1992. It was on a five-year
contract that allowed most of my money to come in during the last
two years. The first two years were spent trying to figure out how
to integrate and work in a corporate environment since I had never
done that before. It took me the whole first year to figure out how
to function plus concentrate my efforts on building the business.
My identity was still in this business even though someone else
now owned it.

By the end of 1994 I did for them something I would never have been able to do for myself. For the 1994 calendar year, my net profits in that division of fourteen trucks was $975,000. That was even after sharing expenses from other divisions such as promotional designs, buildings, and investments. I would never have been able to achieve that level unless I was working for someone else. I'm an excellent worker and employee when left alone, but if someone tries to control me, I get an attitude and something inside me rebels. Knowing how to be an excellent employee will make you a much better employer.

What event stands out as a major stumbling block that you needed to overcome as an entrepreneur?

Self-confidence has really been my biggest limiting factor. As a child, I had very low self-esteem and growing up was pretty rough. I had a speech impediment when I was young, and since it was embarrassing for me to talk, I tried not to talk in public. If you don't interact with people, you end up in a little box because life is all about relationships with people. You learn so much more by talking with people as opposed to reading a book or watching anything. If you are not a good communicator, it sets you back. I did not lose my speech impediment until I was about eighteen, and didn't gain my self-confidence until I was in my second year of marriage. That finally happened when I broke the apron strings, so to speak, with the domineering side of my father. My father is a very strong-willed man. He was also the root of my confidence problems, and I learned so much from my father about how not to do things. If you've got a very good source of information showing you how not to do things, you need to align yourself with other people that show you how to do the right things. People like accountants and bankers think with their brain. Entrepreneurs think with their mind. Your mind is much more awesome than your brain. Your brain can only hope to achieve what your mind does every day. I do believe that an entrepreneur functions with his mind, not with his brain.

What advice could you give someone who has aspirations of becoming an entrepreneur?

Figure out what you want to do; not what your father or other people or the latest survey tells you to do. The surveys told everyone ten years ago to become software experts, so everyone went to school for that, and the market is now saturated with computer software people. We all have to make a living and make payments, and that's where basic education comes into play. I'm not a college kind of guy, but I can tell you that there are a lot of negative things about college. I think that those years that you spend in college teach you a lot about people. The most successful students can socially interact and are well spoken. These are the people that companies want to hire. College helps form you for what business and life is all about—relationships with people. Again, you have to figure out what you want to do and then start building toward that; focus on something. You need the same basics no matter what you decide to do in life, and college provides the social interaction that is more important than just the academics alone. So get educated.

Describe your current enterprise.

In 1976 I was first introduced to the armored business at the age of seventeen working construction. Times were really tight in the late 1970s and early 1980s, and there was a devastating building market along the Front Range. To earn cash, I would go down to the Denver Mint where bags of coin came up on conveyor belts out of the basement, and tractor-trailers would back up, and we would grab the bags and put them on pallets, forty to a pallet, and wheel them up to the truck. The truck drivers didn't want to work that hard so they would hire people to load. I hired on and in two-and-a-half hours I could make $75–$100 cash. At that time you could load trucks and then could go to your regular job.

My father was a trucker so I was very familiar with the business. The old-time truckers were great. When my father went to work for a company in New Jersey, he leased his truck to them and began to haul coin for them. I would maintain my father's truck on the weekends. He bought two more trucks and was working as a lease operator when he was suddenly taken ill. He asked me to run his trucks for him until he recovered, but his health deteriorated. I enjoyed the business, so I started focusing my attention on the armored truck business. I built it from three trucks to seven trucks with fourteen or sixteen employees.

When the company we leased our trucks to declared bankruptcy, we discussed going into business for ourselves, and I was granted the first new authority in thirty-five years to haul money from the U.S. Mint. Over the years I had met the head traffic officer at the United States Mint office in Washington, DC, and he knew that he could rely on me. He had learned he could trust me and therefore was willing to sponsor me in order for me to get my authority. We had the business running by September 1989. However, due to poor communication between my dad and I, he insisted we shut down the business when debts were increasing rapidly before profits were realized. He owned the trucks, but I had the authority. I contacted a company in Denver to see if they might be interested in buying the company intact. Dad got $500,000, his health insurance, and a token job; I got a management job. A closing date was set in January. However, a week before Christmas my father called and wanted to call off the sale of the company. I tried to explain to him that all he owned were the trucks, and he couldn't sell the business without my authority. Western Distributing decided they didn't need our trucks, just my authority, and they paid me a weekly retainer while the deal was negotiated.

Meanwhile, Dad's deal to sell the trucks fell through, and he was headed for bankruptcy. The bank proposed that if Dad could convince me to come back with my authority, and I would agree to run the business, the bank would allow me to assume the notes and debts without any down payment. So I agreed and made the phone call to Western Distributing that I was not going to go through with their offer. By November we were running at a monthly profit of 11 percent, which is a reasonable profit. I bought my father out, and he got $250,000 so he had cash to live on. My philosophy to make the company profitable was to haul money out, but never dead-head back. I didn't limit myself to just the armored car business.

By March 1992 I sold the company to Western Distributing and went to work for them on the five-year buyout plan. From April 1992 to May 1995 I had three of the best years of my life. During that time I thought working for somebody else was great; it gave me security and less stress. However, in May 1995 my supervisor walked up to me and handed me my termination form and told me the boss wanted me fired. He had fired me because he said I still thought of the company as my own and that was a problem. When I asked him how he was going to pay me what he owed me, he said he wasn't going to pay me anything and would see me in court. I had $1,700 in savings and checking, two kids, a car payment, a house payment, and no job. I loaded up my things from my office and headed for the nearest phone booth and called a banker acquaintance of mine who works with truckers. I told him I needed $2 million to start another armored truck business. I went down to meet with him, and he told me if he got me the money, I would have a 50 percent silent partner. That was a high cost of money, but it looked like a future to me.

By July 5, I had hauled my first load of coin out of the Denver Mint as American Armored Transport. In about forty-five days I had assembled the entire business. Twenty-eight of the thirty-two drivers, including the dispatch and billing clerk, had quit or were terminated and all came to work for me. We were in competition with three multimillion-dollar organizations, and by the end of 1996 I was $1,286,000 in the red. The reason we lost money was that we had to lower the rates in order to keep market share. There's no question that you can operate at a loss for a period of time as long as you keep enough volume to stay ahead of the impending doom. We kept running and cut revenues from $1.75 per running mile to $1.03, which is way below cost. By the end of 1998 I had paid all my debt, and I actually showed a profit of $250,000 for that year. Through this whole thing, my accountant was begging me to plan what type of bankruptcy I was going to choose. The bank didn't even know my name, but I had people believing in me.

Today American Armored handles over 93 percent of all ground transportation, interstate basis, for the United States Treasury, Bureau of the Mint, Bureau of Engraving and Printing, and all bullion and raw material. We are also a domestic air transporter for the government, as well as for private industry, and an international transporter for the government and for private industry. We're also in the jewelry show division. We have terminals and/or offices in Denver, Philadelphia, Los Angeles, New York City, and San Francisco.

Describe your feelings toward your enterprise. Would you sell your enterprise? Would you work for a new owner? Would you take on a partner?

Yes, if I had a lucrative offer, I would sell my business. With stipulations, I would work for a new owner. However, I would be very up front with the new owner about how to work with me successfully. As for taking on a partner, you have to remember that I've had a 50–50 silent partner. Many people say to not take on a partner and never take on a 50–50 partner because someone has to have the control. I've had a 50–50 partner now for six years, and he is the best person with which I could have aligned myself. There has been moral, financial, and personal backing. He has supported me when I was worried and always backed my decisions. However, I realize that is not always the case, so today I would probably sell up to 49 percent but never 50 percent. Or I would sell 90 percent but no less unless it went to 49 percent. I will sell a controlling interest because I built the business big enough. I'd still have a job and a future. I'd sign a noncompete for five years, but after that I'd come back out.

How do you stay competitive with other firms in your industry?

Don't always believe what other people think is right. I still treat the Mint like a customer, not a cash machine. The competition seems to treat the industry like they are the only game in town.

What innovations have you implemented to improve your enterprise?

Instead of limiting ourselves to what the Mint and the federal government needed, we've kept our focus on where the profit comes from. A lot of the profit comes from hauling bottled water from Los Angeles, bolts and nuts from Chicago, and textiles from Texas. So we have trucking terminals with an armored facility within the confines, but it's not our whole endeavor. We have our own shops and terminals, so we function like a transportation company. We don't call ourselves exclusively an armored company; we're a transportation company, and we make innovations to stay in line with general commodity backhaul. We build and maintain personal relationships. You must build respect and never take a customer for granted.

Notes

1. Eric von Hippel, *The Sources of Innovation* (New York: Oxford University Press, 1988), Chapter 1.
2. Joseph A. Schumpeter, *Capitalism, Socialism and Democracy*, 3d ed. (New York: Harper and Row, 1950).
3. Kenneth J. Arrow, "Economic Welfare and the Allocation of Resources for Invention," in *The Rate and Direction of Industrial Activity: Economic and Social Factors*, National Bureau of Economic Research (Princeton, NJ: Princeton University Press, 1962), pp. 609–625.
4. Ibid., pp. 609–625.

11

The Entrepreneur in the American Economy

Summary and Conclusions

For almost 300 years the entrepreneur has been recognized as a part of the economy. In the early part of the Industrial Revolution, the entrepreneur was viewed as someone who changed the state of resources or helped resources become more productive. That view is still accurate today although the activities of the present-day entrepreneur are more detailed and integral to a healthy, vibrant, and growing economy.

The Industrial Revolution brought about major changes to the daily activities of virtually all humans, but especially the entrepreneur. The Industrial Revolution offered many more implements to the entrepreneurs in their never-ending search to find ways to change the way things are done. The increased ability of the entrepreneur to make changes in products and production processes has transformed society from one of a subsistence lifestyle to one of unheard-of ease of living and luxury just one generation ago. At the center of this ever-increasing standard of living and ease of life is the entrepreneur. Innovations, the successful result of entrepreneurial efforts, are the lifeblood of this ease with which most of the free world carries out their daily lives.

Although the entrepreneur is not ingrained in the vast majority of economic theory, it is central to the long-term viability of a healthy economy. One reason for this lack of presence in economic theory is the confusion between capitalists and entrepreneurs. In many instances these two terms are used interchangeably, which further confuses their separate domains. Risk is one concept that can be used to define separate realms for each segment in a market economy. The risk of the capitalist is a financial risk, with the possibility of profits if the endeavor is successful. Juxtaposed to the financial risk is the entrepreneurial risk—that is, a risk to change the way things are done in order to make the product or process better. Therefore, many entrepreneurs are or become capitalists, but far fewer capitalists ever become entrepreneurs.

As Joseph A. Schumpeter pointed out almost seventy years ago, the entrepreneur is a sociologically distinct individual. The act of the entrepreneur is innovation, and it is the entrepreneur who takes an idea and applies it to a product or industrial process, and the result demonstrates the presence of an innovation. The important ingredient in innovation is commercialization or, in other words, production for sale in the marketplace. The acid test for innovation is commercialization and this separates innovations from inventions. These innovations are focused differently and lead in different directions depending on the type of market that prevails for the product, but commercialization is still the objective whether the product is offered for sale in a competitive market or a monopolistic market.

There are as many different entrepreneurs as there are different businesses that offer opportunities for innovation. However, there seems to be a core of characteristics that are common to most entrepreneurs. Among these characteristics are self-confidence, determination, persistence, optimism, creativity, focus, insight, and the willingness to push ahead and accept the resulting consequences. All entrepreneurs are distinct individuals, but some special characteristics seem to be present in most entrepreneurs.

These characteristics are utilized in varying degrees by entrepreneurs as they move through the act of creating new products and production processes. These stages through which ideas flow to become new products and production processes can be formalized into research, development, demonstration and commercialization, but oftentimes these more formal stages get blurred as the process becomes one of trial and error, repeating stages until a final product or production process has been achieved. Whether the search is more formalized or very informal in a small fabricating shop or production floor, the process is played out again and again by the myriad of entrepreneurs operating on a daily basis to make changes in order to make better products and production processes.

Although much of economic theory is devoid of explicit entrepreneurial activity, much of economic principles can be of great aid in the attempt of the entrepreneur to reach commercialization of products and production processes. Successful commercialization can be better achieved with a firm understanding of the principles of costs of production, marginal analysis, stages of production, returns to a factor, price elasticities, and income elasticities, as well as many other economic principles as they apply to the specific commercialization project at hand. As Joseph A. Schumpeter outlined, an entrepreneur who innovates and creates a new product has attained a temporary monopoly control of other producers of products. Understanding the economic principles of monopoly can greatly enhance the position and longevity of the product developed by the successful entrepreneur.

Once this temporary monopoly position has been established by the entrepreneur, there is an ongoing effort to standardize the product and streamline the production process for increasing volumes of production, to develop efficient production processes as well as increased efforts to lower the per-unit cost of the product. These efforts include the continual drive to change inputs and input combinations in the production process. The changes made in inputs and input combinations can lead to a smoother production process and a more uniform product. These efforts continue to enhance the commercial status of the product or process.

The search for a smoother, more rapid production process is a logical drive in the integration of the product and the production process. Economics can again lend a helpful approach to this drive toward integration. The more formal analyses of economies of scale, economies of scope, and economies of integration can be informalized and applied to a specific product or a specific production process. Although economics is most often taught in a more formalized fashion, the principles and concepts can quite easily be applied to a specific product or production process. This interweaving of economics and entrepreneurship can greatly enhance the commercial success of new products and new production processes. It can also enhance the understanding of the life cycle or timeline of products and production processes. This understanding allows the entrepreneur to accept the inevitable decline in the usefulness of a product or process and the inevitable rise of a new product or process.

In addition to using the principles of economics as an aid to entrepreneurship, the integration of technology and management can also greatly enhance the success of the entrepreneur. In the process of creating new products and production processes, there are inevitable time lags that slow this creation of new products and production processes. In addition, there are many so-called blind alleys and dead ends that consume much time in the search for successful new products and production processes. These time-consuming lags can be greatly reduced and/or eliminated with the integration of (at a minimum) technology, economics, and management. This interdisciplinary approach to innovations can both reduce the time lags in product and process development and enhance the success and longevity of the usefulness of those products and processes.

To complete the understanding of the role of the entrepreneur in the American economy, it is important to understand the origins of the innovations. Many, if not most innovations are user led, although the manufacturer usually gets credit for the innovation. A common procedure is to place a prototype product in the field and allow a user to field test the product or process and suggest changes that might enhance the performance of the product or process. It is commonly acknowledged that the end user is often the source of innovations although those users rarely if ever get credit as the actual source of the innovation. As a result of the field test, the manufacturer redesigns the product or process and attaches a manufacturer's label on the innovation. Therefore, most observers assume that the actual innovation was done by the manufacturer because the new product is so labeled.

One major outcome of this common assumption that innovations are producer led and producer induced is to federally fund producers to research and develop new products and processes. The result is to often waste federally funded research and development funds by financially supporting individuals and companies that are not the actual innovators of new products and processes. There is a great need to restructure federal support for research and development toward the actual innovator in order to produce greater results for the federal expenditure. The ultimate outcome of any publicly or privately funded research and development should be to allow the entrepreneur to commercialize the innovations.

The entrepreneurial biographies at the end of each chapter are an attempt to show the diversity as well as some common traits that exist with the sociologically distinct type of individuals known as entrepreneurs. Their excitement, drive, determination, and passion for their work will hopefully be evident as the reader explores the series of eleven entrepreneurs. These entrepreneurs are not today's world-famous people. Rather they are hard-working, innovative individuals who get excited about what they are contributing to society and the economy. They are individuals who go to work each day with a special eagerness to continually search for new ways to get things done and new avenues to make changes in order to make better products and better production processes. These examples of entrepreneurs have thousands of counterparts in the American economy who collectively form the driving force that makes life more comfortable for society. Entrepreneurs remain the lifeblood of the American economy.

Entrepreneurial Biography 11: John Freeman

Name:	John Freeman
Company:	Architecture One
Number of Employees:	8
Annual Sales:	$750,000

What events and/or people were present in your youth or early adulthood that you now realize influenced your becoming an entrepreneur?

I don't feel there was anything remarkable or dramatic in my youth. I grew up in Iowa and am a typical Midwestern personality, though not a farm boy. The greatest influence on my career and my work habits comes from my father. My dad, Bob Freeman, was the son of a middle-class, middle-income insurance salesman in Iowa City. Bob was a jock at heart, a basketball star, intelligent but poor, and uncaring academically. He married the cute cheerleader, my mom, and they're still together fifty years later. The thing that he excelled at and that he passed on to me is the ability and desire to work hard. Dad said he didn't take work seriously (which I don't believe) until he saw the face of his firstborn child. My dad worked his way up from a small-town insurance salesman and eventually became CEO of three consecutive, different insurance companies. He still sits on the board of his last company having retired six or seven years ago. It must be from him that I learned to work hard. He worked at home and lots of evenings at the office. I probably didn't see nearly enough of him as I was growing up, though I don't recall being concerned about it at the time.

I worked as soon as I was old enough and mowed lawns, etc. I worked as an assistant at the Des Moines Art Center when I was fourteen. I worked lots of summers and some vacations at a nearby factory when I was fifteen and sixteen (I lied on the job application about my age). I worked in a lumberyard for two or three summers during college. I tried food service for three days once and quit because I couldn't stand the work. Similarly, I tried a couple of different graveyard shift jobs in school but couldn't get the sleep schedule worked out. I quit each of these, exhausted after three days. I worked all the time. I don't think I worked these jobs for the money although that was probably the nominal reason at the time. Money has never been a strong motivation or concern to me. I think I worked because I thought it was what you were supposed to do.

Describe some of your early efforts at entrepreneurship.

Early entrepreneurial experiences include going to my first university to study art. It was an idea of an overly enthused youth. I was a free spirit in the age of the hippies, and art was a great vehicle for that. I dropped out of school after three years and a marriage because I couldn't see clearly how I might make a living as an artist. I might have been vaguely fearful or shy or maybe just lost the enthusiasm for art.

I hacked around as a carpenter and painter. I remember once writing a letter offering homeowners my (fictional) expertise as a house painter, and wouldn't they like me to paint their house? I still have a copy of the letter somewhere. I distributed four of these letters and got one call. I painted that house and then their neighbor's and then one of the neighbor's friend's. This was a kind of footloose period that I guess was entrepreneurially formative. I didn't worry much about the long-term future; I just went out and got some work whenever I got through with the last job. I fixed up barns and did odd jobs at a local hog farm. I helped a framer on a new house for a friend of one of my uncles. I think the only tool I owned at that time was a hammer. I decided I could do carpentry and began to freelance fix-it, painting, and repair jobs. I learned as I went and bought a small collection of tools. I remember two different jobs in neighboring houses where the lady clients thought I was a finish carpenter, and I didn't know enough to say I wasn't.

What awful things I must have wrought in their houses.

I decided during this two-year period to go back to school to become an architect. It made sense as a combination of art and carpentry. We moved to the other university town in Iowa, and I enrolled in school. I was now older than most of my classmates and enjoyed the schoolwork though it wasn't easy. Architecture school is an exercise in attrition of all but the most highly motivated students. Three in a row all-night work sessions are common, and then the professor will come by your desk and trash the basic concept of your project with just a couple days to the deadline. The working industry is similar, I guess; lots of deadlines, stress, and confused directions from the clients. I also worked part-time during school and in the summers as a carpenter. I ran a roofing business one year though I don't know where I found the time. We were also extremely poor but still young enough that it didn't matter. Those were some fun times. I never thought about quitting school. I guess that once I made a decision, I just went through the course until it was done. I think that's true of a lot of my decision making on major and minor issues; I don't backtrack or reconsider or anguish over a past decision.

The other notable part of my personality, besides being hard working, was my lack of concern for money and financial security. When I was young, I had no money and didn't worry about it. Now I have lots of it, and I still don't worry about it. Every few years, though less lately, I find an uncashed check that I used as a bookmark in the back of a desk drawer. I have a good level of self-confidence and always feel that the money will work itself out. I know now that I am risk tolerant. I've always been a great money saver, which is good. My lifestyle is relatively modest, and whatever money doesn't get spent just goes to savings.

What were some events or projects that were not successful, but contributed to your success as an entrepreneur?

I guess I have as many failures as anyone must, but none of them are memorable. I felt a deep and depressing failure when my marriage broke up but don't think this is exceptional. That was shortly after we moved to Colorado, and I was working as a young architect. Also, in the course of five years I was fired by both the small architectural firms in town; once because of the tough economy of the 1980s, and the other because of my single-guy barfly habits after my divorce. At each of these times, although I was personally crushed, I took a month off before looking for another job. I always had an easy time finding the next job with a minimum of effort.

What project stands out as one of your major entrepreneurial successes?

The second time I got fired was the start of a success story. There weren't any other architectural firms in town, and I had never commuted, so I approached the owner of a large engineering firm, Landmark, and asked him to let me start an architectural division within his company. This worked and it didn't take long. I don't remember how long it took but think that it was nearly zero time before I had enough work to keep me busy. In about two years, I had a staff of four employees and was making a good business from referrals and walk-ins.

What event stands out as a major stumbling block that you needed to overcome as an entrepreneur?

The owner of the above firm was impressed by my work ethic though unimpressed with my single lifestyle. I think that in order to be successful as an entrepreneur you must be content in your personal life. This owner was, however, somewhat of a scrooge as far as pay, bonuses, flexible working policies, etc. So I knew I wanted to do something else. If I'd stayed there much longer, I might have flipped out and gone traveling or become a bum as I've sometimes thought of doing. I'm glad I didn't. One of my attributes of success in a small town is that I've just been working away here for twenty-four years now and [have] become a fixture.

Anyway, my relationship with Landmark was broken like a cheap watch when a friend who had just split up with my last employer approached me with, "Why don't we give it a try?" The rest, as they say, is history. He's been my partner now for the last seventeen years.

What advice could you give someone who has aspirations of becoming an entrepreneur?

My advice would be work hard, don't worry, be lucky . . . and be honest.

Describe your current enterprise.

We started Architecture One with nothing. I was getting married at the time. We each borrowed $3,000 from our parents, rented some cheap space, and bought some furniture. We didn't get paid for about six months. I recall being nervous if I thought about what I was doing, so I made a point not to think about it too much. I was in love, anyway, and that probably distracted me. We started in 1984, which was just before the deepest part of a national recession and the consequent idling of most architectural businesses. We were hard-working, poor, and lucky in some respects. The business and our incomes grew slowly at first but have advanced almost every year.

We employ eight people now and for the last few years. We have an income that would be envied by our cohorts in same-size or larger firms. We do not advertise, do not turn down much work, do not spend time writing proposals for work that we do not feel we can get, and we stay out of court. Our most profitable work is small jobs like house plans and back porch remodels. This is work that other architects shun. We make less profit on the bigger projects with large fees, projects that other architects strive for. I don't know why that is, but at least we have recognized what works for us. We could be characterized as a low-tech operation. We didn't rush to get on the popular CAD drafting systems. We still have hand draftsmen, which is unusual. We work on several hundred small projects a year unlike our competitors who may work on ten or more larger projects. I personally put in real time on three or more projects each day if not consumed with talking on the phone or running around. I enjoy the diversity.

Describe your feelings toward your enterprise. Would you sell your enterprise? Would you work for a new owner? Would you take on a partner?

Would I sell the business? You bet, in a heartbeat. Unlike my dad, I would love to be retired, although small architectural firms are traditionally impossible to sell. My partner (bless his heart) is resistant to giving minor partnership interests or other incentives that might allow a next generation ownership of the business. Would I work for a new owner? I would hope not. Would I take on a partner? Not again. I love my partner like a brother, but in small ways my views and his differ. This is not a big concern, but after being together for seventeen years, those little things niggle, just like the little things your wife does after that long.

How do you stay competitive with other firms in your industry?

Boy, that's a hard one. I guess the competitive edge is that I'm happy to live in a small town. I've come to be one of the good old boys, which is okay with me. We run a low-tech business that provides for a need that is not being satisfied by the larger high-tech firms.

What innovations have you implemented to improve your enterprise?

We are sprinters, not long-distance runners. Our product is what our community, a typical bedroom, coupon-cutting town, will support. We have been fortunate over the years to employ some great help who are capable and efficient. We delegate as much of the work as possible to our employees. We pay them well and try to treat them as equals when we can. We have the honor of a good reputation in the community so that people can find us even though we don't advertise. And mostly, we work hard to keep our customers happy.

Suggested Readings

Abernathy, W.J., K.B. Clark, and A.M. Kantrow. 1981."The New Industrial Competition." *Harvard Business Review* (September–October): 68–81.

Abernathy, W.J., and P.L. Townsend. 1975. "Technology, Productivity, and Process Change." *Technological Forecasting and Social Change* 7: 379–396.

Abernathy, W.J., and J.M. Utterback. 1978. "Patterns of Industrial Innovation." In *Strategic Management of Technology and Innovation*, R.A. Burgelman and M.A. Maidique, eds. Homewood, IL: Irwin, 141–148.

Abernathy, W.J., and K. Wayne. 1974. "Limits of the Learning Curve." *Harvard Business Review* (September–October): 109–119.

Achilladelis, B., A.B. Robertson, and P. Jervis. 1971. *Project SAPPHO: A Study of Success and Failure in Industrial Innovation*, 2 vols. London: Centre for the Study of Industrial Innovation.

Acs, Z.J., and D.B. Audretsch. 1987a. "Innovation in Large and Small Firms." *Economics Letters* 23: 109–112.

———. "Innovation, Market Structure and Firm Size." 1987b. *Review of Economics and Statistics* 69: 567–575.

———. 1988. "Innovation in Large and Small Firms: An Empirical Analysis." *American Economic Review* 78: 678–690.

———. 1989. "R&D, Firm Size, and Innovative Activity." Wissenschaftszentrum, Berlin, Discussion Paper No. FS IV-89xx.

Aldrich, H., and C. Zimmer. 1986. "Entrepreneurship Through Social Networks." In *The Art and Science of Entrepreneurship*, D.L. Secton and R.W. Smilor, eds. Cambridge, MA: Ballinger.

Allen, Robert C. 1983. "Collective Invention." *Journal of Economic Behavior and Organization* 4, no. 1 (March): 1–24.

Arrow, Kenneth J.1962a."Economic Welfare and the Allocation of Resources for Invention." In *The Rate and Direction of Industrial Activity: Economic and Social Factors*, A Report of the National Bureau of Economic Research. Princeton, NJ: Princeton University Press, 609–625.

————. 1962b. "The Economic Implications of Learning by Doing." *Review of Economic Studies* 29 (June): 155–173.

Arthur, W.B. 1989. "Competing Technologies, Increasing Returns, and Lock-in by Historical Events." *The Economic Journal* 99, no. 1 (March): 116–131.

Ayres, R.V. 1986. "Computer Integrated Manufacturing and the Next Industrial Revolution." In *Competitiveness Through Technology*, J. Dermer, ed. Lexington, MA: Lexington Books, 11–24.

Baily, M.N., and A.K. Chakrabarti. 1988. *Innovation and the Productivity Crisis*. Washington, DC: Brookings Institution.

Bairstow, J. 1986. "Automated Automaking." *High Technology* (August): 25–28.

Barrett, D. 1985. "Technology: The Permanent Wave." *Business Quarterly* (Spring): 43–52.

Barrett, F.D. 1980. "Tools and Tricks for Innovators." *Business Quarterly* (Winter): 57–62.

Barrier, Michael. 1994. "Innovation as a Way of Life." *Nation's Business* 82, no. 7: 18–27.

Baumol, W. 1968. "Entrepreneurship in Economic Theory." *American Economic Review* 58: 64–71.

————. 1990. "Entrepreneurship: Productive, Unproductive and Destructive." *Journal of Political Economy* 98, no. 5: 893–921.

————. 1991. "Entrepreneurial Theory: Existence and Inherent Bounds." Paper presented at the Entrepreneurship Theory Conference, University of Illinois at Urbana-Champaign, October.

Bell, D. 1976. *The Cultural Contradictions of Capitalism*. London: Heinemann.

Berger, Alan J. 1975. "Factors Influencing the Locus of Innovation Activity Leading to Scientific Instrument and Plastics Innovation." SM thesis, Sloan School of Management, MIT, Cambridge, MA.

Betz, F. 1987. *Managing Technology: Competing Through New Ventures, Innovation, and Corporate Research*. Englewood Cliffs, NJ: Prentice-Hall.

Binswanger, A. 1974. "A Micro Economic Approach to Induced Innovation." *Economic Journal* 84 (December): 940.

Binswanger, H.P., and V.W. Ruttan. 1978. *Induced Innovation: Technology, Institutions and Development*. Baltimore, MD: Johns Hopkins University Press.

Bird, Barbara J., D. Hayward, and D. Allen. 1993. "Conflicts in Commercialization of Knowledge: Perspectives from Science and Entrepreneurship." *Entrepreneurship: Theory and Practice* 17, no. 4: 57–77.

Blaug, M.1963. "A Survey of the Theory of Process Innovations." *Econometrica* (February): 13–32.

Boulding, K.E. 1991. "What is Evolutionary Economics?" *Journal of Evolutionary Economics* 1, no. 1: 9–17.

Boyden, Julian W. 1976. "A Study of the Innovative Process in the Plastics Additives Industry." SM thesis, Sloan School of Management, MIT, Cambridge, MA.

Bozeman, Barry, and Michael Crow. 1995. "Federal Laboratories in the National Innovative System." Georgia Institute of Technology, School of Public Policy.

Brown, K.A. 1988. *Inventors at Work: Interviews with 16 Notable American Inventors*. Redmond, WA: Tempus Books.

Browne, J., K. Rathmill, S.P. Sethi, and K.E. Stecke. 1984. "Classification of Flexible Manufacturing Systems." *The FMS Magazine* 2, no. 2: 114–117.

Bullinger, H., H. Warnecke, and H. Lentes. 1985. "Towards the Factory of the Future." In *Towards the Factory of the Future*, H. Bullinger, H. Warnecke and H. Lentes, eds., New York: Springer-Verlag, xxix–liv.

Burgelman, R.A., and M.A. Maidique. 1988. *Strategic Management of Technology and Innovation*. Homewood, IL: Irwin.

Burgelman, R.A., and L.R. Sayles. 1986. *Inside Corporate Innovation: Strategy, Structure, and Managerial Skills*. New York: Free Press.

Bygrave, W.D., and C.W. Hofer. 1991. "Theorizing about Entrepreneurship." *Entrepreneurship Theory and Practice* 16, no. 2: 13–22.

Bylinsky, G.1984. "America's Best Managed Factories." *Fortune*, May 28, 16–24.

Campbell, A.1987. "Improving Productivity Is Becoming Vital for Survival on World Scene." *The Globe and Mail*, November 9, B9.

Carland, J.W., F. Hoy, and J.A.C. Carland. 1988. "Who Is the Entrepreneur? Is the Wrong Question." *Entrepreneurship Theory and Practice* 16, no. 4: 33–39.

Carsrud, A.L., and R.W. Johnson. 1989. "Entrepreneurship and Regional Development." *A Social Psychological Perspective* 1: 21–32.

Clarke, Roderick W. 1968. "Innovation in Liquid Propellant Rocket Technology." Ph.D dissertation, Stanford University, Stanford, CA.

Coase, R.H. 1937. "The Nature of the Firm." *Economica*, N.S. 4: 386.

———. 1960. "The Problem of Social Cost." *The Journal of Law and Economics* 3: 1–44.

Cohen, S., and J. Zysman. 1987. *Manufacturing Matters: The Myth of the Post-Industrial Economy.* New York: Basic Books.

Cohen, W.M., and D.A. Levinthal. 1989. "Innovation and Learning: The Two Faces of R&D." *The Economic Journal* 99: 569–596.

Cohen, W.M., and R.C. Levin. 1989. "Empirical Studies of Innovation and Market Structure." In *The Handbook of Industrial Organization*, Richard Schmalensee and Robert D. Willig, eds. Vol. II. Amsterdam: North-Holland, 1059–1107.

Council of Economic Advisers. 1981. *Economic Report of the President*. Washington, DC: Government Printing Office, 211–213.

Craig, R., and H. Noori. 1985. "Recognition and Use of Automation: A Comparison of Small and Large Manufacturers." *Journal of Small Business and Entrepreneurship* 3, no. 1: 37–44.

Crain, R. 1966. "Fluoridation: The Diffusion of an Innovation Among American Cities." *Social Forces* (June): 467.

Dasgupta, P., and J. Stiglitz. 1980. "Industrial Structure and the Nature of Innovative Activity. "*Economic Journal* 90, no. 2: 266–293.

David, Paul A., 1975. *Technical Choice Innovation and Economic Growth: Essays on American and British Experience in the Nineteenth Century.* London: Cambridge University Press.

———. 1992. "Analyzing the Economic Payoffs from Basic Research." *Economics of Innovation and New Technology* 2: 73–89.

Davies, Stephen. 1979. *The Diffusion of Process Innovations.* Cambridge and New York: Cambridge University Press.

Denison, E.F. 1962. *The Sources of Economic Growth in the United States and the Alternatives Before Us* (Research Report) (13). New York: Committee for Economic Development.

Dosi, G. 1988. "Sources, Procedures and Microeconomic Effects of Innovation." *Journal of Economic Literature* 36: 1126–1171.

Drucker, P.F. 1971. *The Age of Discontinuity: Guidelines to our Changing Society.* London: Pan Books.

———. 1985. "The Discipline of Innovation." *Harvard Business Review* (May–June): 67–72.

Edwards, Keith L., and Theodore J. Gordon. 1984. "Characterization of Innovations Introduced on the U.S. Market in 1982." The Futures Group, U.S. Small Business Administration, Contract No. SBA-6050–0A-82, March.

Enos, John Lawrence. 1962. *Petroleum Progress and Profits: A History of Process Innovation.* Cambridge, MA: MIT Press.

Evenson, Robert E. 1984. "International Invention: Implications for Technology Market Analysis." In *R&D, Patents, and Productivity*, Zvi Griliches, ed. Chicago: University of Chicago Press, 55–70.

Falconer, T. 1986. "WRSM: Cutting the Cost of CAD." *Canadian Business*, May, 82–89.

Florida, Richard L., and Martin A. Kenney. 1990. *The Breakthrough Illusion: Corporate America's Failure to Move from Innovation to Mass Production.* New York: Basic Books.

Ford, Cameron M. 1996. "A Theory of Individual Creative Action in Multiple Social Domains." *Academy of Management Review* 21, no. 4: 1112–1142.

Foster Associates. 1978. *A Survey of the Rates of Return to Innovation.* Washington, DC: National Science Foundation.

Foxall, Gordon R., Francis S. Murphy, and Janet D. Tierney. 1985. "Market Development in Practice: A Case Study of User-Initiated Product Innovation." *Journal of Marketing Management* 1: 201–211.

Freeman, C. 1979. "The Determinants of Innovation." *Futures* 11, no. 3: 206–215.

———. 1982. *The Economics of Industrial Innovation*, 2d ed. Cambridge, MA: MIT Press.

———. 1986. "The Diffusion of Technical Innovations and Change of Techno-Economic Paradigm." *Conference on Innovation Diffusion*, Venice, Italy, March, 17–21.

———. 1988. "Japan: A New System of National Innovation?" In *Technical Change and Economic Theory*, G. Dosi, C. Freeman, R. Nelson, G. Silverberg, and L. Soete, eds. London: Pinter, 401–431.

Freeman, C., J. Clark, and L. Soete. 1982. *Unemployment and Technical Innovation: A Study of Long Waves and Economic Development.* London: Pinter.

Futia, C. "Schumpeterian Competition." 1980. *Quarterly Journal of Economics* 94, no. 4.

The Futures Group. 1984. *Characterization of Innovations Introduced on the U.S. Market in 1982.* Washington, DC: U.S. Small Business Administration, Office of Advocacy.

Gannes, S. 1988. "The Good News About U.S. R&D." *Fortune*, February 1, 48–56.

Gartner, William B. 1990. "What Are We Talking About When We Talk About Entrepreneurship?" *Journal of Business Venturing*, January, 15–28.

Gatewood, Elizabeth. 1993. "The Expectancies in Public Sector Venture Assistance." *Entrepreneurship: Theory and Practice* 17, no. 2: 91–95.

Gellman Research Associates. 1976. *Indicators of International Trends in Technological Innovation*, Report to the National Science Foundation.

———. 1982. *The Relationship Between Industrial Concentration, Firm Size, and Technological Innovation*. Washington, DC: U.S. Small Business Administration, Office of Advocacy.

Gerwin, D. 1985. "Organizational Implications of CAM." *International Journal of Management Science* 13, no. 5: 443–451.

———. 1982. "Do's and Don'ts of Computerized Manufacturing." *Harvard Business Review* (March–April): 107–116.

Gibbons, Michael, and Ron Johnston. 1974. "The Role of Science in Technological Innovation." *Research Policy* 3: 220–242.

Glynn, Mary Ann. 1996. "Innovative Genius: A Framework for Relating Individual and Organizational Intelligences to Innovation." *Academy of Management Review* 21, no. 4: 1081–1111.

Gold, A. 1984."Small Is Beautiful Now in Manufacturing." *Business Week*, October 22, 152–156.

Gold, B. 1982. "CAM Sets New Rules for Production." *Harvard Business Review* (November–December): 88–94.

Goldhar, J.D. 1984. "What Flexible Automation Means to Your Business." *Modern Materials Handling* 39, no. 12: 63–65.

———. 1987. "Evolution in Manufacturing—The Inevitability of Strategic Impacts of CIM." In *Computer Applications in Production and Engineering: Proceedings of the Second International IFIP Conference on Computer Applications in Production and Engineering*, Cape '86, Copenhagen, Denmark, 20–23–May, 1986, ed. by K. Bø, et al. Amsterdam and New York: North-Holland, 3–14.

Golding, A.M. 1971. "The Semiconductor Industry in Britain and the United States: A Case Study in Innovation, Growth and the Diffusion of Technology." Ph.D. dissertation, University of Sussex, England.

Goodwin, R.M. 1991. "Schumpeter, Keynes and the Theory of Economic Evolution." *Journal of Evolutionary Economics* 1: 29–47.

Graham, John R. 1994. "Seven Keys to Innovative Thinking." *Managers Magazine* 69, no. 8: 26–27.

Griliches, Z. 1957. "Hybrid Corn: An Exploration of the Economics of Technological Change." *Econometrica* 25: 501–522.

———. 1979. "Issues in Assessing the Contribution of R&D to Productivity Growth." *Bell Journal of Economics* 10: 92–116.

———. 1988. "Productivity Puzzles and R&D: Another Non-Explanation." *Journal of Economic Perspectives* 2, no. 4: 9–21.

———. 1990. "Patent Statistics as Economic Indicators: A Survey." *Journal of Economic Literature* 27: 1661–1707.

———. 1992. "The Search for R&D Spillovers." *Scandinavian Journal of Economics* 94, no. 3 (Supplement): 529–547.

Griliches, Zvi, and Jacob Schmookler. 1963. "Comment: Inventing and Maximizing." *American Economic Review* 53, no. 10 (September): 725–729.

Grossman, L. 1984. "Economic Transformation: Technological Innovation and Diffusion in Ontario." Ministry of Treasury and Economics, March.

Groover, M.P. 1987. *Automation, Production Systems, and Computer-Integrated Manufacturing.* Englewood Cliffs, NJ: Prentice-Hall.

Groover, M.P., and J.C. Wiginton. 1986. "CIM and the Flexible Automated Factory of the Future." *Industrial Engineering:* 75–85.

Gupta, A.K., S.P. Raj, and D. Wilemon. 1985. "The R&D-Marketing Interface in High-Technology Firms." *Journal of Productivity and Innovation Management* 2: 12–24.

Haas, E.A. 1987. "Breakthrough Manufacturing." *Harvard Business Review* (March-April): 75–81.

Hansen, Eric L., and Kathleen R. Allen. 1992. "The Creation Corridor: Environmental Load and Pre-Organization Information-Processing Ability." *Entrepreneurship: Theory and Practice* 17, no. 1: 57–65.

Hanusch, H., ed. 1988. *Evolutionary Economics: Application of Schumpeter's Ideas.* Cambridge: Cambridge University Press.

Hayes, R.H., and S.C. Wheelwright. 1984. *Restoring Our Competitive Edge: Competing Through Manufacturing.* New York: Wiley.

Institute for Defense Analyses. 1976. *The Effects of Patent and Antitrust Laws, Regulations, and Practices on Innovation.* 3 vols. Arlington, VA: National Technical Information Service.

Hebert, R.F., and A.N. Link. 1989. "In Search of the Meaning of Entrepreneurship." *Small Business Economics* 1: 39–40.

Herron, Larry, and Harry J. Sapienza. 1992. "The Entrepreneur and the Initiation of New Venture Launch." *Entrepreneurship: Theory and Practice* 17, no. 1: 49–55.

Hofer, Charles W., and William D. Bygreve. 1992. "Researching Entrepreneurship." *Entrepreneurship: Theory and Practice* 16, no. 3: 91–100.

Iwai, Katsuhito. 1984a. "Schumpeterian Dynamics: An Evolutionary Model of Innovation and Imitation." *Journal of Economic Behavior and Organization* 5: 159–190.

———. 1984b. "Schumpeterian Dynamics, Part II: Technological Progress, Firm Growth and 'Economic Selection.' " *Journal of Economic Behavior and Organization* 5: 321–351.

Jackson, John E., and Gretchen R. Rodkey. 1994. "The Attitudinal Climate for Entrepreneurial Activity." *Public Opinion Quarterly* 58, no. 3: 358–380.

Jewkes, John, D. Sawers, and R. Stillerman. 1961. *The Sources of Innovation.* New York: Norton.

Johnson, B.R. 1990. "Toward a Multidimensional Model of Entrepreneurship: The Case of Achievement Motivation and the Entrepreneur." *Entrepreneurship Theory and Practice* 14: 39–54.

Juhasz, Andrew Anthony, Jr. 1975. "The Pattern of Innovation Exhibited in the Development of the Tractor Shovel." SM thesis, Sloan School of Management, MIT.

Kagan, Daniel. 1995. "Why Entrepreneurs Ignore Good Advice: A Study in Non-Linearity and Ego." *Human Systems Management* 14, no. 4: 327–333.

Kamien, Morton I., and Nancy L. Schwartz. 1972. "Timing of Innovations under Rivalry." *Econometrica* 40, no. 1.

———. 1975. "Market Structure and Innovation: A Survey." *Journal of Economic Literature* 13, no. 1 (March): 1–37.

———. 1982. *Market Structure and Innovation*. Cambridge and New York: Cambridge University Press.

Kantrow, Alan M. 1980. "The Strategy-Technology Connection." *Harvard Business Review*, 58, no. 4 (July–August).

Kingston, William. 1997. *Innovation: The Creative Impulse in Human Progress*. London: John Calderj.

Kirchhoff, Bruce A. 1991. "Entrepreneurship's Contribution to Economics." *Entrepreneurship: Theory and Practice* 16, no. 2: 93–112.

Kirchhoff, B.A., and B.D. Phillips. 1989. "Innovation and Growth Among New Firms in the U.S. Economy." In *Frontiers of Entrepreneurship Research 1989: Proceedings of the Ninth Annual Babson College Entrepreneurship Research Conference*, Center for Entrepreneurial Studies, Babson College, Wellesley, MA, 1989, 173–188.

Kirkland, R.I. 1988. "Entering a New Age of Boundless Competition." *Fortune*, March 14, 40–48.

Kirzner, I.M. 1979. *Perception, Opportunity, and Profit: Studies in the Theory of Entrepreneurship*. Chicago: University of Chicago Press.

Kline, S.J., and N. Rosenberg. 1986. "An Overview of Innovation." In *The Positive Sum Strategy: Harnessing Technology for Economic Growth*, R. Landau and N. Rosenberg, eds. Washington, DC: National Academy Press.

Knight, Kenneth E. 1963. "A Study of Technological Innovation: The Evolution of Digital Computers." Ph.D. dissertation, Carnegie Institute of Technology, Pittsburgh, PA.

Kumpe, T., and P.T. Bolwijn. 1988. "Manufacturing: The New Case for Vertical Integration." *Harvard Business Review* (March–April): 75–81.

Kuznets, Simon. 1962. "Inventive Activity: Problems of Definition and Measurement." In *The Rate and Direction of Inventive Activity: Economic and Social Factors*, National Bureau of Economic Research. Princeton, NJ: Princeton University Press, 19–43.

Kwasnicki, Witold, and Halina Kwasnicka. 1992. "Market, Innovation, and Competition." *Journal of Economic Behavior and Organization* 19: 343–368.

Lancaster, K. 1966. "Change and Innovation in the Technology of Consumption." *American Economic Review*, Supplement (May): 14–23.

Langan-Fox, Janice, and Susanna Roth. 1995. "Achievement Motivation and Female Entrepreneurs." *Journal of Occupational & Organizational Psychology* 68, no. 3: 209–218.

Lee, T., and L.L. Wilde. 1980. "Market Structure and Innovation: A Reformulation." *Quarterly Journal of Economics* 94: 429–436.

Lehmann, Walter G. 1975. "Innovation in Electron Microscopes and Accessories." SM thesis, Sloan School of Management, MIT.

Levin, Richard C. 1978. "Technical Change, Barriers to Entry, and Market Structure." *Economica* 45 (November): 347–361.

———. 1986. "A New Look at the Patent System." *American Economic Review* 76, no. 2 (May): 199–202.

Levin, Richard C., and Richard R. Nelson. 1984. "Survey Research on R&D Appropriability and Technological Opportunity. Part I: Appropriability." Working Paper, July, Yale University, New Haven, CT.

Levin, R.C., et al. 1987. "Appropriating the Returns from Industrial R&D." *Brookings Papers on Economic Activity*, no. 3. Washington, DC: Brookings Institution, 783–820.

Link, Albert N., and John Rees. 1990. "Firm Size, University-Based Research, and the Returns to R&D." *Small Business Economics* 2: 25–31.

Lionetta, William G., Jr. 1977. "Sources of Innovation Within the Pultrusion Industry." SM thesis, Sloan School of Management, MIT, Cambridge, MA.

Loury, G. 1979. "Market Structure and Innovation." *Quarterly Journal of Economics* 93, no. 3: 395–410.

Machlup, F. 1962. "The Supply of Innovations and Inventions." In *The Rate and Direction of Inventive Activity: Economic and Social Factors*, R.R. Nelson, ed. Princeton, NJ: Princeton University Press.

Mackenzie, Lynn Ryan. 1992. "Fostering Entrepreneurship as a Rural Economic Development Strategy." *Economic Development Review* 10, no. 4: 38–44.

Maidique, M.A. 1980. "Entrepreneurs, Champions, and Technological Innovation." *Sloan Management Review* (Winter): 59–76.

Mansfield, Edwin. 1968a. *The Economics of Technological Change*. New York: Norton.

———. 1968b. *Industrial Research and Technological Innovation: An Econometric Analysis*. New York: Norton.

———. 1972. "Contribution of R&D to Economic Growth in the United States." *Science*, February 4, 487–494.

———. 1981. "How Economists See R&D." *Harvard Business Review* (November–December): 98–106.

———. 1985. "How Rapidly Does New Industrial Technology Leak Out?" *Journal of Industrial Economics* 34, no. 2 (December): 217–223.

———. 1988. "Industrial Innovation in Japan and the United States." *Science*, September 30.

———. 1991a. "Academic Research and Industrial Innovation." *Research Policy* 20: 1–12.

———. 1991b. "Estimates of the Social Returns from Research and Development." In *Science and Technology Policy Yearbook*, M. Meredith, S. Nelson, and A. Teich, eds. Washington, DC: American Association for the Advancement of Science.

———. 1992. "Academic Research and Industrial Innovation: A Further Note." *Research Policy* 21: 295–296.

———. 1995. "Academic Research Underlying Industrial Innovations: Sources, Characteristics, and Financing." *Review of Economics and Statistics* (February): 55–65.

Mansfield, Edwin, et al. 1971. *Research and Innovation in the Modern Corporation*. New York: Norton.

———. 1977. "Social and Private Rates of Return from Industrial Innovations." *Quarterly Journal of Economics* 91 (May): 221–240.

Marquis, D.G. 1982 [1969]. "The Anatomy of Successful Innovations." In *Read-

ings in the Management of Innovation, compiled by Michael L. Tushman and William L. Moore. Boston: Pitman, 42–50.

Martin, Kenney. 1986. "Schumpeterian Innovation and Entrepreneurs in Capitalism." *Research Policy* 1 (February): 21–33.

Martin, M.J.C. 1984. *Managing Technological Innovation & Entrepreneurship*. Reston, VA: Reston.

McCune, Jenny C. 1995. "The Entrepreneur Express." *Management Review* 84, no. 3: 13–19.

McDougall, G.H.G., and H. Munro. 1984. "The New Product Process: A Study of Small Industrial Firms." *Journal of Small Business: Canada* (Fall): 24–29.

McGinnis, M.A., and M.R. Ackelsberg. 1983. "Effective Innovation Management: Missing Link in Strategic Planning." *The Journal of Business Strategy* 4, no. 1: 59–66.

McGrath, Rita Gunther, Ian MacMillan, and Sari Scheinberg. 1992. "Elitists, Risk-Taking, and Rugged Individualists: An Exploratory Analysis of Cultural Differences Between Entrepreneurs and Non-Entrepreneurs." *Journal of Business Venturing* 7, no. 2: 115–135.

McMillan, C.J. 1987. "The Automation Triangle: New Paths to Productivity Performance." *Business Quarterly* 52, no. 2: 61–67.

Meadows, Dennis L. 1967. "Accuracy of Technical Estimates in Industrial Research Planning: Data Appendix." Working Paper No. 301–67, Sloan School of Management, Cambridge, MIT, Cambridge, MA.

———. 1968. "Estimate Accuracy and Project Selection Models in Industrial Research." *Industrial Management Review* 9, no. 3 (Spring): 105–119.

Meredith, J. 1987a. "The Strategic Advantages of New Manufacturing Technologies for Small Firms." *Strategic Management Journal* 8: 249–258.

———. 1987b. "The Strategic Advantages of the Factory of the Future." *California Management Review* 29, no. 3 (Spring): 27–39.

Mill, J.S. 1950. *Philosophy of Scientific Method*. New York: Hafner.

Miller, R.E. 1971. *Innovation, Organization and Environment: A Study of Sixteen American and West European Steel Firms*. Sherbrooke: Institut de recherche et de perfectionnement en administration.

More, R.A. 1986. "Developer/Adopter Relationships in the Adoption of CAD/CAM Systems: Implications for Operations Management." *National Center for Management Research and Development*, Working Paper Series No. NC86–02, July.

Mowery, D., and N. Rosenberg. 1979. "The Influence of Market Demand on Innovation: A Critical Survey of Several Recent Empirical Studies." *Research Policy* 8: 102–153.

———. 1989. "The Growing Role of Science in the Innovation Process." In *Technology and the Pursuit of Economic Growth*, David C. Mowery and Nathan Rosenberg, eds. Cambridge and New York: Cambridge University Press, 21–34.

Myers, S., and D.G. Marquis. 1969. *Successful Industrial Innovations: A Study of Factors Underlying Innovation in Selected Firms*. NSF 69–17. Washington, DC: Government Printing Office, 59.

Myers, S., and E.E. Sweezy. 1978. "Why Innovations Fail." *Technology Review* (March–April): 40–46.

Nasar, S. 1988. "America's Competitive Revival." *Fortune*, January 4, 44–52.

Nathan, R.R. and Associates. 1978. *Net Rates of Return on Innovations*. Washington, DC: National Science Foundation.

Nelson, Richard R. 1959. "The Simple Economics of Basic Scientific Research." *Journal of Political Economy* 67, no. 3 (June): 297–306.

———. 1982. "The Role of Knowledge in R&D Efficiency." *Quarterly Journal of Economics* 97, no. 3 (August): 453–470.

———. 1987. *Understanding Technical Change as an Evolutionary Process*. Amsterdam: North-Holland.

Nelson, R.R., and G. Wright. 1992. "The Rise and Fall of American Technological Leadership: The Postwar Era in Historical Perspective." *Journal of Economic Literature* 30: 1931–1964.

Nelson, Richard R., and Sidney G. Winter. 1974. "Neoclassical vs. Evolutionary Theories of Economic Growth." *Economic Journal* 84: 866–905.

———. 1977. "In Search of Useful Theory of Innovation." *Research Policy* 6: 36–76.

———. 1982a. *An Evolutionary Theory of Economic Change*. Cambridge, MA: Harvard University Press.

———. 1982b. "The Schumpeterian Tradeoff Revisited." *The American Economic Review* 72: 114–132.

Nordhaus, William D. 1969. *Invention, Growth, and Welfare: A Theoretical Treatment of Technological Change*. Cambridge, MA: MIT Press.

———. 1973. "Some Skeptical Faults on the Theory of Induced Innovation." *Quarterly Journal of Economics* 87 (May): 208.

Osborne, Richard L. 1994. "The Myth of the Renaissance Man: The Balance Between Enterprise and Entrepreneur." *Review of Business* 15, no. 3: 36–40.

Pakes, Ariel, and Mark Schankerman. 1987. "An Exploration into the Determinants of Research Intensity." In *R&D, Patents and Productivity*, Zvi Griliches, ed. Chicago: University of Chicago Press.

Pavitt, K. 1971. *Conditions of Success in Technological Innovation*. Paris: OECD.

Peck, Merton J. 1962. "Inventions in the Postwar American Aluminum Industry." In *The Rate and Direction of Inventive Activity: Economic and Social Factors* (a Report of the National Bureau of Economic Research). Princeton, NJ: Princeton University Press, 279–298.

Peters, Donald H. 1969. "Commercial Innovations from University Faculty: A Study of the Invention and Exploitation of Ideas." Working Paper No. 406–69, Sloan School of Management, MIT, Cambridge, MA.

Peters, T. 1988. *Thriving on Chaos*. New York: Knopf.

Peters, T.J. and R.H. Waterman, Jr. 1982. *In Search of Excellence*. New York: Warner Books.

Qualls, W., R.W. Olshavsky, and R.E. Michaels. 1981. "Shortening of the PLC—An Empirical Test." *Journal of Marketing* (Fall): 76–80.

Quinn, J.B. 1985. "Managing Innovation: Controlled Chaos." *Harvard Business Review* (May–June): 73–84.

Rahmeyer, F. 1989. "The Evolutionary Approach to Innovation Activity." *Journal of Institutional and Theoretical Economics* 145, no.2 (June): 275–297.

Reinganum, J.F. 1985. "Innovation and Industry Evolution." *Quarterly Journal of Economics*: 81–99.

Rice, Mark P. 1995. *Growing New Ventures, Creating New Jobs: Principles and Practices of Successful Business Incubation*. Westport, CT: Quorum.

Rice, Ronald E., and Everett M. Rogers. 1980. "Reinvention in the Innovation Process." *Knowledge: Creation, Diffusion, Utilization* 1, no. 4 (June): 499–514.

Robert Nathan Associates. 1978. *New Rates of Return on Innovations: Report to the National Science Foundation*.

Roberts, E.B. 1974. "A Simple Model of R&D Project Dynamics." *R&D Management* 5, no. 1 (October): 1–15.

———. 1977. "Generating Effective Corporate Innovation." *Technology Review* (October–November): 26–33.

Rogers, Everett M. 1962. *Diffusion of Innovation*. New York: Free Press.

Rogers, Everett M., with F. Floyd Shoemaker. 1971. *Communication of Innovations: A Cross-Cultural Approach*, 2d ed. New York: Free Press.

Roman, D.D., and J.F. Puett, Jr. 1988. *International Business and Technological Innovation*. New York: Elsevier.

Romer, Paul M. 1990. "Endogenous Technological Change." *Journal of Political Economy* 98: S71–S102.

———. 1993. "Implementing a National Technology Strategy with Self-Organizing Industry Investment Boards." *Brookings Papers on Economic Activity: Microeconomics* 2. Washington, DC: Brookings Institution, 345–399.

Rosenberg, Nathan. 1974. "Science, Invention and Economic Growth." *Economic Journal* 84, no. 333 (March): 90–108.

———, ed. 1983. *Research on Technological Innovation Management and Policy*. Greenwich, CT: JAI Press.

Rosenbloom, Richard S. 1978. "Technological Innovation in Firms and Industries: An Assessment of the State of the Art." In *Technological Innovation: A Critical Review of Current Knowledge*, P. Kelly and Melvin Kranzberg, eds. San Francisco: San Francisco Press.

Rothwell, Roy, and Walter Zegveld. 1981. *Innovation and the Small and Medium Sized Firm*. Hingham, MA: Kluwer-Nijhoff.

Sage, Gary.1993. "Entrepreneurship as an Economic Development Strategy." *Economic Development Review* 2, no. 2: 66–67.

Sahal, D. 1981. *Patterns of Technological Innovation*. Reading, MA: Addison-Wesley.

Scherer, F.M. 1982. "Demand Pull and Technological Invention Revisited." *Journal of Industrial Economics* 30: 225–237.

———. 1984. *Innovation and Growth: Schumpeterian Perspectives*. Cambridge, MA: MIT Press.

Schmookler, Jacob. 1962. "Changes in Industry and in the State of Knowledge as Determinants of Industrial Invention." In *The Rate and Direction of Inventive Activity: Economic and Social Factors* (a Report of the National Bureau of Economic Research). Princeton, NJ: Princeton University Press, 195–232.

———. 1966. *Innovation and Economic Growth*. Cambridge, MA: Harvard University Press.

Schonberger, R.J. 1987. "Frugal Manufacturing." *Harvard Business Review* (September–October): 95–100.

Schultz, T.W. 1980. "Investment in Entrepreneurial Ability." *Scandinavian Journal of Economics* 82: 437–448.

Schumpeter, Joseph A. 1950. *Capitalism, Socialism and Democracy*, 3d ed. New York: Harper & Row.

————. 1954. *History of Economic Analysis*. New York: Oxford University Press.

Science Policy Research Unit. 1972. *Success and Failure in Industrial Innovation: Report on Project Sappho*. London: Center for the Study of Industrial Innovation.

Senia, A. 1987. "Companies Turn Old Ideas into Profits." *High Technology Business* (December): 36–39.

Shaver, Kelly G. 1995. "The Entrepreneurial Personality Myth." *Business & Economic Review* 41, no. 3: 20–23.

Shaw, Brian. 1985. "The Role of the Interaction Between the User and the Manufacturer in Medical Equipment Innovation." *R&D Management* 15, no. 4 (October): 283–292.

————. 1986. "Appropriation and Transfer of Innovation Benefit in the U.K. Medical Equipment Industry." *Technovation* 4, no. 1 (February): 45–65.

Shimshoni, Daniel. 1966. "Aspects of Scientific Entrepreneurship." Ph.D. dissertation, Harvard University, Cambridge.

Shell, Karl. 1966. "Toward a Theory of Inventive Activity and Capital Accumulation." *American Economic Review* 56, no. 2 (May): 62–68.

————. 1967. "A Model of Inventive Activity and Capital Accumulation." In *Essays on the Theory of Optimal Economic Growth*, Karl Shell, ed. Cambridge, MA: MIT Press.

————. 1973. "Inventive Activity, Industrial Organisation and Economic Growth." In *Models of Economic Growth*, James A. Mirrlees and Nicholas H. Stern, eds. New York: Wiley.

Sokoloff, Kenneth L. 1988. "Inventive Activity in Early Industrial America: Evidence from Patent Records, 1790–1846." *Journal of Economic History* 48 (December): 813–850.

Sokoloff, Kenneth L., and Z. Khan. 1989. "The Democratization of Invention During Early Industrialization: Evidence from the United States, 1790–1846." Working Paper, University of California–Los Angeles.

Stearns, Timothy M., and Gerald E. Hills. 1996. "Entrepreneurship and New Firm Development: A Definitional Introduction." *Journal of Business Research* 36, no. 1: 1–4.

Stevenson, H.H., and D.E. Gumpter. 1985. "The Heart of Entrepreneurship." *Harvard Business Review* (March-April): 85–94.

Stevenson, H.H., M.J. Roberts, and H.I. Grousbeck. 1985. *New Business Ventures and the Entrepreneur*. Homewood, IL: Irwin.

Taylor III, A. 1987. "Lee Iacocca's Production Whiz." *Fortune*, June 22, 36–44.

Tisdell, C.A. 1971. "Commonwealth Industrial Research and Development Grants: Economic Evaluation." *Economic Analysis and Policy* 2, no. 2: 124–129.

Trajtenberg, M. 1990. *Economic Analysis of Product Innovation: The Case of CT Scanners*. Cambridge, MA: Harvard University Press.

Tushman, M.L., and W.L. Moore, compilers. 1982. *Readings in the Management of Innovation*. Boston: Pitman.

U.S. Department of Commerce. 1967. *Technological Innovation: Its Environment and Management.* Washington, DC: Government Printing Office.

Utterback, J.M. 1971. "The Process of Technological Innovation Within the Firm." *Academy of Management Journal* (March): 75–88.

———. 1974. "Innovation in Industry and the Diffusion of Technology." *Science*, February 15, 658–662.

Utterback, J.M., and L. Kim. 1985. "Invasion of a Small Business by Radical Innovation." In *The Management of Productivity and Technology in Manufacturing*, P.R. Kleindorfer ed. New York: Plenum Press.

Valery, N. 1987. "Factory of the Future." *The Economist*, May 30, 3–18.

Von Hippel, E. 1976. "The Dominant Role of Users in the Scientific Instrument Innovation Process." *Research Policy* 5, no. 3 (July): 212–239.

———. 1977. "Transferring Process Equipment Innovations from User-Innovators to Equipment Manufacturing Firms." *R&D Management* 8, no. 1 (October): 13–22.

———. 1978a. "Users as Innovators." *Technology Review* 80, no. 3 (January): 3–11.

———. 1978b. "A Customer-Active Paradigm for Industrial Product Idea Generation." *Research Policy* 7, no. 3 (July): 240–266.

———. 1980. "The User's Role in Industrial Innovation." *TIMS Studies in the Management Sciences* 15: 53–65.

———. 1982. "Appropriability of Innovation Benefit as a Predictor of the Source of Innovation." *Research Policy* 11, no. 2 (April): 95–115.

———. 1985. "Testing the Correlation between the Functional Locus of Innovation and Appropriable Innovation Benefit." Working Paper No. 1688–85, Sloan School of Management, MIT, Cambridge, MA.

Von Hippel, Eric, and Stan N. Finkelstein. 1979. "Analysis of Innovation in Automated Clinical Chemistry Analyzers." *Science and Public Policy* 6, no. 1 (February): 24–37.

Walker, J. 1969. "The Diffusion of Innovation among American States." *American Political Science Review* 63 (September): 880.

Walsh, V. 1984. "Invention and Innovation in the Chemical Industry: Demand Pull or Discovery Push." *Research Policy* 13: 211–234.

Williamson, Oliver E. 1965. "Innovation and Market Structure." *Journal of Political Economy* 73, no. 1 (February): 67–73.

Yorsz, Walter. 1976. "A Study of the Innovative Process in the Semiconductor Industry." SM thesis, Sloan School of Management, MIT, Cambridge, MA.

Index

About the Author

Bruce A. McDaniel is chair of the Economics Department at the University of Northern Colorado. Dr. McDaniel has earned a B.S. degree in Business and Economics from Manchester College, an M.A. degree in Economics from Ball State University, and a Ph.D. in Economics from Colorado State University. He has taught at Anderson College, SUNY–Genesee Community College, Indiana University–Purdue University at Indianapolis, and Marquette University. Dr. McDaniel has eighteen years of teaching experience and eight years of experience in the private sector owning and managing small businesses. In addition to consulting work, he has published several articles in professional journals.